DUTY
of CARE

*To Samira, Haydon, Yasmina, Mum,
my brothers Stuart and Ian, and sister Liz.*

*And to the Australian people who were so
magnificent in their tireless support and
continual faith in our innocence.*

DUTY
of CARE

Steve Pratt

SIMON & SCHUSTER
AUSTRALIA

DUTY OF CARE

First published in Australia in 2000 by
Simon & Schuster (Australia) Pty Limited
20 Barcoo Street, East Roseville NSW 2069

A Viacom Company
Sydney New York London Toronto Tokyo Singapore

© Steve Pratt 2000

All rights reserved. No part of this publication may be reproduced, stored in a retrieval system, or transmitted, in any form or by any means, electronic, mechanical, photocopying, recording or otherwise, without the prior permission of the publisher in writing.

National Library of Australia
Cataloguing-in-Publication data

Pratt, Steve.
Duty of care.

   Includes index.
   ISBN 0 7318 1010 4 (HB)
   ISBN 0 7318 1006 6 (PB)

   1. CARE Australia – Biography. 2. Humanitarian assistance – Political aspects – Serbia – Kosovo. 3. Prisoners of war – Australia – Biography. 4. Prisoners of war – Serbia – Kosovo – Biography. 5. Kosovo (Serbia) – History – Civil War, 1998 – Personal narratives, Australian. I. Title.

361.763092

Cover images courtesy of AAPIMAGE
Cover and internal design by Greendot Design
Typesetting by Asset Typesetting Pty Ltd

Set in 11/14 Sabon
Printed in Australia by Griffin Press

10 9 8 7 6 5 4 3 2 1

The names of a number of individuals referred to in this book have been changed at the author's request.

CONTENTS

Foreword by the Rt Hon. Malcolm Fraser, AC CH		vii
Acknowledgments		xiii
Prologue		1
Chapter One	Early Days	6
Chapter Two	Into CARE	23
Chapter Three	From Iraq to Yemen	47
Chapter Four	An African Trial	63
Chapter Five	Zaire	77
Chapter Six	To Yugoslavia	95
Chapter Seven	Kosovo — Crisis and Response	112
Chapter Eight	Grim Expectations	131
Chapter Nine	Closing Down Kosovo	144
Chapter Ten	NATO's War	157
Chapter Eleven	Arrest	170
Chapter Twelve	The First Twenty-Four Hours	187
Chapter Thirteen	Under Threat of Death	201
Chapter Fourteen	Military Non-Intelligence	218
Chapter Fifteen	The Confession	229
Chapter Sixteen	A New Nightmare	243
Chapter Seventeen	First Light	260
Chapter Eighteen	The Trial	276
Chapter Nineteen	Duty of Care	302
Epilogue		314
Index		319

FOREWORD BY
THE RT HON. MALCOLM FRASER AC CH

This is Steve Pratt's story, told largely through his experiences as a CARE Australia worker providing humanitarian assistance in times of emergency.

Steve's work in northern Iraq, Yemen, Africa and Yugoslavia gives an insight into one aspect of CARE Australia's international operations — that of emergency relief. It is challenging work, sometimes dangerous, always physically and emotionally draining. Witnessing people enduring intolerable hardship, experiencing the trauma of loss, attempting to merely survive another day; this is too often the lot of CARE Australia workers in times of emergency.

That men and women from Australia and around the world are prepared to come forward to work in such conditions and to attempt to provide relief amidst humanitarian distress is worthy of the highest commendation and praise. That there is a need for them and their work is unfortunately self-evident. Somalia, Rwanda, the Congo, Ethiopia, Angola, Bosnia, Albania, Macedonia, Yugoslavia, Iraq — the list goes on. As I write this foreword, CARE Australia is preparing to assist some of the 16 million people facing the threat of starvation in the Horn of Africa. That effort will once again save lives.

While Steve Pratt has experienced the work of CARE Australia in emergency contexts, he has by no means experienced the full breadth of the organisation's activities. He knows little of the work of CARE Australia's long-term development projects in other parts of the world.[1] Steve has not, for instance, been part of CARE's efforts to introduce new cash crops and agricultural methods for impoverished farmers in Vietnam, to protect forests and watersheds through Asia, to address the scourge of HIV/AIDS in Cambodia and the provision of clean water and sanitation facilities in Mozambique and central and southern Iraq. Steve has also not been party to the continuing dialogue between CARE Australia and groups such as AusAID, the World Bank and other major development players — dialogue which often centres around issues such as poverty alleviation, debt relief, good governance practices, gender equity and the promotion of civil society.

Steve Pratt's story is, however, no less real or valid as a result of his lack of involvement in the full gamut of CARE Australia activities. His is not an attempt to reflect on the many and complex factors which give rise to, and perpetuate, the suffering of millions of innocent people. It is instead the story of one Australian. Based on his own experiences, it provides us all with a valuable insight into the reality of those experiences.

The arrest, detention, trial and imprisonment of Steve Pratt, Peter Wallace and Branko Jelen in Yugoslavia in 1999 caught the attention of the world. It was a major focus of Australian public attention throughout the year. That three good men, working to provide aid and assistance to Serbian refugees in Yugoslavia during the lead-up to the early days of war, should be arrested, tried for and convicted of charges relating to espionage, seemed totally inexplicable. Surely, thought many, there must be more to the story. To depart the twentieth century as it had begun, with another war in the Balkans, was itself hard for people to comprehend. But to have three aid workers, two of them Australians, accused of being spies in that conflict — how was that to be explained?

Within the pages that follow, Steve Pratt spells out his own explanation. Read this story and understand that good, ordinary people, undertaking extraordinary humanitarian work, became pawns in a much larger international struggle. For their efforts in providing assistance to those in need, they paid a terrible price.

So what have we learned? What can CARE Australia, all international non-government organisations and the entire international humanitarian community learn from this experience? I offer the following brief thoughts.

Firstly, in a period where the term 'new world order' has quickly gained, and is just as quickly losing, credibility as a concept, regional disorder has become an accepted reality. Our world continues to

FOREWORD

change and to evolve. Much of that change and evolution is painful; often it is chaotic and results in tragic human suffering. While governments and international institutions such as the United Nations respond at an official level, there is a clear and vital role for 'people's organisations' — non-government organisations such as CARE Australia which are strictly neutral. They do not play a role in the implementation of national policies but rather respond to the humanitarian imperative of people caring for one another, wherever we reside on the face of this planet.

During the detention of Steve, Peter and Branko, I was once again humbled as I watched the response of CARE Australia to the needs of the hundreds of thousands of people fleeing the war in Yugoslavia, including Kosovo, and moving into Macedonia and Albania. At a time when CARE Australia management and staff were dealing with the imprisonment of their colleagues and going to extraordinary lengths to secure their release, they were also mounting a huge emergency relief effort. Refugee camps in Macedonia, such as Stenkovic II and Cegrane, were staffed and operated by CARE Australia and served for many months as temporary homes for over 120 000 people. Following the war, many of those same CARE Australia staff accompanied refugees returning to Kosovo and set up programs to assist them as they attempted to re-establish their lives. There is indeed a very real need for organisations such as CARE Australia.

Second, to the men and women who come forward to serve their brothers and sisters in times of need, we owe an obligation of greater protection. Organisations such as CARE Australia will continue to be called on to assist people in areas of conflict, including armed conflict. There is an urgent need for the development and adoption of internationally agreed protocols recognising the impartial, non-political, nonpartisan work of the men and women working with such organisations. I have spoken with the Secretary-General of the United Nations, Kofi Annan, about the need for such protocols. The Secretary-General thoroughly agrees and himself draws attention to, and is greatly alarmed by, the diminishing respect for and protection provided by internationally recognised symbols such as the blue flag of the United Nations and the famous Red Cross and Red Crescent.[2]

Ideally we can work to establish a convention through the United Nations to which all nations will be asked to subscribe, just as they theoretically subscribe to the Geneva Conventions in the conduct of war. The new convention acknowledging the need for protection of humanitarian workers would have criteria which organisations must meet in proving their humanitarian credentials, and may consider a new, internationally recognised common symbol by which they can be identified.

We must act to achieve this level of protection for those who seek only to serve.

The final lesson I will put to you is of my own experience as Chairman of CARE Australia and as the Special Envoy of the Australian Government to Yugoslavia, charged with the task of securing the release of the CARE workers. I witnessed and was part of an extraordinary effort involving close cooperation between CARE Australia management, the Australian Department of Foreign Affairs and the CARE International network. We received advice and assistance from the Serbian community in Australia. I sought and received willing support and intervention from a range of internationally recognised individuals. Such people included former South African President Nelson Mandela, President of Finland Martti Ahtisaari, Secretary-General of the United Nations Kofi Annan and the United Nations' High Commissioner for Refugees Mrs Ogata, to name a few. I am aware of representations to the authorities in Yugoslavia from many different national governments, from Djibouti to China, our own Australian Government, the Governor-General of Australia[3] and many state and regional leaders.

During the period in which we were seeking the release of the three CARE workers, I and others working with me met with anyone who could, with any degree of credibility, claim to exercise some level of meaningful contact or influence with the Government of Yugoslavia. The lesson I offer is that while such contacts are sometimes useful in providing information, it is official representations showing due courtesy and respect for national laws and international protocols which bring about results.

At the end of the day it was the decision of the President of Yugoslavia to grant clemency which resulted in the release of Steve

FOREWORD

Pratt, Peter Wallace and Branko Jelen. There were no secret deals, agreements or commitments. Despite fanciful theories to the contrary, it was adherence to the legal process and the practice of international diplomacy which brought our people home, and in the case of Branko Jelen, to his family's new home in Australia.

I commend to you Steve Pratt's story. It is the story of one man, one humanitarian worker, one captive. While Steve Pratt's story is now confined to these pages, the stories of a thousand more humanitarian workers are being played out as you read, and will continue to be played out for many years to come.

Value life and work for a world of security, human dignity and shared responsibility.[4]

Malcolm Fraser
May 2000

---

[1] CARE Australia currently maintains operations in China, Vietnam, Cambodia, Laos, Myanmar (Burma), Jordan, Yemen, Iraq, Macedonia, East Timor and Yugoslavia. Australia is one of ten member nations which make up CARE International, the others being Austria, Canada, Denmark, France, Germany, Japan, Norway, the United Kingdom and the United States of America. CARE International works in over 60 countries providing relief and development assistance.

[2] See 'Report of the Secretary General to the Security Council on the Protection of Civilians in Armed Conflict', 8 September 1999.

[3] Governor-General Sir William Deane is also the Patron of CARE Australia.

[4] Taken from the CARE Australia Vision of 'A world which values security, human dignity and shared responsibility and promotes the opportunity for people to shape their lives'.

ACKNOWLEDGMENTS

I wish to pay a tribute to Branko and the Jelen family, and to Peter Wallace and the Wallace family (who kindly stayed in touch with Samira throughout), who shared in our terrible ordeal.

Samira, whose dedication and steely determination gave me strength to see the ordeal through, and for her patience, backroom support and measured advice these last four months of writing.

Stuart Pratt, for his tireless campaigning on our behalf, his assistance to my family and his very diligent and detailed background preparation of records of events which contributed to the writing of this book. To Mum and Ian and Liz for remaining so strong and patient, the knowledge of which also helped me worry a little less.

The CARE Australia team: those with whom I had the honour to work in the field these last seven years; the tireless and unthanked souls at Canberra head office, led by Charles Tapp; the team which supported my country office so effectively and then bled for all three of us throughout this debilitating episode. And to the ex and current CARE colleagues who kindly gave me feedback while I wrote, particularly my old field colleague and boss. Also, too, to CARE International their national and country mission offices around the world for their support to us, particularly CARE USA and CARE UK.

Malcolm Fraser for his courageous and determined efforts to secure our release and for his initial encouragement in commencing the book project.

Our British friends Joan and John and Ambassador Mark Heggie and wife Zoe who were relentless in their support for Samira and must have suffered 'burn out' under those extraordinary circumstances. To my first wife Kaye and her husband Geoff who generously took Samira in during the dark days.

Old mates from my youth and the Gosford district, who despite the many years of separation quickly rallied to help, particularly the remarkable Marika Souri, the indefatigable Gabi Hollows and my classmates from Gosford High.

Australian leaders, the Governor-General Sir William Deane, Prime Minister John Howard, Tim Fischer and Alexander Downer, who believed in and pushed the cause and kept up a correspondence with us and our families. Also to Murray Cobban and the wonderful DFAT team who never wavered in their support or their belief in our innocence.

The community of Casino and others of the Northern Rivers who rallied behind my mother and the family.

The Australian Serb community leaders who were to come on board and contribute so importantly to our release.

Class mates from Officer Cadet School, Portsea, and army chums who kindly sought me out on return to reassure me. And so too old mates and mentors Peter Truelove, Bob Singh, Lt Col Peter Murphy who also assisted in the return home and recovery process. And to the many old chums who have called me and who I have failed to get back to in the rush of these past months.

Those media workers who objectively pursued the story and who by their efforts kept the focus on, or then later brought some sanity to the story, particularly Mark Colvin, who was unrelenting in seeking the truth; and Greg Wilesmith, Katy Cronin, Liz Jackson and others.

The many people around the world who prayed in their mosques, churches and temples for us.

Angelo Loukakis for his passionate belief, his wisdom and his hosing down of a sometimes too emotional writer, as well as his willingness to commit Simon & Schuster to the story; Trish Lake for her initial recognition of the story, her literary insight and her guidance in turning it into reality; Sarah Shrubb for her editorial contribution.

And to little Yasmina who during those early days in Budapest kicked her mummy into a better frame of mind. And then later, on my return, focused my recovery.

PROLOGUE

They're coming again, more interrogation probably. It's been at least six hours since the last session, the longest break since I arrived. After five days in here I am dog tired. I have lost weight significantly; my jeans are beginning to slip down. Lost weight through nervous exhaustion and constant fear. Don't mind admitting that most of the time I am shit scared and not feeling particularly brave, nor confident about what I have done or how I am coping. Just plain shit scared. Cannot see a thing in this three-quarter dark, dingy, dank basement cell, nothing to do, nothing to read, plenty of time to think and to be afraid, to ponder on these bastards' threats to do me in. If I disappear will anybody in my family or my organisation, CARE Australia, ever know what has happened to me?

Here they come alright. I recognise the footfalls of the doorman as I call him. He at least smiles, doesn't beat me, feeds me, even seems sympathetic. The keys crashing through three or four locks on two doors, the inner one opaque. Paranoid bastards these military agents. Do they think I have the strength to escape after the way they have worked me over for the last four days? In they come, the two plain-clothes military intelligence goons, torches flashing, taking no chances, their billy clubs at the ready, checking to ensure I am not behind the door. Are they kidding? I am stuffed. And even if I did overpower these three blokes, where am I in Belgrade? Where to run to in broad daylight, holding up my grotty jeans and trying to keep my laceless shoes on? They prod me back to the wall, muttering in Serb. These blokes speak very little English, which is surprising given that I would seem to be their prize captive — doesn't the Yugoslav Military Intelligence have sufficient English-speaking agents to at least provide someone?

I am hooded and handcuffed and this immediately heightens my fear. Jesus, my fear levels spring up and down and all over the place by the hour; can the system put up with this for much longer, I wonder? The two agents guide me out of the cell. Where the hell are they taking me? Is this it? Have they decided I am of little use to them? Are they going to top me, to get me to disappear? They have told me daily I am on the 'missing' list and that I will be lucky to live — but if I co-operate, perhaps I might live, perhaps I will see my family. I sweat heavily. I can hear the pulse belting in my temples at about 160 to the minute. My head is down as I try to keep my balance, try not to trip, try to maintain whatever dignity I have left. I am guided not too gently along a pathway outside the cell and I get the impression I am out in sunlight. No, they wouldn't kill me in the daylight. I know how these regimes work. They take their extrajudicial executions away in the small hours of the night, down to some marshy and forested foreshore along the banks of some river.

Brought into a large office on what appeared to be the third floor of this interrogation centre, I am unhooded. Immediately I recoil from the bright morning light flooding into the place through wide windows. I am seated next to a desk, surrounded by six agents. Opposite me sits Chief, sleeves of his tracksuit top rolled up. Looks like a bloody home-grown friendly GP, but this fatherly appearance masks a sinister, nasty piece of business. Peering owlishly over his half-eye spectacles he hands me a one-page summary, a summary of my so-called confession.

From the corner of my eye I see the one I know as Scarface seated close to me, maybe a metre and a half away, his chair backwards. He is focusing on me intently. On the table next to him and pointed in

PROLOGUE

my direction sits an 8.5mm Mikarov service pistol, standard fare in Eastern European countries. At the doorway is a Police Militia policeman in camouflage blues with an AK47 assault rifle. The guns I know from my military days, but the behaviour is so totally foreign to my experience I wonder if this is really happening to me, Steve Pratt, at all. The others are scattered around the room, chain-smoking and/or chewing gum as usual. All stare at me quietly.

There is an air of expectation. Chief says to me that my life remains in the balance. He demonstrates — as he has ad nauseam over the past four days — what this means. He places one hand vertical to the other, indicating something upright. I must now read and memorise my 'confession' — a summary of four days of interrogation. It is pure unadulterated crap, a fabrication of incredible proportions. I say I refuse, as I have from time to time over the last four days, and Chief says, through a woman interpreter, 'Major Pratt, I am running out of patience. We know you are a spy. You are expected to co-operate and tell the truth. We are not interested in the untruth. If you do not co-operate, Major, I tell you again, I have the discretion and the authority to liquidate you today. These men here will take you away, you will be shot.'

One of them hits me a wide arcing backhander across the side of the face. My right ear rings. It reminds me of being belted in a rugby game, so I fantasise on this and try not to show pain. Another blow comes from behind straight into the back of my head, knocking me forward onto the desk. Both ears are ringing now. I try to stay calm, try to think — what is next, what do I have to assess, what mood am I judging here? I know I am exercising my wits to survive, I feel rightly or wrongly that perhaps death is looming — then think maybe I am overly worried, that it can't happen. I don't know. With four nights of little sleep, I am not thinking too clearly. Whack! Another open-hander straight across the face. Bloody Scarface, the little weasel. I reckon five years younger and I could do him, if it were just him and me.

The miracle is I haven't broken down. I'm just sitting quietly waiting for whatever. Chief breaks the silence: 'Major, as I said to you on our first interrogation, we can either do this the easy way, like gentlemen, or we beat you. Until I decide you will die, that is.' In the distance the air raid sirens start calling in chorus, five or so of them across the city. That mournful, deeply resonating moan, a sound which hasn't changed since World War II. This unfortunately does not break the moment for me. What I am facing is a statement betraying myself, my organisation, and my country. Something which it turns out will become a worldwide televised 'video-confession'.

Blue Uniform cocks his rifle, the clash of metal ringing chillingly across the room. Scarface hits me again. Now my knees are knocking. My breath is coming in short gasps. My ears ring, the sting of the hits lingers. I try with all my determination not to display any fear, but God I am shit scared. At least I do not whimper like a dog, and for this I am extremely grateful. That I am making no sound actually comforts me, so narrow is my focus. I pray to God over and over again, and wonder about the seeming hypocrisy — while I am and have always been a believer, prayer and open worship of the Almighty have never been my strong point. It occurs to me what a strange debate this is to be having with myself at this precise time. Whack! Scarface again, what a mongrel! Will I see Samira again? Haydon, my brave young boy? What about the baby, Samira's pregnancy? Mum — God she'll drop dead with shock! And there is Chief, peering at me very closely, watching me over his half-glasses.

How the hell did I, Steve Pratt, CARE Australia country director for CARE International operations in federal republic Yugoslavia, wind up in this incredible mess? On the 'missing' list, hidden away in one of many military camps around the country, with NATO air raids in progress around the clock and facing what appears to be a fairly short-term program to death? In the hands of a ruthless bunch of military intelligence people and secret police who know nothing about CARE International — and could care even less — but who themselves are in fear of the bombing, indeed extremely angered by the bombing and seeking their revenge.

I had no time to consider such a question then, while I was being brutalised and interrogated and living from moment to moment. Only since my release and being reunited with my family in Australia have I been able to reflect on and try to make some sense of my experience. The pages which follow represent my record of the events as well as my attempt to come to terms with them. After I began this process late in 1999, I came to understand that I cannot tell of the predicaments or the triumphs of 1999 without going back to the beginnings and tracing the steps, one at a time.

CHAPTER ONE

Early Days

I grew up in a rather old-fashioned way, wanting to serve my country. I was influenced from an early age, I am sure, by my father's sense of service and duty, as well as by his strong belief in pursuing justice. Having developed a keen sense of duty fairly early in life, I first pursued a professional army officer's career and then, twenty-three years later, moved into international aid work, work increasingly associated with international human rights. Perhaps it was the collision of these values with the circumstances I found myself in while working with CARE Australia that was to land me in some of the dramatic events of more recent years.

Born and raised on the northern NSW coast, my early years were spent in country New South Wales when it was still largely bush. My father was the Deputy Shire Clerk of Grafton Shire, apparently serving with distinction during the terrible floods of '54. I can still recall, over many nights during the floods, Dad coming home late in the evenings to my anxious mum. He made quite an impression on the little fellow that I was in his grey felt hat and heavy raincoat, dripping water all over the house. The mighty Clarence had broken its banks and Ben Pratt was out with the men, although I had no idea what he was up to. Dad was transferred to Gosford as Deputy

Shire Clerk again in 1958 and so we all moved, my two brothers, Mum and I excitedly travelling down on the old Grafton Flyer, one of the fastest steam trains in the country, to meet Dad, who had gone ahead.

My brothers and I for years maintained very close contact with our relations up in the Northern Rivers district, and two to three times a year we would travel north to stay with Grandma, Dad's mother, in Casino. We always loved going north, and well into our young teens we still preferred to see ourselves as Northern Rivers boys. Grandma was a solid Presbyterian church lady whose gentleness and lovely dry humour were underlaid with a solid foundation of old Scottish ethics, particularly fairness and integrity. Many of her values were to rub off on me — or at least I have strived to live up to them, with mixed success, through my life.

Grandma and the gaggle of families that made up the Pratt, Gillett and the more distant Boyd clans of the Northern Rivers strongly influenced my upbringing. They were people who had pioneered the then 'wild' country, settling from the Tweed to the Clarence. As boys we would sit around on warm Casino evenings (before television had arrived on the scene to turn our brains to mush), yarning to Grandma, and listening to her stories about the families. The only family member she was reticent about was her husband, Grandad Bede, who had died almost immediately after the Great War. It was years later that I was to piece together the incredible story of Bede Pratt. The Boyds had settled on the Tweed as cedar-getters in 1838. They settled in the 'Big Scrub', the great forest that Captain Cook had remarked on in his log during his passage northwards. Here the Boyds cut the mighty trees along the Richmond and its tributaries, floating them down for collection. The Boyds owned land in Sydney. John had a lovely 100 acres of orchard at old Turramurra; they also owned a large timber mill down on the harbour which received this beautiful cedar, much of which lines the grand old sandstone buildings in Sydney to this day. Old Tom Pratt, a convict who had gained his trusteeship comparatively quickly in the 1820s, was to move to the Hunter, farming and then running horse stock there and later in the New England country. His descendants, George Pratt and his sons, would eventually move down from the tablelands into the

Northern Rivers, take up farming and marry into the Boyd family, by then well established. The Gilletts, my mother's ancestors, of Huguenot French/Irish background (they fled to Ireland in 1610) had settled along the Clarence in the 1840s as boatbuilders, and were to become well known in New South Wales in boating and seafaring businesses. The sloop *Kathleen Gillett*, now on display at the Maritime Museum, was typical of the Gillett creations.

Grandma knew a little of this history. Years later, inspired by her yarns, I was to track down much of the detail through my father. He finally agreed to put together a useful manuscript, 'Tales of the Pratts', about those pioneers. Wonderful old Norm Keats, my Dad's cousin, was my other source. He wrote an incisive text about the early history of the Northern Rivers and pioneering families, titled 'Wollumbi'.

I took enormous pride in these families and all the other pioneering families of the north. Their lives and values were important touchstones for me as I grew and developed my own sense of who and what I wanted to be. Of particular influence was my grandfather, Bede, who had landed at Gallipoli with the 9th Battalion of the 3rd Brigade (I was to realise years later that this battalion was the first battalion ashore and suffered terrible casualties on that fateful first day). He was wounded in the late afternoon of the day that was to become known as Anzac Day, but returned to see out the campaign. The official war record painting depicts my grandfather's company storming the heights on Anzac Day. He went on to France and served in some very difficult actions, which are recorded in the battalion history. Grandad came home to Casino very ill, but continued his job as a stockman. Ever the larrikin, he even continued his famous habit of riding his horse on Saturday afternoons into the South Casino pub. Bede, however, was to die within a year or so of his return from the Great War.

My father, like so many fine young men of the Northern Rivers, went off to New Guinea in 1943, where he fought with the 9th Division at Milne Bay and then south of Kokoda. He was to become seriously ill in that terrible place, and after three long years he too came home in very poor shape. Like many veterans, Dad had become a heavy smoker in those jungles, and along with recurring bouts of malaria, he was often ill through the years because of that. Dad did not suffer fools, and was always keen to pursue the truth. In 1961, as Deputy Shire Clerk, he blew the whistle on corrupt practices in the Gosford Shire and became a state witness in the state-run inquiry into Gosford Council. The entire council was stood down and a number of the officers of the executive were suspended as a consequence of that inquiry. My father, who had to make moral decisions about where he stood in relation to what he had uncovered, was under immense pressure for almost eighteen months, the length of the inquiry. This pressure was not to dissipate when the affair was over — he had to carry the baggage for years.

We were very proud of Dad and admired his no nonsense approach, despite getting the occasional boot in the bum. This admiration carried right through the years when Dad ran the shire as Shire Clerk. Although he spent little time with the family — he was too taken up with his job — we knew he was widely respected as a good administrator and a wise counsellor on all matters to do with the Shire, golf and rugby. As my father watched my developing keenness for the military during my formative years, his great fear was that I would go off to the Vietnam War. I did have a desire to go — not that I told him — as I wanted to follow in his and Grandad's footsteps.

In those early years in Gosford we boys, Stuart, Ian and I, were blessed with good mates in our neighbourhood — the Baileys and the Plumbs — and together we raised merry hell. Our sister Liz, the youngest of us all, had unfortunately to suffer this male-dominated circus. We were also blessed with an abundance of bush. The hills around East Gosford where we lived were our playground as little kids and remained so up into our junior teens. The bush was marvellous, and we had kilometres of it, ridgelines and valleys, to run up and down. We built forts, outposts and secret trails through the place, and threw rocks and threepenny bungers wrapped in clay at those rotten kids from West Gosford who dared to breach our territory. We were very privileged, I believe, compared with the young these days. We lived among wildlife and developed a healthy respect, admiration and I think love for nature and the Australian bush. Dad was forever taking us on weekend picnics up into areas of further adventure in the high country west of Gosford, in the region of Mt Mangrove — we often found Aboriginal carvings and boiled the billy on the banks of Mangrove or Poplan Creek. Pushed on by both Mum and Dad, I learnt at an early age to draw and paint (they reckon I had a talent). On some of Dad's inevitable weekend picnics (he was passionate about the bush, Australian folklore and poetry) I would paint watercolour bush landscapes, my favourite medium and subject. While they were pretty ordinary and probably had Stu and Ian in stitches, I grew to love the habit.

During my formative years, and like many other young people, I looked up to and was influenced by the likes of Robert Menzies and Roden Cutler, by the exploits of Churchill and other wartime heroes and great Australians — pioneers, pioneer airmen and community leaders. At school my interests ran to history, English (in which I did well), rugby league and cricket, while maths and science fell by the wayside; from age thirteen the School Cadets also loomed large among my interests.

All the kids in our little cadet unit had a great time; we learnt much about teamwork, leadership, dealing with 'mother nature's' adversities. We took on physical challenges, personal discipline in all of its positive meanings, and were encouraged to respect and take responsibility for people and property. I rose through the ranks over the years so that by the time I left school I had reached the dizzying heights of Cadet Under Officer. I was also, in my later teen years, to join the local citizens' military forces (CMF) Support Company 17 Battalion, Gosford Depot. The atmosphere in which we trained as young part-time soldiers back then was of course dominated by the Vietnam War. Our weekends were spent manoeuvring in the hills around Gosford. Sometimes around the edges of Gosford Golf Club, scaring the bejesus out of golfers (including Mum, who was a great golfer and captain of the club's ladies' team). Springing out of the tea tree scrub on the edge of the fourteenth hole firing blanks, on our way to clean out the 'Vietcong bunker' dominating the thirteenth hole. On one occasion, after a magnificently executed platoon attack, Mum unfortunately recognised me, resplendent in my baggy 'jungle greens' ('camou' had not been invented); despite my face being daubed in black tree soot, she knew who it was and chased me off the fairway, shaking an eight iron.

Youthful pranks aside, we were growing to be serious young men then, patriotic and committed to our country. Those were the years when there was much talk about the 'Domino Effect', a theory about political phenomena which proposed that there was a threat to all the countries of South-East Asia through the advances of communism. It was argued that a wide range of communist insurgencies springing up like wildfires through the late 1950s, 1960s and carrying through to 1970 were being co-ordinated at the geopolitical level through a Russian/Chinese/North Korean/North Vietnamese conspiracy. Socialist movements in democratic countries were seen to be a part of that conspiracy. There was certainly then abundant evidence of deep sympathies towards these regimes in the Western socialist movements, including within the communist and socialist movements of Australia, but there was no evidence then (nor has it surfaced since) to suggest any co-ordinated strategic tie-in between Western (and Australian) political movements and the communist world aimed at bringing about an Asia/Pacific takeover. There was a fair degree of paranoia about the issue in those days, but while the dominoes did not fall, a communist takeover was the perceived threat of that day. My later teens and early adolescence had as a backdrop this climate of concern, as well as the ongoing debate about whether the United States, Australia and their allies should have become involved in the Vietnam War (confronting the line of falling dominoes, as it was seen).

The political fallout resulting from our involvement in the war — the demonstrations and political attacks against our own country, its establishments, its soldiers, the portrayal of ours as 'a divided society' — was for me profoundly disturbing, and it made me angry. I was enormously proud of the Australian Army's involvement and its conduct in that war, despite the farce and sad comedy of the prosecution of the war by the Americans. One thing was abundantly clear to me: until the point when it became untenable for the Australian force to continue in Vietnam, the Australians had achieved all their military and political aims in the provinces allocated to them, including the curtailment of terror and the improvement in the lives of the communities there. Military infrastructure in the south, however, was another issue.

I graduated from Gosford High School in 1968, not to see some of my schoolmates again for years to come. It would be with a bursting heart that in June 1999 I would read of the campaign put together by Marika Souri, an old classmate from Gosford Primary and then High School, as well as Clark and many others, in support of my release from Belgrade prison. But back then I went off to the Officer Cadet School at Portsea, where I joined the Australian Regular Army, at the time a lean, fit and very professional army. The army had been continuously deployed in South-East Asia since the Korean War of the 1950s, fighting one insurgency after another, in support of Australia's neighbours. Officers and soldiers were then uncompromisingly tough and I thought it an honour to be selected to undertake officer training.

I had my ups and downs and nearly did not survive the first two months of training. I thought as an ex-CMF soldier I knew it all, but I most certainly did not. I remember facing my company commander in the first six weeks and being told by him that it appeared I was 'not up to it'. Before his unrelenting gaze it was humiliating to be told that I was a heartbeat away from getting thrown out of the college. I had to really take stock of myself, and with the strong support of classmates I managed to pull through that first orientation phase.

After that, I did not look back. We forged close bonds at the college. Our first and ferocious encounter with a tough senior class man was with one Les Hiddens, a Vietnam veteran who would later become famous as ABC TV's irrepressible 'Bush Tucker Man'. Harry Healey (Damian) was a very close and supportive mate and another good soldier. Greg Platt, something of a rebel as a cadet, became a damn good officer and, years later, CARE Australia's deputy project manager in Cambodia.

Training in the winter conditions of Portsea peninsula, without respite from the blowing winds and rains straight up from the South Pole, and then being driven on for more by very tough men, was incredibly beneficial. The emphasis placed on physical endurance would stand me in good stead. Whenever I felt down or was facing

EARLY DAYS

adversity I would often think back to those Portsea days and remind myself to buck up, to get a grip. This memory would play an important and sometimes vital role in my eventual ordeal in Serbia. Supremely fit, full of jumping beans and ready to take on the communist enemies of democracy, I was off and running.

I graduated and was posted to the 6th Infantry Battalion, Royal Australian Regiment, then based in Townsville. The battalion had just returned from its second tour of South Vietnam. I found myself at barely twenty years of age commanding a platoon of twenty-five mostly veteran Vietnam fighters. It was one of the most defining moments of my life, and a challenge with which I struggled. I had very good non-commissioned officers — that is, sergeants and corporals — and they carried me in many ways and for a long time in that battalion. We trained hard in the tropical heat of North Queensland, and got used to patrolling in the rugged high country that dominated that part of the world. This was the old army still. Few trucks, few armoured vehicles to carry soldiers and few bloody choppers. It was a walking army, and a fat soldier in the 1960s and early 1970s was a rare sight. The Australian Army had for thirty years walked the length and breadth of the rugged mountain ranges of South-East Asia, East Asia and the Pacific. I would ponder often on the absence of trucks as we would hike it for another 20 kilometres or so with the kitchen sink on our backs. They were good days.

The 6th Battalion went to Singapore for garrison duties and was to remain there for two years. In my second year with the battalion my professional performance suffered and I found myself distracted by the wonderful new experiences associated with living in Singapore. The rugby is good, as is the cricket, and we threw ourselves into sport with a gusto. I was by now a Rugby Union convert, and greatly enjoyed playing night matches on the Padang, in the centre of town, beers on the sideline and then over to the old Raffles for yet more post-match beers. Then down to the colourful 'car park' makan stalls near the 'Cold Storage' for a bowl of noodles. The music of the day for me was the Beach Boys, Santana and Mick Jagger's 'Brown Sugar'. 'Santana Abraxas' album was the most magical of all and became my favourite for all time. It was a great life. Rich Singaporean girls with their father's patronage at the Singapore Cricket Club, the discos of Orchard Road and the balmy colourful relaxed mood of tropical living. I had my old $500 1959 Jaguar, an old ex-Brit estate car, and a flashy batik shirt made down at Changi shops by Fong Yu the tailor for five bucks. Not to mention a pair of wretched powder blue, high-waisted, ridiculously flared bum-hugging disco trousers (locally made of course), bought for about seven bucks. While I was careful to keep out of trouble, this life nevertheless took its toll. Crashing back to earth I was posted earlier than expected out of the battalion, a very disappointing experience, and returned to Australia, where I moved to the Recruit Training Battalion at Wagga Wagga in the Riverina. Not Singapore, but the best thing that could have happened. Stung by the shame of being disciplined, I decided to pull up my socks.

On promotion to Captain, in early January 1975, I was posted to the 5th/7th Battalion Royal Australian Regiment. Within hours of arriving at Holsworthy I was thrown onto a Hercules by the battalion second in command, Phil Davies. From there I was flown to Darwin, where the battalion had been since it had been urgently mustered and dispatched around Christmas in response to the devastating Cyclone Tracy. I was to spend three months there as an acting Company Commander commanding 130 troops providing administrative and logistical support to the battalion. This was to be another one of those defining moments in my professional career. A brand new captain thrown into the deep end of a major's job. I make the most of it and professionally find the experience very rewarding, as much as one is able to amid the devastation of cyclone-flattened Darwin. I shared accommodation (a half-ruined dormitory room) with the company commander of A Company, Captain Peter Cosgrove MC. He was about three years senior to me and awaiting imminent promotion to major. Over the next year and a half I was to mainly work indirectly with Peter, though occasionally closely with him, which was always interesting and a good learning experience. He was a role model for all the captains and lieutenants in the battalion — a gentleman, tough but fair, and pretty clever. He loved his rugby and when it was not time to be serious he had an effervescent sense of humour. In Darwin he whipped his new company into shape, as we all did our various companies. The battalion performed magnificently and tens of thousands of house sites were cleared, the area cleaned and prepared for the return of the evacuated community. We worked six and a half days a week, my job being primarily to provide the vehicles and other resources to the companies, and ensure that all logistical support was available to the troops.

I was soon involved in armoured vehicle training, preparing the battalion to convert from its traditional walking role to a mechanised role. The whole battalion of 780 troops was to be equipped with armoured vehicles, with the officers and soldiers trained in new tactical and technical skills associated with armoured operations. This involved battalion second in command Ian Guild and me visiting the United States at the end of 1975, to study US Army mechanised battalion theory and practice. The battalion became mechanised, and over a further year under our new Commanding Officer, Lieutenant Colonel Murray Blake MC (who some wily and clever soldier good-naturedly called 'Blake the Snake', because he did not let the soldiers get away with any tricks), the battalion perfected new battle and manoeuvre concepts. Murray Blake, when he strutted around the battlefield, reminded me of that Colonel in the movie *Apocalypse Now* who says, 'I just love the smell of napalm in the morning.' He cracked the whip, and over the year the battalion was forged into a new fighting force — the soldiers loved him.

Over the next few years, postings were to Headquarters First Task Force and then to the Adelaide University Regiment. A significant event for me was the CHOGM security operation of 1978. In response to the Hilton Hotel bombing incident in which two council workers and a policeman were killed, another policeman and a garbage collector grieviously wounded, Prime Minister Malcolm Fraser called out the troops, the first such emergency in Australia for many years. I was the staff officer responsible for air support operations, and for the first time in my life I had the strange experience of carrying arms in the streets of western Sydney. My Headquarters was responsible for co-ordinating and commanding the movement of 3000 troops to cover and secure the expressway from western Sydney to Bowral, in the southern highlands. There were no further incidents, but for the best part of a week we had been well and truly on our toes, charged with preventing any assassination attempts on the lives of the Commonwealth's Prime Ministers.

In 1979, posted as Adjutant to the Adelaide University Regiment (AUR), I enjoyed the responsibility for the training of university student officer cadets, members of the Army Reserve. It was here I met my first wife, Kaye. By the end of the year we were living together and we married in 1981. We had some very happy years in Adelaide. We travelled through the wineries regularly, and to the Hahndorf hills, a time of very pleasant socialising. Kaye is a very determined woman and she proceeded with officer cadet training, which she completed in Sydney a couple of years later. Meanwhile I was now married, had just been promoted to a new position in Papua New Guinea, and was about to embark on a path of 'middle management' in my army career.

In January 1982 I was posted to the 2nd Battalion, Pacific Island Regiment (2PIR), a Papua New Guinea Defence Force (PNGDF) unit in Wewak. Promoted to major, I was appointed Operations Officer — practically speaking, senior adviser to the Papua New Guinean Commanding Officer. We were 150 kilometres from the border with the Indonesian territory of Irian Jaya, and 2PIR was the PNGDF unit then responsible for border security in the troublesome zone on the northern side of PNG.

2PIR patrols were in constant contact with Free Papua Movement (OPM) rebel groups along the border. These were rebels from Irian Jaya who would seek safe haven on the PNG side. The OPM rebels were not a nice bunch at all, certainly not the romantic lot they were portrayed as by idealists in Australia at the time. They did, however, pursue a noble cause. It was clear from where we stood that the Indonesian 'transmigration' of hundreds of thousands of Javanese into Irian Jaya was having a devastating effect on both the country and the West Papuan culture. The Australian Government at the time turned a blind eye and said nothing.

The Indonesians would often come over the border in 'hot pursuit', and this would be chaotic for the local citizens. Both OPM and Indonesian forces would steal from the gardens of the locals, taking from their essential livelihood. We were constantly monitoring both OPM and Indonesian movement on our side of the border to protect the local inhabitants as best we could. Our patrols were too weak to pick a fight with the Indonesians, who operated in company-sized groups (around 100 men). Frankly, the PNGDF was in no position to pick a fight with the Indonesian forces operating along the border regions of Irian Jaya. The best we could do, therefore, was maintain a patrolling presence and hope to deter the movement of these interlopers. Our patrols witnessed atrocities committed by both Indonesians and OPM against local civilians and by the Indonesians against OPM and their civilian followers. Indonesian 'Ranger Battalion' patrols would cut off the heads of OPM rebels killed, and we thought, from the evidence available to us, that most rebels were killed — they were not captured unless they were considered important. The heads were carried back to Jaya Pura, their base for border operations, for bounty collections. Ranger Battalion patrols were thus often seen carrying copra bags, apparently for this purpose. Such was the crude administration of justice by the colonising forces in Irian Jaya.

For the next three years, for my sins, I was posted to Army Office (Department of Defence) at Russell Hill in Canberra. This place was headquarters for the Australian Army. Ripped out of the jungles of Papua New Guinea, I found myself shining a chair in the bureaucracy which is Defence — a hell of a transition. I quickly appreciated the difficulty of administering a defence force within the constraints which typify the Australian political scene. While army officers, particularly infantry types such as myself, tended to deride Defence public servants and even career army staff officers who excel in these places, I soon began to understand that things were not that simple. However, I never fell in love with the unwieldy bureaucracy that was and still is Defence in this country.

Kaye and I bought our first house in the suburb of Latham, and we had a lot of fun developing the place. In 1984 our son Haydon was born. In this period, while serving in Canberra, I was to attend the US Army's Logistics Staff College at Fort Lee, Virginia USA. As the first Australian student to attend a 'Matériel Acquisition and Management' course (as only the Americans could describe and title it), I was also to find myself the only foreigner on the course, indeed the first one accepted by the college for this particular course. There were three other Australians — two students and one exchange instructor — in the place as well. I was a bit of an oddity on this course, in a group of sixty-four civilian public servants, military captains, majors and colonels. I was to become the course mascot. It was a great time and a very useful one professionally — although the taking home to my own army of 1000 rote-learnt American acronyms was no great achievement. Six months later I graduated with a B1 pass and speaking like a goddammed American. Kaye and little Haydon were to join me for a surprisingly pleasant tour of the States (something I had never before envisaged). I had picked up a broad range of logistical skills which would serve me well in the army postings which were to follow, and also later in aid work. Ironically though, during my imprisonment in Belgrade in 1999, my captors would cynically accuse me of attending this military course for CIA training.

In 1987 I was transferred back to Sydney, this time for service with the Sydney University Regiment, where I spent three years in a rewarding job, rubbing shoulders with the famous 'Rum Corps'. The Rum Corps is the quaint term for the old 'Sydney Order', that part of society that has its roots in the administrative, legal and military elements of early colonial Sydney life. No convicts in these ranks. The students and officers of the regiment were undergraduates or past graduates of the university, with a strong presence in the ranks of law students and lawyers. Kaye and I had rented a house in Turramurra, about 45 minutes by train from the university. Being the keen young infantry major I was, I would each morning 'train it' halfway and walk the rest of the way to the regiment, carrying a heavy pack for endurance training. It took about an hour. It was at this time too that I joined the Liberal Party, South Turramurra Branch, the president of which, a larrikin by the name of Peter Truelove, became a firm friend and mentor. My decision to join a political party was at that time rather strange for an army officer. Army officers tend to feel they must demonstrate political neutrality, as part of their professional persona, and I think that is by and large the right approach. Personally, I had always been a bit of a political agitator and political moaner. It seemed to me at the time that the country was losing its way, educationally and socially. There were also questions on Australia's defence policy and foreign policy brewing away. These were matters passionately close to my heart, although ones I knew that as a serving army officer I could do little about publicly. Most political parties to me were the same, but it seemed then that the Liberal party philosophy was closer to my thinking than any of the alternatives.

In 1989 I was preselected by the Liberal Party to campaign against the federal member for Banks (in south-west Sydney), Darryl Melham. We campaigned for a full year in that seat, and with a solid core of forty volunteers made good headway, campaigning in any one of the seven shopping centres each Saturday morning and forever doorknocking. But the house came down, at least in terms of the Banks campaign, when Howard was rolled by Peacock for the federal opposition leadership in late May 1989. Peacock was not nearly as respected by the swinging voters of Banks as Howard had been. Howard was then, in my opinion, very appealing to the war veterans and a significant batch of voters of other persuasions. In early 1990 we lost the campaign. We managed, however, to achieve a swing of 2 per cent, something to be proud of, given that there was a 2 per cent swing against the federal liberals in New South Wales and a 2.5 per cent swing against them nationally.

The most shattering and bitter experience of this period of my life, however, was my separation from my wife and son. The toll of electioneering, the incredible personal burden of Hawke and Keating's 18 per cent interest rates and my foolish pre-occupation with work/politics over marriage brought our marriage down. Kaye and Haydon moved away, and I reacted by hurling myself deeper into my soldiering and political campaigning. Our 6-year-old boy was confused and very unhappy; he was the true victim of our rupturing disagreements. I was to experience that 'knife through the chest' feeling of guilt each time I subsequently looked into the little boy's big, confused blue eyes. While irretrievably separated, I was to be grateful that Kaye and I quickly buried our differences and unlimited access to my boy was allowed.

In late 1991 the Government decided that our already sadly depleted defence force needed to be cut further. Administrative and logistics services had been slowly privatised over recent years and a number of heavy rear echelon units had disappeared from the organisational chart. Some of these privatisation and subcontracting initiatives had made sense, although I was still dubious. But I thought now, in 1991 through 1992, that the Government was simply going too far. Defence capability was being cut to the bone; this sort of capability had taken decades to acquire, to build, and would not be able to be reinstated quickly should the need ever arise (which proved to be the case in 1999 for East Timor).

Land Command seemed to me the only sane part of the Defence Force left, and I was enjoying my soldiering there. However, and despite my great love for the army, I was tired of the deaf ear being turned by politicians of all colours to our good commanders. And I was tired of the kowtowing of some of our senior officers to the Government. I retired. At age forty-three it was also the right time, if I was going to undertake a transition to civilian life and find a meaningful role for myself elsewhere.

I then immediately went to work as a logistics consultant for a commercial company named AVIO, a company which was well established throughout South-East and East Asia in the airport infrastructure building and support business. They had decided to get involved in running a logistics support service for the Cambodia UN transition authority, UNTAC, and were responding to a tender that had been called. By word of mouth they had heard of my military logistics experience and my involvement in staff officer work relative to Cambodia. They rightly assumed that I could help them, and I did. I had an invigorating eight months with the company, which included for me the strange experience of working from my own home, my little flat in Woollahra. I would travel to head office in Melbourne for planning sessions and do the 'think tanking' at home. I had plenty of good mates in the military who kindly helped me out with the finer technical details, which I was then able to plug into my new work.

In October 1992, only days after retiring from the force, I flew off to Cambodia with the AVIO MD to conduct a reconnaissance and liaison exercise with the UN logistics staff. The objective was to establish a vehicle fleet support service for the UN civilian vehicle fleet, which numbered 6000 four-wheel drives scattered all over the country, including in some of the more isolated and dangerous northern and north-west provinces. We had put together a very good but not cheap plan incorporating the deploying and building of a base workshop, a series of field workshops and mobile repair teams. It was an organisation unashamedly designed along military lines, the only sort of organisation that was ever going to work under those conditions. In Phnom Penh the MD and I found ourselves arguing the toss with the UN people over fairly essential issues; our outline concept had impressed the UN logistics people but they sought to screw us down on fundamentals. This was my first dealing with the UN and I did not much like what I saw. It was apparent to me that their approach ran only as far as providing ridiculouly small and meaningless budgets for very serious affairs — token 'tick the box' efforts which would be meaningless on the ground.

AVIO decided that we would plough on with the project proposal, the preparation of the tender bid, but we had to wait months for any response. We continued to finetune the plan and regularly responded to UNTAC queries, confident that we were the best of the rumoured five bidders. In Sydney on his fleeting visits home I would meet Bob Singh, one of the directors and partners of AVIO. It seemed to me he was constantly in the air pursuing business. I found myself therefore often briefing Bob on the golf course. He was a fanatical golfer, had very little free time and so between flights in and out we would squeeze in a game or two and discuss business at the same time. Bob was an emotional golfer. Gruff and always in a hurry, he was a real dynamo, an ideas man, with a broad knowledge of business and political issues across the whole of the region.

Working with AVIO was a starkly new and interesting experience. As it turned out, we were not successful in the tender, and in April 1993 we ceased wasting our time. Nobody won the tender. Curiously, UNTAC decided they would cancel the plan and have no country-wide support services but instead would rely on the Japanese Government to replace all vehicles as they broke down. This struck me as terribly wasteful and a misuse of valuable and scarce donor-provided resources. I was to reflect some years later (this was not consciously apparent in 1992/1993) that the valuable

AVIO experience was a bridge from my military life to the new world of emergency humanitarian work. I had taken military logistics experience and skills with me and applied them to a commercial company seeking to undertake a humanitarian support program; this had probably imbued in me the notion that old soldiers like me could make very worthwhile contributions in the field of emergency humanitarian work.

CHAPTER TWO

Into CARE

Within a week of finishing with AVIO I had answered a job advertisement for CARE Australia, looking at a position for an 'Operations Manager'. Operations management seemed to me relatively close to my experience profile. The advertisement mentioned that the position required some logistics experience — something I had — and would be in CARE's operation in either Yugoslavia or northern Iraq. This was a time when CARE Australia was expanding quite rapidly. I knew a little about CARE Australia, and while I did not initially think that humanitarian work was absolutely my cup of tea, I had sufficient understanding of the type of work to know a field managerial position would be a meaty and challenging one. I enjoyed management, I very much enjoyed working in the field; after all, I mused, that had been my entire working life. While I felt compassion towards those in desperate plight around the world, I frankly had little time for some I had seen in the humanitarian business; generally there seemed to me too many idealists who were naive in political and practical terms. I did, however, respect the business of getting humanitarian aid out to where it was needed, having seen this in action regularly over the years during my military experience.

It seemed to me that the type of managerial challenges, resource management exercises, planning and problem-solving in humanitarian organisations such as CARE Australia were, conceptually speaking, very similar to those in the business of soldiering. That was part of the attraction. Serving overseas too, and being able to run an operation that was going to do some practical good and perhaps save lives also very much appealed to me at the time; it also appealed to my old-fashioned sense of adventure, of which I had an abundance. I proceeded with the application.

I was interviewed, and then, at seven that night I received a phone call indicating that I had been accepted and asking whether I could move within the week! They were desperate. In a weak moment — and I think possibly pulled by some siren song promising adventure — I said yes. I agreed to a six-month contract, stored everything and went away with CARE for six and a half years.

After various briefings, orientations and meetings, I arrived in northern Iraq about 30 May 1993. We were briefed in Jordan by the CARE Australia Middle East Office, CARE Australia's regional office then in charge of four Middle East missions, if you were to include the north and the south of Iraq as two. This four-day holdover was fascinating for me, my first ever taste of the Middle East. A trip to Petra, in the south of the country, while waiting for our visas to be approved for entry to Iraq, to see the marvellous ruins and deeply significant religious sites, was a memorable experience. As a keen student of history, ancient and modern, I was up to my armpits in it there. The Roman amphitheatre in Amman, the capital of Jordan, and the Roman ruins at Jurash, north-east of the city, were my first sightings of ancient ruins in the northern hemisphere. These were the ruins of civilisations which to me have been the most important to ponder. Dressed for the occasion in chino dungarees, rough bush shirt, Akubra and boots I felt right in my element.

With a band of ten or so new CARE recruits I crossed the great Iraqi desert, keen to get at it. The human resources office had promised me a program officer's job in Amman, running assistance for the Kurds, and I was told I might be looked at for management positions later on in my contract. I was satisfied with that, happy to fit in anywhere. A contract of six months was not too long if it all turned out to be a farce, I thought.

I travelled across the desert with a motley crew of good people, most of whom I was to establish close friendships with, friendships as close as I had experienced anywhere else. As we motored across the desert, 1000 kilometres to Baghdad, I became friendly with a pharmacist, Trevor, from South Australia, who was to take responsibility for the management of the medical warehouse that CARE would run on behalf of the UN children's fund (UNICEF). He would end up, however, taking up a logistics position in Suleimaniyah. Trevor's introduction to the desert and the Middle East was a severe case of Delhi Belly for the entire journey across that inhospitable, featureless and billiard table-flat desert. Poor Trevor needed to stop on the hour every hour, and it was 40°C all the way. His stoicism and unfailing sense of humour, perspiring and ashen-faced though he was, were admirable. We were soon to find out that his misfortune would be nothing unusual. Sickness of this kind was to become a commonplace affair among the Australian team, living as we were under less than ideal conditions.

On the afternoon of the second day of our demanding journey, and with Trevor still pretty sick, we arrived at the line of control, about 20 kilometres west of Erbil. For fifteen or so kilometres as we raced across the plains towards Erbil we had passed heavy concentrations of Iraqi military forces. This was for all of us a very sobering sight. These quite impressive forces, made up of tanks, artillery, infantry units and anti-aircraft batteries (Kurds did not have aircraft but the Western coalition forces did), were in position facing the line of control. At Aski-Kalak we passed under watchful, suspicious, hostile eyes as we crossed the river marking the frontier, driving past the burnt-out wreck of a destroyed truck draped against the bridge railing (apparently left there by the Iraqis for decoration and as a warning).

On the other side we were met by about thirty of CARE's Peshmerga guards, our first sighting of these impressive warriors — and warriors they were, as war was what they lived for. They greeted us warmly and with great curiosity. We noticed that many of their number were not on the road with us but up in the tree line above, manning their weapons and carefully watching the Iraqis on the heights dominating the other side of the river. Very tense, very watchful, but not melodramatic. Seeing so many armed men was another jolting and sobering step in our initiation. Nobody in our briefings along the journey from Canberra (or in Canberra) had ever explained the reality of this heavy fighter presence, and I wondered what the other members of my party thought about it all.

We arrived in Erbil, the capital of Kurdish (northern) Iraq. We were all spellbound. Old concrete Middle Eastern houses, some of them quite grand, amidst broken and run-down streets. Inquisitive Kurdish children were all about us. And the guards — guards were everywhere, by the dozens, surrounding us. They were an intimidating sight for most of the new Australian staff, who I am sure were wondering what the hell they had let themselves in for. We then went on north to the outer suburban village of Ain-Kawa, our eyes bulging out of our heads. This was the home of the United Nations/ Non-Government Organisation (NGO) community, a veritable fortress. Guards, sandbagged walls, barbwire everywhere. My colleagues, totally buggered after another hot day's drive, were silent as we approached the CARE Australia headquarters.

We met the project manager, a man in his mid-thirties whom I thought too young for this mission. I had known him years earlier. He was a clever fellow, deeply committed to humanitarian operations, a bit of an adventurer. He had climbed in the Himalayas — and during a quiet moment months later I was to discover that he had had some seriously dangerous and life-threatening experiences there. This was his second tour to northern Iraq. I was to change my mind about him very quickly — he was a capable and effective project manager doing an unenviable task. He took us up the stairs of this large concrete block-style building, which was crudely built, but clean and spacious. We sat on hard metal chairs in a circle in his large sparse office and he briefed us ten new chums, bluntly. He indicated we would all for the first month be attached to various mission teams for orientation and to see where we might best fit into the team. The program manager, as mission head, briefed us on the mission that afternoon. His grip on minute detail over this very broad and challenging mission was impressive, and he demonstrated to me and the others (we of course all compared notes in the corner of the bar that night) that he had a clear and strong conviction about where he and we as a team ought to be going. A fairly intense, no nonsense bloke, his rather eloquently worded but precise briefing of the general humanitarian operation was regularly laced with references to security and safety. He was very blunt about the latter; clearly these were issues which worried him, as much as his concerns that the mission achieve its humanitarian objectives and do it in a 'best practices' fashion.

The CARE Australia objectives in northern Iraq were to sustain the severely disadvantaged members of the Kurdish community, across the whole of the Kurdish north, by providing food, heating oil (in the winter) and medical supplies. The Kurdish beneficiaries CARE was directly or indirectly benefiting numbered about five million people, a population seriously incapable of sustaining itself. The fledgling Kurdish Coalition Government, appointed under UN patronage, lacked the money, the administrative resources and the experience to feed, heat and provide medicine for its population. Additionally, it was significantly distracted by Iraqi-backed insurgents and other interlopers hell-bent on destabilising the Kurdish coalition and embarrassing the UN/international NGO community in northern Iraq.

CARE was the implementing partner, with UN World Food Programme (UNWFP or just WFP), for the collection, storage and distribution of staple foods. CARE was also the implementing partner with UNICEF for the collection, storage and distribution of the heating oil, as well as for the storage of the medical supplies imported by the UN. Further, CARE was the implementing partner, with UNHCR (UN High Commission for Refugees), for the supplying of basic necessities — clothing, blankets, fundamental cooking and hygiene items — to those Kurdish refugees who managed to return to the north from neighbouring Kurdish enclaves in bordering countries. This last program was a relatively small one, as little more than a trickle of poor refugees were able to find the means and the courage to take the hazardous journeys across mountain passes back to Iraq; nevertheless it was an important program, headed up by program officer Andrew, a young, clever and caring man who was, even when I arrived, a veteran in the mission.

The CARE operation in northern Iraq was divided into three area 'sub' missions, representing the three Kurdish provinces: Dohuk in the far north, Erbil in the centre and the romantically named Suleimaniya (a variation on 'Solomon') in the south. Each area sub-mission had its head office in a provincial capital and full delegation to decide both the actual humanitarian need in its area and how to implement distribution within the area. Central control exercised by the project manager was strategic in the sense that the project manager laid down the program parameters and program and administrative policy, and set and supervised the overall budgets, and the three area managers got on with their operations within those parameters.

Some thirty-two Australians, the maximum at any one time in country, were spread across the three areas, with the majority in Erbil, a smaller number in Suleimaniya and a still smaller number in Dohuk. In my tour of duty for CARE I was to be the area manager for Erbil, and I was area manager for Suleimaniya later. We had up to fifteen hundred Kurdish staff across the whole of the north, all contracted through the agency Al-Kalah. Al-Kalah also contracted about one thousand Peshmerga guards. The Peshmerga (meaning 'he who serves') and Christian guards were subcontracted deliberately at 'arm's length' from the organisation; therefore, in principle they were not directly employed as CARE staff. But such was the warmth and trust between CARE and the guards that, practically, the relationship was (and had to be) much closer. The mission head office for northern Iraq stood adjacent to but entirely separate from the Erbil area office. This mission structure seemed to work fairly well. CARE's mission consisted of a massive infrastructure: fuel depots, warehouses, engineering plant to clear roads and mountain passes in winter, the running of large convoys (these were subcontractor run), and the operation of a wide network of field staffs.

CARE ran three large fuel depots, those in Erbil and Suleimaniya being particularly large operations by any international standard. The Iraqi economy had been a very significant oil/fuel-based economy, so oil/fuel production and storage infrastructure was impressive. CARE's great challenge was to prop up damaged and neglected facilities so as to be capable of supporting a fuel operation storing tens of millions of litres of fuel and sometimes distributing millions of litres daily, an operation with little margin for error. To give some idea, the perimeter of the Erbil fuel depot was a couple of kilometres. Keeping the fuel clean (the Turkish fuel tanker convoy drivers were a hell of a challenge to us in terms of guaranteeing purity and correct quantity on delivery), and maintaining non-leaking facilities and non-corrupted fuel lines within those facilities, was a constant struggle.

It was at this time that I met Peter Wallace, who had been in the country about eight months already. In weeks to come we were to work together — I would be his team leader as the newly appointed area manager for Erbil province, Erbil area office. Peter would be appointed as the fuel logistics officer for Erbil area office. We were years and interests apart but we sorted all that out early and worked well together. I can remember having long debates with him at the bar well into the night over issues such as Australia's South Vietnam involvement and geopolitics in general. He was clever and liked a good argument. He proved to be diligent and effective as a fuel logistics officer, displaying an excellent mind for numbers. Like my ex-lieutenant colonel mate Phil, with whom Peter has a close technical working link, Peter was to suffer badly and continually from giardia, a very stubborn disease that struck a significant number of our staff. They all grinned and bore it in very uncomfortable circumstances — our sanitation facilities were very basic and ordinary.

The warehouses were of the same magnitude as our fuel depots, if not even larger. A number of rugby fields would fit alongside each other in each of these facilities. Iraq had been a significant grain producer, particularly in the north, where the country is green. The warehouses would store all manner of food produce — packaged and tinned, and also grain stored loose to be bagged. A young Australian program officer in the blazing heat of day, boots, Akubra (fairly commonplace amongst the teams) and sensible bush shirt, could walk for hours through his warehouse storage bays, checking and counting stock, berating his national staff to get on with the repacking and prepositioning of stocks, perhaps in anticipation of the next distribution.

There is a myth in the general community that aid work is all emotion, the tearful handing out of loaves of bread. It is in fact a tough and demanding business requiring a wide range of logistical and accounting skills, among many others. You must account for every little litre and gram distributed, you must register and confirm the bona fides of every beneficiary. You must subject yourself to regular inspection and be prepared for significant audits to be conducted on your organisation, perhaps even a few years later — and by then your organisation had better be able to produce receipts, way-bills, dockets, operational running sheets for vehicles and convoys, staff payments and subcontractor payment documentation, and detailed program activity reports, among other things. If the aid organisation does not meet these basic but stringent requirements its reputation suffers and the organisation can kiss further corporate, government and even private donations goodbye. CARE Australia's Australian and locally engaged staff usually learn these responsibilities and administrative constraints on the job. Managers at all levels have a serious responsibility to teach these skills to new Australian staff very quickly, usually in the hurly-burly of ongoing operations.

Food distributions in our area were organised by CARE field teams and delivered by trucks in convoy. Distributions were then 'post-monitored' (monitor teams following some days later) to ensure that the beneficiaries received what they were entitled to. Daily the convoys, consisting of locally contracted Kurdish truck companies, rolled out of the warehouses. To save time, the previous day was spent loading, while other convoys were out distributing elsewhere. The basics were distributed — flour, sugar, cooking oil, chickpeas; nothing exotic, nothing perishable. The local diet was hardly appetising. The ration delivered was not sufficient for the whole month; it usually covered only about half. People were able to acquire basic items from struggling markets and to grow some of their own. In winter the ration was increased to compensate for the decreasing availability of locally grown or acquired food. CARE would go around the small towns and villages dotted through the rolling grassy plains and higher mountain reaches to prepare its schedule of deliveries. This pattern of planning applied to both fuel and food distributions.

CARE field staff, mainly young educated Kurds accompanied by a couple of Australian program officers, would scour the place to find and select local community agents. These agents would be contracted to receive, store and then progressively distribute the food stocks to their villagers. Distribution day would see, for example, ten to twenty 15–20 tonne trucks lumber up muddy or dusty tracks to selected villages and towns, off-load the stocks to the agents and their own hired labourers, all of this overseen by Australian program officers with their knowledgable and wily Kurdish staffs, who could pick ringers a mile away. Corruption, regrettably, was forever present and it was a constant battle to cope with it.

The advantage of, and therefore essential reason for, the presence of Australian program officers in the field at distributions was to referee all brawls, of which there were plenty. They could back up and protect their field staff (who knew the locals and knew exactly what was going down). Significantly, they would then take the tough decisions which perhaps their field staff might be reluctant to take. However, I was to find throughout my years working with CARE that my rather military-style ethos of requiring staff to conduct regular field visits and closely supervise — and encourage — field staff was to run me foul of some Australian co-workers. There was a tendency for some to spend inordinate amounts of time hobnobbing in local UN offices, sometimes canvassing for better-paid UN jobs, or just enjoying the airconditioning.

In the first month of my orientation, a period in which we new chums were all assessed by the project manager, I was appointed to a short-term project to assess the mission's security and security procedures. CARE was taking over a new facility, a medium-sized warehouse, perhaps one football field in size. This would be the stock holding area for medicines which CARE would import and hold for safekeeping. Security had been beefed up since the tragic death of a CARE Australia worker and the grievous wounding of another Australian and a Kurdish driver some five months before I arrived, but it was time for another review. Thus I was to find that my first real task in a humanitarian organisation was not to learn how to be a program officer and implement aid program activities, but instead to apply my old military skills. Given the Byzantine nature of the place, though, and the incredible mosaic of factions, gangs, brigands, feuding families, political parties, smugglers and other unsavoury types, all in conflict with one other, it would not be right to say that the Iraqis were responsible for all the troubles in 1993 and 1994. Additionally, strong Iranian and Turkish cross-border interference was evident, and it was paramount in destabilising the Kurdish enclave. It was in this hothouse that CARE Australia had determined it would get on with its operations, despite the wide-ranging and steadily growing threats.

We were obliged to put some extraordinary security procedures in place; the fact that they were necessary and were rigorously implemented demonstrates the severity of the situation. All Australian staff travelled in the field (anywhere outside of the three major provincial towns, that is) with a minimum of two vehicles and a minimum of five Peshmerga guards. Vehicles were large four-wheel drives: Landcruisers, Nissan Patrols, Austrian PUKs and a variety of other similar types. Australian staff were to be split between vehicles to allow no more than two per vehicle if possible. Guards always sat in the front seats with drivers, weapons facing out through windows. Vehicles were ordered to travel at appropriate intervals, about 75 to 100 metres apart, depending on the nature of the countryside, so as to minimise casualties should machine gun, rocket grenade or mortar ambush occur. Travelling after sunset was not permitted. Vehicles and staff were not permitted to leave hard tack road surfaces or well-known/well-used dirt tracks, for fear of landmines and unexploded bombs, which literally littered the place.

Every CARE staff house would have a shift of three Peshmerga guards or nightwatchmen, protected by a wall of sandbags. These men went into action about a dozen times in my experience. CARE offices, warehouses and fuel depots were also manned by heavy weapon-carrying Peshmergas. Armed men were posted at important places behind sandbagged walls and on top of prominent rooftops through all facilities in the north. Later in the year, as conditions further deteriorated, we introduced escort vehicles which were open-tray Landcruisers, V8 Ford or Chevrolet pick-ups, carrying extra guards with heavy weapons. These would travel at the rear of truck convoys or at the rear of large field staff vehicle convoys. Two of these vehicles went into action during my experience. Soon after I departed the mission another incident occurred in which one of these escort vehicles broke up an ambush just south of the Erbil/ Suleimaniya province line when a field staff vehicle in front was ambushed. The ambush was broken up by suppressing machine gun fire — two of the ambushers, rebel Kurdish fighters, were killed. CARE Australia had three Kurdish staff wounded in two road ambushes.

We knew that our security policy did not look very humanitarian. We debated whether our extraordinary and tough security procedures degraded the humanitarian impression, but continually felt, given the number of security incidents impacting on other organisations, as against CARE's relative safety, that our policy was vindicated, and vindicated regularly. We debated this continually through 1993. CARE Australia vehicles operating across the north stood out as being well prepared for trouble. Which is why we attracted far less trouble then other NGOs, UN agencies and other international organisations. It is also why CARE Australia was able to continue delivering its aid and getting about the countryside to monitor and plan its humanitarian programs.

There are many well-documented occasions, in UN and other reports received by the UN, that show that during periods of security disintegration throughout 1993 and 1994, CARE Australia was often the only NGO on the road doing its job. There were other NGOs, particularly the French (and noticeably Médecins Sans Frontières), who criticised CARE for taking such strident and supposedly non-humanitarian measures; indeed, for being so visible. They, however, were to take casualties — at least five international staff from European NGOs and an unknown but not insignificant number of their Kurdish staff were to die or be wounded on main roads in ambushes in the space of about eighteen months. Most other NGOs supported CARE's approach and adapted their procedures accordingly. The irony was that the UN often relied on CARE Australia to lend its Peshmerga fighters to assist UN Guards in the carrying out of their protection tasks. No wonder they were prepared to fund CARE's security capability.

The Australian staff had understandably mixed views on these security measures. New staff, who arrived every one to two months, would be shown the procedures, attend a demonstration of the procedures. They would then be put through the drills associated with, for example, 'ambush procedure'. How were they to behave in the event of an incident? They would undoubtedly be grabbed by the scruff of the neck at the hands of a burly Peshmerga and led to safety. There were some Australian staff who did not take the 'no travel after sunset' measure seriously; more than likely because they had found it difficult to organise themselves to finish the day's fieldwork on time so as to be able to return to base on time. These habits changed rapidly after a number of fuel truck convoy sunset ambushes occurred on the road to Suleimaniya in September 1993. Most staff then accepted, grudgingly but with quiet relief, that they were stuck with such security measures.

Why did Australians stay to do the job, given these circumstances and given these stringent procedures? Why did we all not simply take the next jumbo home, particularly after experiencing these horrible incidents involving the shooting of our staff, the night shooting raids on our houses (three attacks on my own, being the greatest number of all attacks in Erbil), the death of other international staff and later the outbreak of civil war and heavy fighting around us? Such questions were often discussed around the bar at the infamous CARE Erbil Club, but nobody had a satisfactory answer. Clearly, the major reason was the magnitude of the humanitarian operation, supporting millions of Kurds in essentially life-saving programs. Then there were the basic values and commitment of the Australians, our fondness for the Kurds, who were a stoic, dignified and uncomplaining lot — all important factors. Further, there was something in the air, the spirit of the place, the desert and mountain country that is Kurdish Iraq, which I believe appealed to a significant number of our Australians and touched their adventure nerve. Finally and importantly, there was the camaraderie within the organisation, among both Australians and Kurds. The camaraderie in this mission, more than any other mission that CARE Australia had ever conducted (and, I believe, has since conducted), was another reason for such a strong retention of Australians in the mission, despite the dangers.

After my orientation month, I was selected as the new area manager for Erbil province, having completed my project of revamping CARE's safety and security procedures. In addition to being area manager, I was to retain a secondary responsibility as CARE's security officer for the entire mission. I did not need nor relish the added responsibility. Then, around Christmas 1993, I participated in the six-monthly ritual of preparing new project proposals, the exercise of renewing the existing, massive programs and balancing the budgets to prepare for the next programming semester. This was always a gruelling and rigorous set of tasks. Among other things, the project manager would be obliged to call in the Kurdish subcontractors, with whom we would again negotiate our partnered operations. Terrible talks would follow, with difficult negotiations. This drama would play out for a week. Then CARE would trot down to the UN offices in Ain-Kawa (Erbil) and the same exercise would run again there.

The UN tried to put the screws on CARE in different ways. Why were we not bringing more Australian funds to the table? Why did we need so many international staff? Robert Yallop, CARE Australia's director for Middle East operations, was in the country with us. But he nearly didn't make it. His visa was only approved at the last minute and some staff he badly wanted to bring with him to assist in this exercise had not got through. I remember Robert, puffing madly away on that infernal pipe and staring through the smoke haze at the senior UN programming director, responding with 'Rubbish, we could not accept that crap!' And so the negotiations twisted on, with Robert and the project manager eventually threatening that CARE Australia could simply not continue under the arrangements proposed and would have to consider pulling out immediately.

Meanwhile, over in the infamous CARE Erbil Club the rumours were running hot. We were around the bar wondering whether we would all be packing up to leave within days. What about the Kurdish people? What about those dedicated 2000-odd staff? The only jobs for them were in NGOs. Their contract with CARE Australia was valuable, the experience was valuable; they felt the job was unfinished and they must stay. The club was famous in the international aid community in Erbil. Most UN and other NGO workers would come down to the CARE Club a couple of times a week. Just to watch the bloody Australians, observe that irreverent behaviour and that off-the-wall, dry and gritty sense of humour, which only the Irish can outdo.

Beer was flowing, music booming away on batteries, all of it soothing for cold, tired, homesick workers. Dried mud on boots and smears of it on heavy parkas. The old blow heaters struggling to keep that bitter winter out of the club, damn blackout, old smoky lanterns and candles. Where was that useless bloody mechanic and what was he doing about the bloody generator? Lots of good-natured exchanges about the poor blighter — he was innovative and he kept the place ticking along. This was where the de-stressing took place, in a big way.

Meanwhile, back at the project office and bathed in the half-light of the lanterns, negotiations with the subcontractors got under way. They were an evil bunch, I was to decide. Saddam moustaches, scars cutting over weathered faces, would probably kill their grand-mothers for a few Iraqi dinars. Large flashy rings on fingers. Just as menacing, though, were Hardi, our chief Peshmerga, and his brother Mardi, patrolling outside the conference room in full view of the contractor and his snaky staff. At just the right moment, as chief snake is elaborately clearing his throat to lie, Hardi cocked his weapon, ostensibly checking it, routine really, 'Forgive me, chaps, for interrupting the conference.' Robert puffed away, his pipe smoke this time welcome above the lantern fumes. Quietly assessing things. Snake in his oily voice crooned away, one side of his face lit by lantern amber, the other deep in shadow. His eyes flashed as only Kurdish eyes could. The brightest eyes in the world.

Why did we put up with these subcontractors? Because they were the only credible game in town, and we did not have the luxury to stuff around, experiment with unknown subcontractors and start over again once the program was in full swing. Besides, in terms of the inalienable principle by which CARE must operate, the current subcontractors looked like coming in again as the best, lowest, firmest and fairest bid on the tender. By midnight, this last day in the week during a cold Christmas, negotiations were completed. In the centre of the CARE Australia compound there in Erbil the late-night owls celebrate with a few whoops in the bar over at the club. CARE was to continue in the business of doing something towards saving these people. A new round of negotiations would swing around again five months later.

In late February 1994 it was also decided that as Suleimaniya province was then hotting up to be the most unstable of our three areas I was, because of my experience, to be transferred there. Amman decided that I was to be formally appointed second hat: deputy project manager for the northern Iraq mission. Suleimaniya was a vastly different place from Erbil. A low-key civil war between the factions was developing into something more permanent, and soon the PUK, the dominant faction in the southern province, began cleaning out its KDP rivals. Their officers were attacked in Suleimaniya city, with full-blown street battles erupting in the most public of places. Our programs were not interrupted by the fighting, though; we seemed to be able to skirt any trouble or potential trouble. We were still able to roll our truck convoys out of the warehouse daily through most of the troubles. Our strong guard contingents meant that most fighters left us alone.

The UN chief for Suleimaniya called a crisis conference in early April. I was now included in UN provincial security meetings. Partly because CARE was recognised as one of the larger NGOs operating in the province, but also, importantly for the UN, because we had the widest spread across the province. We were therefore capable of being their eyes and the ears in assessing the humanitarian situation. That situation was now rapidly changing. We joined with the UN in developing contingency plans for an expected massive refugee movement of farmers and rural villagers out of the south-eastern districts. It was anticipated that these people would surge towards the provincial capital of Suleimaniya city, about 100 kilometres west-north-west. About 10 000 resettled refugees, a UNHCR caseload in a UNHCR-built housing complex at Said Sadiq, 15 kilometres north of the district capital, would need to be evacuated, and they would join the anticipated mass exodus. The housing complex area had already caught the odd artillery shell coming over from the Iranian border, mercifully without any hits on the houses. CARE accepted responsibility for all this, and was tasked by the UN to establish 'way stations' along the main highway and the secondary channelling routes leading into the highway from the frontier. We would erect water points and sanitation, and provide emergency food distribution and first aid, in conjunction with Médecins du Monde. The UN did not want these way stations to become long-term stayover choke points, but they would be essential to 'resuscitate' exhausted refugees.

CARE had no free funds immediately available to allocate to this unforeseen emergency. I pressured the UN Suleimaniya office for funding and it was agreed to. Meanwhile, the CARE Iraq mission had urgently sought from our Middle East office the launching of an appeal to donors for the ongoing funding of this new emergency program, in the event that the crisis became long term. I felt comfortable that we had sufficient funding promised from the UN, and this confidence allowed CARE Suleimaniya area office staff to go out to our subcontractors to prepare for food stockpiling and way station and water point construction.

Due to other leave requirements and delays in 'end of contract' Australian staff changeovers, I found myself alone in terms of international staff for some weeks as the crisis built. As I was to experience so many times working with CARE over the years, I found myself running on adrenaline. The mission did not seem to be able to find anybody else to detach to my area office, due partly to overstretch in other areas and partly to the fact that the road down to Suleimaniya from Erbil those days was increasingly cut by the fighting, which was spreading from Suleimaniya northwards to Erbil. CARE was now facing the threat of fighting and consequential disruption to humaniatarian programs on a number of fronts across the north. But I had good, loyal Kurdish staff and figured we would get along just fine until my Australian colleagues were able to return.

The UN chief, his senior staff, his UN Guards commander and myself undertook a series of humanitarian assessments in the south-east districts, as far as we dared go given the fighting, and given our lack of confidence in defining exactly where the fighting was. The refugee problem was worsening, and there were strong signs of PUK troop movements and movements of other Kurdish factions. We could hear the artillery thundering in the distance along the towering mountains that define the rugged border country while our planning continued, and it was not clear to us where people were. We feared that tens of thousands of farmers and villagers must be trapped between the dominating lake, the border mountains and the fighting, unable to pass into Said Sadiq, the town sitting at the main crossroads. It could be that anticipated refugee flows were blocked, but could suddenly surge when a break in the fighting allowed escape. Would they overwhelm the planned resources?

An incident occurred during this period of civil war and preparation for refugee contingency operations where I found myself thrust into a human rights witnessing role, quite by accident. It was also a particularly dangerous experience. For three days I had not heard from my Kumul warehouse. I had directed that all staff call in twice daily from these outposts with situation reports, by way of their Codan HF radios. We also needed to know the state of the warehouse stocks there, as these would be vital for the refugee contingency plan we were trying to put into place. The warehouse was stocked with some 'dry ration' emergency food stocks, blankets, emergency shelter materials, clothing and essential cooking items. The stocks had been there for more than a year, wisely put in place by my predecessors for just such purposes, as well as for equipping returning refugee families.

We travel down the highway to the southeast, to update the refugee situation and check the Kumul warehouse situation. I am the only international staff member in the south-east, as it turns out, on this day. With me are three CARE vehicles, carrying a strong contingent — seven senior and experienced field staff and about fifteen Peshmerga guards. We pass a trickle of refugee families and count up to 150 cars and trucks on the road, carrying large passenger loads and overloaded with household effects and sometimes livestock. The refugee crisis has worsened significantly in the three days since the UN assessment team and I have last been down in this district.

I radio in the information to the UN chief, and do so again a number of times through the morning. We carefully count the refugee vehicles, stop and talk to people and gradually build a picture of where they have come from and which areas are the hardest hit. We have to be careful not to be misled by exaggeration, and often we have to cross-check information to see whether a poor old farmer's report has been perhaps based on conjecture or on an unreliable second-hand report. But gradually we build a reliable report and the news is disturbing. The fighting is growing in intensity, thereby exacerbating the refugee crisis and seriously prolonging the suffering. This civil war has clearly been prolonged by the meddling of a number of regional foreign powers. Turkey, Iran and Iraq, and perhaps Syria to a lesser extent, are fuelling the fires of this mountainous Kurdish region. They will never leave the Kurdish people to sort out their differences. As our small convoy of three vehicles approaches Said Sadiq, ducking in and out of military vehicles and the swirling of growing troop activity, it is now most evident that the UN and international NGOs would be flat strapped responding to a significant refugee exodus. This info is passed back to the CARE office for immediate forwarding to the UN in Suleimaniya.

In the early afternoon of that day we travel into the Zeman bridge area 15 kilometres east of Said Sadiq. This is a strategic bridge and crossroads in the south-east district. We have discussions with the local PUK military commander and are able to learn a little bit about the fighting, the refugee movements and some news about the CARE warehouse, which the PUK think to be still intact.

We take our leave, and I warmly wish the commander and his soldiers the best of luck — I can remember feeling for them an old soldier's understanding. The country in this border region is stunningly beautiful, although the fires of battle can be seen burning in the foothills of the border ranges. Heading towards Kumul, some 15 kilometres inside the Iranian border, the lake and the interior of Suleimaniya are at our backs. We are heading east towards Kumul, which we can see about 2 kilometres away. The border mountains, beautiful and majestic, loom over us. They are craggy and rugged and stand about 1000 metres in altitude over the plains of Kumul. Sheer mountains, but with a dominating ridgeline that runs down from the backbone of the mountain range.

On arriving at Kumul there is no sign of life anywhere, no sign of our staff. The eerie silence makes me feel very uneasy. The Peshmerga, doing their job so skilfully, have spread out, moving around the village, but are to come upon a grim sight. They have found civilian bodies. Twenty bodies are reported to be scattered along the outskirts of the village in long grass, although I am unable to see them. They have their heads cut off, normally the method of the Pasdar fundamentalists operating in the area. I see two and can see clearly that they are without heads. It is a revolting and nauseating sight; they lie broken in the long grass, like rag dolls, but curiously I cannot see where their heads have gone. The mess is too much and too confusing. Poor devils. The sight is burned into my memory. I take my Peshmergas' word for it and tear myself away from that terrible scene and thank my lucky stars I have not eaten all day. I've seen enough and walk quickly back to the warehouse.

As we move back to the warehouse we are ambushed. Serious trouble. The crack! crack! of bullets flying over our heads, heard before we hear the deep booming reports of the weapons themselves. Faces in the dirt and scrambling for our lives. Heavy weapons fire from positions, we work out later, some 2 kilometres east of Kumul, from that dominating ridgeline. We are pinned down. We remain pinned under desultory fire for some four hours, fearing that we may become directly involved in a serious firefight. In this period I am to place my Peshmerga leader Hajar, a bear-like creature now strangely in his element, in charge of all of us. I am certainly out of my element. Hajar and his Peshmergas are calm and businesslike, while I am as scared as hell. I decide that Hajar, the blighter, actually relishes the dire straits we are in. I am to have a vivid memory years later of this great man, sitting with his back against the dirt mound, checking his weapon, reloading spare magazines and grinning from ear to ear like a kid in a sandbox. We are mortared, and witness the heavy artillery, clearly not the weapons of the local Kurdish rebels, firing deep into Iraqi Kurdistan. And we know that the artillery base is well inside Kurdish Iraq, to allow it a greater reach into Iraq, in support of the Hezbollah Kurd and Pasdar fighters.

The situation has become very dangerous. The Peshmergas believe they can see Kurdish fighters some hundreds of metres away, angling around — perhaps to attack us. My driver is very worried and again insists I take his spare weapon. I do not. It is not necessary: the attack does not materialise. Unable to move anywhere during this extremely tense and frightening time, Hajar, his more experienced fighters, my clever field staff and I are examining that dominating ridgeline east of Kumul, and we establish as many facts as we can about this Iranian Revolutionary Guard battalion presence. I am drawing up a map with sketches from a pocket notebook — a formal 'incident report' is to be prepared and then submitted to the UN chief in Suleimaniya. By nightfall of that wretched day we are able to extricate ourselves from the ordeal.

This incident had been my sixth time under fire, this last twelve months. Three of those were relatively minor — shots fired at my house, with my house guards returning fire. On one occasion I had been marginally injured, when two of my bodyguards and I had been flattened by rocket-propelled grenade exploding metres above our heads at the Suleimaniya UNHCR compound. Although concussed, we had not been seriously injured. But this incident at Kumul had been prolonged — three to four hours trapped, wondering whether we would have to fight off an armed assault. An ordeal which had focused my mind on the dilemma that the code of conduct of humanitarian workers clashed with the principle of personal security and defence of your mates. After twenty-three years of largely war-free service, I had found myself in frantic and scrambling combat-like conditions. It had all been a frightening blur. Metaphorically I had changed my underpants a dozen times and my nose had regularly dug holes in beautiful old Mother Earth. Very strong bonding with my field staff, and our security guards, resulted from this series of events.

But we are resigned to the fact that the Kumul warehouse is now lost, and unsure of where those missing staff have got to. Years later I am to hear that they may have safely turned up, some weeks later, in Said Sadiq.

❖ ❖ ❖

Subsequently I made a detailed report to the UN about the presence and actions of the Iranian force, and the finding of the bodies. The Suleimaniya UN chief investigated further and supported my report. The UN Guards chief requested my company and we visited the area again; I pointed out the presence of the Iranian force. We were accompanied by the CARE project manager, who had managed to break into Suleimaniya in a lull in the fighting further north. The UN Guard commander gathered further facts and confirmed my allegation. Unfortunately, during this witnessing inspection we found ourselves under mortar fire — directed at PUK forces close to us — and were forced to scramble to safety again. UN Suleimaniya reported the presence of the Iranian force and their actions to the UN head office for northern Iraq, recommend-ing that urgent steps be taken politically to force them to cease their activities.

No substantial measures were taken, however; the whole thing appeared to be flushed down the toilet, with a fair amount of ambivalence on the part of UN northern Iraq, it seemed to me (and to other committed NGO leaders in Suleimaniya). Totally dissatisfied and disillusioned with UN northern Iraq I took action with my international NGO colleagues in Suleimaniya. We got together and co-drafted a letter of report and appeal, much of it based on my initial reports and sketches, my 'witnessing' reports included in the submission, which we addressed to the Secretary-General of the UN, Boutros Boutros-Ghali, and rather clumsily copied to President Bill Clinton and British Prime Minister John Major. In effect, going over the top of the heads of the northern Iraq UN mission. The Iranian Revolutionary Guard battalion which had operated 10 kilometres inside Kurdish Iraq, and probably a lot deeper, was clearly and formally identified.

A senior UN officer in Erbil, who had been too long in the country and was perhaps too close to one side in the Kurdish factional brawl, took issue with CARE because of my pivotal role in the research for and preparation of the letter. I was severely rapped over the knuckles by CARE Australia for this indiscretion; that is, the exercising of direct action, and not through the CARE chain of command. I cannot fault the organisational logic in that, and in the end had to take my medicine. I was transferred quickly from northern Iraq, in a sense disciplined.

At the time I was very angry with everybody, including CARE Australia. I had been ripped away from the mission to which I had become deeply committed, and this was really painful. This was a time of greatly disturbing feelings and conflicting emotions about what was right and wrong in the world of international aid. It was some months before I was able to settle down again — and only after much reflection — and that was in the mountains of Yemen. Pragmatism and realpolitik had triumphed again over individuals' human rights, this time those of the Kurdish farmers and villagers in the south-east of Suleimaniya.

CARE's time in northern Iraq had been as gruelling during my thirteen months there as it had been in the period before I was there. The death of a fellow Australian and the Kurdish staff, to whom we had become closely attached, left deep scars on the organisation, no matter that steps were taken later to minimise such risks. The position of the Kurdish people, particularly the 100 000 or so widows, many with families, was devastating. CARE had pushed itself to the limits of budget, capacity, organisational and staff energy and security risk to continue delivering the aid to those remote villages, so many of which were in desperate or inhospitable places.

CARE had been able to continue delivering aid when other organisations had decided it was best to 'take cover' — during times of fighting and general security deterioration. Had we been right to push on? The ability to deliver aid had been dependent on the building of strong security measures. This had been controversial and criticised by some as extreme, but was entirely necessary, in my view. CARE found itself regularly pressured by the UN to provide more resources, to lighten the UN funding burden. But in practical terms this was something CARE could not do, as the Australian public had long ago turned its attention to other concerns. In northern Iraq in 1994, CARE escaped the axe and continued operating as the UN implementing partner, but the pressures would eventually be too much to bear.

CARE's relationship with the UN in northern Iraq in 1993–94 was in my experience mostly positive, with plenty of mutual respect and a close mutual support. However, on a number of occasions, particularly in Yemen two years later, the UN would ditch its major implementing partner, regardless of good performance and for purely budgetary reasons, in favour of an unknown quantity. This involved the selection of an inexperienced international or sometimes a hastily cobbled together local affair. The services, and the effectiveness of aid delivery, would in these circumstances deteriorate dramatically, while the people, the recipients of aid, would suffer. Meanwhile, some clever-dick UN officer would be rewarded for his budgetary initiatives. In Zaire in 1996 and again in Yugoslavia in 1997 I would experience this — pressure exerted by the UN on CARE to significantly cut its costs and capability, to the point where CARE could not have and would not have continued. Erbil in 1994 was my first exposure to the real world of humanitarian administration, and the questions raised there would dog me over the next five years.

Whether CARE should have continued its operations in Kurdish northern Iraq under such extreme security conditions is a point that many will debate. Many CARE individuals might look back and ask whether they should have stayed on in 1994, rather than opting out because the security incidents erupted and continued regularly, with increasing magnitude. It does honour to those extraordinary individuals that, for the most part, they saw the need to take some risk and stay to fight the humanitarian and human rights battle. Besides budgetary constraints and differences of opinion with the UN over implementation and funding, it was the deteriorating security situation which was no doubt the deciding factor in CARE's eventual pullout in 1995.

During my time in northern Iraq, I began to come to the view that where the humanitarian need is extreme (as was the case there), and the UN and the international community is willing to provide satisfactory protection — be it UN troops, UN contingent guards, other international coalition troops — or, as the UN did in the case of Northern Iraq, give the authority and resources to allow an NGO to take whatever security measures are deemed necessary (with a UN check and balance applied), then a capably organised NGO has a moral obligation to continue its work. An international NGO not so organised and not so willing is an inefficient and potentially dangerous organisation, and should not be in the business. With these concepts taking shape in my mind I recovered sufficiently from my exhaustion and found the personal faith to go off to Yemen with CARE in June 1994.

CHAPTER THREE

From Iraq to Yemen

Yemen is a unique little country with a fascinating history and roots in a sophisticated and ancient civilisation. The educated Yemenis know and assert their history, although the country is so racked by poverty and political strife these days that nobody else cares much about their heritage and past values. The demonstration of civilised values as practised in the mountains of Shabwa by the court of the Queen of Sheba thousands of years ago have little bearing on the confused and tumultous situation in Yemen these days. In 1994 Yemen was home to thousands of Somali refugees, who had fled across the Red Sea and Gulf of Aden to settle in wretched camps along the Yemeni coastline. CARE Australia had established a mission, known as CARE Yemen, to partner a refugee operation with the UNHCR by managing a refugee camp at Al-Gahin. Approximately 200 kilometres east of Aden and 30-odd kilometres inland, it was located near the town of Laudar, about 300 metres up into the foothills of the coastal mountain range. The refugees had moved to this place during the Yemeni civil war of early 1994, away from their former CARE Yemen camp at El Khoud, 75 kilometres east of Aden. El Khoud itself had become a final and strategic battleground for the northern forces' second army, which was advancing on Aden from the east. Southern forces trying to defend Aden had fought one of their last desperate battles in this area.

At the time of this battle, as the northern forces' first army was closing in on Aden from the north, the CARE Australia international staff had had no choice but to suspend the mission. They had evacuated via the port of Aden by boat across the Red Sea to Djibouti, on the African coast. The CARE Yemen office, however, somehow managed to stay open, run by its Yemeni staff, during this climactic period of war, as the northern forces pounded Aden with artillery and air strikes and closed in for the kill. The office was powerless, though, to do anything for the Somali refugees who had fled to the mountains, and could only ride out the storm, seeking to protect themselves and their assets. The civil war was a horrendous little affair which developed after the south decided they had been overexploited and disenfranchised from national affairs. The numerically inferior south had bitten off far more than they could chew by unilaterally declaring independence from the more conservative north. Thousands of people were to die — many civilians in the south and many soldiers on both sides of the conflict. It is estimated that the north lost something in the order of 10 000 dead in the earlier stages of the war, during their cumbersome start to proceedings. But it must have always been merely a matter of time before the south was defeated; I was to wonder time and again in Yemen why they had not understood that.

Having joined the mission in Sana'a, CARE Yemen's country headquarters, I was briefed by CARE's country representative, Nagpal, an Indian who had served as CARE's first project manager in northern Iraq. He was an interesting character, clumsy and prickly in his personnel management; clearly he had some difficulty getting used to the Australians and vice versa. But he was a clever man, capable and experienced in the aid business, and had been with CARE USA for many years. Sana'a was a delightfully romantic place in the historical sense. At almost 3000 metres altitude, the city is one of the highest in the world, and requires you to physically adjust to the thinner air. Surrounded by sparse, craggy mountains, it was a thriving place of bazaars and forever jammed traffic trickles. Palaces and military barracks seemed to dominate the place — not pretty in their architecture, but grand in their own way. The place had the life and energy of any modern metropolis, but on closer inspection it was clear that it was very old and very conservative; indeed, beneath a few satellite dishes, it had an almost feudal quality about it. Everywhere people looked poor, and I soon gained the impression that life for many was a real struggle. A dusty, stone-strewn, barren landscape surrounded the city. It was not much better inside; there were few paths, no parks and very little greenery. The old city quarter was fascinating, an old mud and stone structure, with twisting and ancient alleyways. More donkeys evident than vehicles. I left this behind me and drove off to the south in the dying days of the civil war.

Some days later my driver, Muhammad Labani (a Bedouin from Sana'a whom I had nicknamed 'Top Gun' because he drove like a fighter pilot), and I approached Aden from the east, having inspected the remains of the refugee camp at El Khoud. Nothing there was left standing, absolutely nothing except the concrete blocks on which had stood the various administrative buildings. As we drove along the coastal road, wind blowing the sand dunes onto and sometimes across the road, I marvelled at how bloody hot it was. It was 44°C and very, very humid. In the seven months of 'summer', the temperature on the coast would be a constant 44°C, day and night, no variation, and that infernal humidity would never budge in its intensity either. At the end of the seventh month, and not a day before, God would throw the switch and knock it down to a reasonable 30°C for the winter.

Top Gun's old red Landcruiser rattled along, but at least the brakes were excellent. I had on numerous occasions in the previous days thanked God for Top Gun's brakes as we had descended the incredible escarpments, dropping 2500 metres down some of the most dynamic mountains I had ever seen. The British engineers who had built these roads decades before must have been geniuses. Top Gun chewed his gat, something new for me to see. A disgusting green mess crushed in the mouth and held there for hours, made from leaf tips freshly picked that day. The bottom of Top Gun's vehicle was knee deep in discarded leaves. Occasionally he would spit some of the crushed mess out onto the road, where I am sure it would stain forever whatever it splattered on. I felt sick.

I was to discover in my Yemeni education that gat was a stimulant, chewed by 95 per cent of the Yemeni male population, an obsession that was to bring the nation to its knees for four hours every day. As I had driven down from the north with Top Gun, each afternoon we cruised through mountain villages that were dusty and hot but no longer teeming, as they had been in the mornings. They would be adorned by hundreds of men lying along the streets, backs on walls, cars, whatever, chewing and chatting and often, it struck me, oblivious to the broken sewers running across the streets, another feature of town life I was to notice.

We entered the city of Aden — fires were still burning, smoke was still pluming from the war. We had crawled for hours behind elements of the northern army still moving into Aden. Top Gun and I sweltered as we squinted into the afternoon sun. Nobody on the streets except northern soldiers and old soviet T55 tanks. I was stunned by the number of tanks and the size of the army. But the final battle had been tough for them. All along the eastern coastal road the sand dunes were littered with destroyed military vehicles — trucks, mobile artillery trucks and armoured cars. Tank and artillery ammunition cases, brightly shining in the sunlight, littered the edges of the road in their hundreds, testimony to the savagery of the final battle.

We drove past a now largely destroyed airport, burnt-out shells of aeroplanes strewn across the runways, including (judging by the surviving markers on tailplanes), some of the Yemeni domestic passenger fleet. Was it necessary to destroy their precious national assets, I wondered? Tanks were now at every corner, and they were a curious sight to see — most of them (obviously they had been here for a few days) were covered in household furniture and household effects, lashed down to the upper decks. War booty. Aden was now a filthy and damaged city. White concrete block houses, interspersed with brown mud adobes, as far as the eye could see. Broken rusty wired fences, now coated in plastic bags, pinned by the hot moist breeze relentlessly roaring in off the Gulf of Aden. Debris, flotsam and jetsam strewn all over the place, up and down

MAY 1967: Lance-Corporal Pratt (far right), instructing at the CMF 2nd Division basic training course, Holsworthy, NSW.

JANUARY 1982: Operations officer, 2nd Battalion Pacific Islands Regiment, Wewak, Papua New Guinea. The commanding officer, Lieutenant Colonel Roki Lokinap, is handing out military skills prizes.

MAY 1984: As a student at the US Army's Logistics Management Centre, Fort Lee, Virginia.

OCTOBER 1989: Running for federal parliament in the seat of Banks — campaigning with MP Phillip Ruddock in the shopping centre at Riverwood, south-western Sydney.

MARCH 1992: Major Pratt, staff officer, logistics at HQ Land Command, Victoria Barracks, Sydney.

JULY 1993: CARE Australia area manager, Erbil province, northern Iraq. Pictured near Shaklawa with two of my personal Peshmerga guards, who were showing me the battleground of 1991.

SEPTEMBER 1993: Chairing a meeting of local officials and Peshmerga guard chiefs in Erbil. Loyal and honest Salam on my right was my very wise assistant, keeping everyone cool.

MAY 1994: Northern Iraq, with CARE area manager, Suleimaniya (right) and two of my office staff.

OCTOBER 1994: Al-Gahin refugee camp, Yemen. As CARE logistics officer appointed to co-ordinate the UNHCR-sponsored return of Somali refugees, I was involved in organising the first convoy of 500 to Aden Port for the journey over the Red Sea.

OCTOBER 1994: Refugee return operation, Yemen. With my good friend the UNHCR communications officer Ove (left), who ran the challenging communications plan required to coordinate the movement of thousands of refugees.

APRIL 1995: Regional manager for CARE Australia's great lakes region operation, Nairobi. Pictured with Bernard, my driver, and one of the vehicles donated by Land Rover Australia.

APRIL 1995: At Butare, south-west Rwanda, during the Kibeho Camp crisis. The children were separated from their families during fighting the previous week, and were being cared for by our Rwanda team.

JULY 1995: Visiting our Goma team at one of their food distribution sites in Katale Camp, Zaire. With one of our Australian logistics officers and his Hutu and Zairean field staff.

JUNE 1996: Nairobi office, with son Haydon visiting me from Rome during his school holidays.

NOVEMBER 1996: Amman, Jordan. Samira and I in traditional Bedu costume, celebrating our first wedding anniversary.

every street. Skinny foraging dogs, packs of them roaming all over the place.

The buildings were largely intact — war had been merciful — but everywhere there was damage from artillery and tank shells. Despite the large civilian population the northern army had not been averse to dropping shells all over the city. In places you could see where damage had been the result of outright malice. People were scarcely to be seen; they had been kept off the streets due to a military curfew. We were allowed to proceed to the office. Unlike so much else here, we found it was in one piece.

Troops stand in the front yard of the office. Rohit, the international staff member in charge of CARE's Aden office, is there, having returned that day from Djibouti. Manning the office and smiling her incredibly engaging smile is Samira, the administration officer in the CARE Yemen Aden office. She is very pleased to see us. She explains what has been happening. Samira and an Iraqi national have come to the office as often as they could, including during the days of bombing, to simply man the telephones. Northern troops have occupied this office, as they have all offices around the city; Samira and her colleagues have doubled their efforts to visit the office daily, in order to protect it. I wonder whether CARE even knows about or will ever acknowledge this dedication.

A handful of troops occupy the place and have slept and eaten there. Their Kalashnikovs lie all over the place. They have made a mess but the presence of Samira and the four guards has clearly minimised the mess, theft and vandalism. The three CARE vehicles parked out in the closed courtyard are intact; one has a broken side window, but they are generally OK. Samira relates to us an impressive story. Muhammad, the old watchman, had arrived at the office to find soldiers trying to break into and drive away one of the CARE vehicles. Ignoring their levelled rifles he remonstrated with the younger men, shaming them and then lying across the driveway and challenging the soldiers to drive the vehicles over him, the only way out. I shake my head in wonderment, yet again, at the courage and dedication of the local staffs that we find ourselves with in CARE around the world. Do we Australian staff really appreciate these people and the value they bring to the organisation? Reflecting on the memories of northern Iraq and remembering the acts of selfless behaviour there and now what I was seeing here in Yemen, I wonder when was the last time I saw similar examples in everyday life in my own country? In the event, old Muhammad was to receive a CARE commendation for extraordinary service.

CARE's work in Yemen was exclusively the Somali refugee support program. The refugee camp at Al-Gahin, housing 9000 refugees, the mainstay of the CARE activity, was a relatively small affair compared to CARE's northern Iraq program. Some 4000–5000 additional refugees had fled into Aden from the old CARE/UNHCR-run camp at El Khoud during the civil war. These refugees were the lucky ones, getting into Aden before the occupying troops erected barricades denying them entrance. Meanwhile, many others had been killed during the war. The Aden-bound refugees had found various types of accommodation, mainly in the Aden suburb of Basatin; this was an area where those Yemenis who had originally lived in Somalia as traders and who had taken Somali wives now lived after having fled the Somali war. CARE's Aden office used to run a small warehouse in Aden which held a variety of stores, mainly contingency stocks for new refugee emergencies. The warehouse's main role was to run food and essential family item distributions for the Aden-based refugees, who would turn up at routine times for their ration issue. These people were quite content to live as they were and had no desire to transfer to the new refugee camp at Al-Gahin. Somalis are a very hardy lot, sometimes extremely determined, and very, very resourceful. I was to learn over the next seven months that they were a very tough people.

The CARE Australia country representative was seeking funding to conduct additional programs around the country supporting disadvantaged Yemenis, of whom there were a great many in this incredibly impoverished country. Yemen has a population of about fifteen million people, very few resources, a severe shortage of water and little arable land. Oil exploration continues in the east of the country. Some marginally useful discoveries have been made, but unlike its neighbours, Yemen has essentially been left behind in the commercial development race. CARE Australia was finding it extremely difficult to raise funding from anywhere for Yemen. Yemen is the type of forsaken place which has never attracted world attention or sympathy.

In the first three months of my Yemen experience I did a stint helping out the program officer responsible for the refugee program. The program was based in a small mountain town called Lawder, about 15 kilometres from Al-Gahin. Lawder was a CARE sub-office, one floor of a three-storey building block. The office was office and accommodation combined. Louise, the program officer, had worked with CARE in northern Iraq — this was her second tour with CARE. We shared the house with an Ethiopian cook, a cheerful little lady. The house/office was typical (in design) of a large Arab house: very simple and blockish in layout, with tiled floors and simple decoration. But these were the hills of Yemen, and the services were rough — sanitation was a joke, and blockages were a daily affair.

It was punishingly hot at this time and we tried sleeping on the roof but under mosquito nets; the air was thick with them and malaria was not unknown in these parts. Unlike in Aden, in this little mountain desert town at midnight every night you could depend on a small desert breeze coming from the west. It had just enough of a cool edge to it to bring the temperature down by about five to eight degrees and allow sleep. So we would sleep under clear skies, but often (in the first weeks) would be awakened by the terrible noisy entrance into the town of Yemeni military forces. They were returning to their Lawder barracks, a very large military base, in dribs and drabs every two to three nights. As was the custom, the returning triumphant troops in the convoy would fire all their weapons, starting about 5 kilometres out of town. Usually this was at 1 am, and the sound was deafening. Along with the packs of wild dogs roaming through the many rubbish tips surrounding the town and barking crazily all night, the military symphony contributed to what was a perennially noisy town.

We would drive to the camp early each morning, to be greeted by our Somali staff, who themselves were refugees. The staff were divided into maintenance teams and were responsible to Louise for all aspects of camp maintenance and improvements. We would walk daily around the sheds which housed the refugees. The refugees would generally greet us respectfully and with good humour. We would listen to their stories and their requests. Many of these issues were of a political and refugee personnel administrative nature, and were not CARE's responsibility. They were UNHCR's responsibility, except that UNHCR Aden office rarely attended to these issues.

We experienced a number of nasty incidents in this camp, usually generated by some tenaciously argumentative elements among the refugees. On arrival one particular morning at the camp, Louise and I separated, to attend to different matters. She was surrounded in the dusty centre of the camp by about thirty Somali refugees, some of them committee members, the rest, from information pieced together later, members of the supporting clans. Louise was bowled over in a wild melee. Rioting Somalis stumbled over the volcanic rock outcrops that dotted the place and picked up chunks of the loose stuff and hurled them everywhere. Tough action by Yemeni police and Bedouin staff led by my driver Labani was required to restore order. Louise was shaken, and it was some days before her confidence was rebuilt.

Our Somali staff were ashamed of this incident. They hung their shaking heads, 'Oh Mr Steve, Mr Steve ...' But they need not have, it was not their fault. Many Somali refugees discreetly passed on their sympathy and sorrow, but were too intimidated to confront the all-powerful camp committee of tribal elders. The tall and graceful women in their flowing colourful sarongs and matching head covers, their almond-shaped eyes bright as always, came to us and mumbled their apologies. It was an interesting and new insight for me into Somali behaviour. Tempers had cooled and there was contrition everywhere. This committee was a thorn in our sides, rather than the help it should have been, and we were powerless to rectify the issue as they were, curiously, protected by the UNHCR Aden office field officers.

The concept of having refugee committees to run daily affairs was sensible and quite essential to good camp management, but it was not working there, and indeed was counterproductive to effective and humane management. Dealing with the committee took an incredibly disproportionate amount of CARE Yemen's time. Members of the committee were not averse to intimidating certain refugees. UNHCR had not ensured cross-representation in the selection of committee members, and only the most powerful clans were represented. Some Yemeni police who belonged to the small camp garrison were cleverly manipulated by these crafty old committee elders. Prostitution occurred occasionally, to which a blind eye was turned. There were many other problems like this.

The job could be a young program officer's nightmare, if he or she were not equipped and prepared; I thought that of all CARE Australia's programs around the world, this must be one of the most difficult. The Somalis in Yemen were the toughest, the most unbending, the most playful, and the most ungrateful of the recipients of aid I was ever to experience in CARE's work. I was often to question the wisdom of continuing our role in the face of the hostility we were experiencing there.

During September I took up the logistics officer position for the country program and was based in Aden. Mercifully the heat had abated, but it was still very hot. In these early days I made myself unpopular with the myriad local subcontractors we had providing services to the office and to the refugee program. When they came with a wink in their eye and looking for automatic extensions of contracts, I slapped on the 'tendering process requirements'. They were a little put out. It was easy to see who was really fair dinkum, I thought at the time.

CARE Yemen decided to put together a landmine clearing program. A project proposal was to be prepared for submission to a number of donors and the UN. Landmine clearing had been identified by Rohit and me as a major and urgent activity needed in the south of Yemen, particularly in the 100 kilometre stretch of country north to south approaching Aden. Aden had been ringed by minefields during the war. At this time landmine clearing was seen as a radical activity for international humanitarian NGOs but I argued passionately for it, with Nagpal in Sana'a and with the CARE Australia Middle East Office (CAMEO) in Amman. I reckon there is nothing more humanitarian than clearing landmines, not only in order to minimise death and injury but also to free communities up to return without fear to their community activities — commerce, farming, worship, and general community living.

I was to spend four weeks in the desert stretches around Aden and out into the 'Sahara lanes', a 100 kilometre stretch of sand dunes running east of Aden, along the foothills of the coastal mountain range, an area which was a major trading and movement route for camel-borne supplies and for the movement of livestock. We visited all villages, collecting anecdotal evidence on where mines were known to have been laid and information on where mine incidents had occurred in recent times. We discovered there had been scores of civilians and soldiers killed since the end of the war. In one horrific incident three days before our visit a truck with eight landmine-clearing engineer soldiers was destroyed, killing all aboard, on a small farming track that followed the major north/south wadi, close to the main Aden highway. Then there was a family in a Landcruiser pick-up blown up here, with deaths and serious injuries. Then a goat farmer over there.

The army truck — now a twisted, blackened hulk — lay across the road as a grim reminder. We had to stop and clear ourselves a detouring track to get around it. Probing in the hot sand, it took an hour just to clear 10 metres of track. We did it the old-fashioned way: we used long, pointed probes and 'felt' for any mines, my driver, two field staff and I sweating profusely as we probed. There was no magical scientific answer to safe and thorough checking and clearing. We were sweating not only from the merciless sun but also from a healthy level of tension. Thankfully on that occasion we were not to find any mines. However, we were soon to dramatically and quickly curtail our wadi and track running, even along hardened and clearly defined tracks, due to the ever-present threat. We found evidence of mines shifting in the sand dunes, due to wind action. Crossing the dominating wadi that parallels the Aden highway on the western side we could see landmines sticking out of the sand. It was obvious that when the wadi had begun to run with the first of the end of summer rains the landmines were swept along and onto hitherto safe wadi crossings. A hideous business, I thought at the time. And so in this fashion we travelled around the desert and wadi country, identifying where the major threats were.

Over these weeks we defined the scope of the huge Aden landmine belt problem. Sometimes the army cheerfully and enthusiastically helped us with information, but quite often it was ambivalent — a puzzling response at the time, but one we were to later understand better. We sifted our information and were able to define where the problem was just helplessly out of control — in other words those areas we would need to simply quarantine for the foreseeable future.

We assessed risk areas across the district, and identified (and put in priority order) those communities where we believed we could make a major impact, where we would be able to clear, fence off and say to the community in question, 'These areas inside these newly erected and signposted fences, around your bazaar, your goat grazing areas, your wells and water points and district pump stations are clear. Do not step over those fences. You are responsible for keeping your fences intact and you are responsible for ensuring that your clean zones remain free of landmines.' This was the heart of the concept; it was very dependent on a high level of co-operation and also on villager involvement in the landmine clearing program.

The Dutch government aid agency in Sana'a was enthusiastic about our program. We submitted to them and to the UN Development Program (UNDP) a project proposal of thirty-two pages, consisting of analysis, argument and concept, implementation plan, maps and sketches. Support was generally there, so we proceeded to pursue government approval. Disappointingly we did not get this, yet some weeks earlier, when we first embarked on this project, we had received a cautious but positive response from the government. I was shattered — this was my first serious foray into the world of major humanitarian analysis and project definition work. Four weeks of effort down the drain! The proposal package, though shelved, was at least an example of how we might put together such programs in the future; it seemed to become a useful model for CARE Australia and CARE International in terms of pursuing the concept. Later, in 1997, I was to find that a UN colleague, keen to support our program, in fact had taken the CARE program package and adapted it to a new UN de-mining program proposal.

There was a major question and concern: that the risks of running such a program as a directly controlled activity (ie, through a CARE country office 'de-mining unit') were beyond the scope and capacity of an ordinary humanitarian NGO such as CARE. This was a very fair point, one which was to focus our minds at the time. The risks of committing to such programming, in terms of your own staff safety and the guarantees you might be able to give to the assisted communities, are very high. But they are manageable risks. Should CARE develop its own de-mining capability, given the scope of the landmine problem?

CARE Australia and CARE USA were to later run de-mining programs in Cambodia and Africa, so the commitment by CARE to de-mining did happen. These programs would be subcontracted through small, technical de-mining units who otherwise would not have the capacity to launch their own programs.

I had a wide cross-sectional friendship with the staff in the Aden office. It was nothing like the close, bonded, tightly knit friendship of northern Iraq between myself and my Kurdish colleagues, though. The chaos of that place had created dependencies which were razor edged. In Yemen I was finally able to unwind and settle in to a program where although the humanitarian need was deeply worrying, there was no pressure of war. I was able to think more creatively and to thoroughly enjoy a more relaxed set of friendships. But as in northern Iraq, I was to refrain from getting too close to staff, and still carried, some time after my military life, an old-fashioned but entirely proper approach to staff matters — arm's length, firm but fair and friendly.

Samira and I had nevertheless become firm friends. I depended greatly on her knowledge of the culture and the law as it was practised in this place. During negotiations with subcontractors she was indispensable. With the disputes that we invariably had with contractors, businessmen and government officials she was the brightest and most able person, and always hurled herself with an almost religious fervour into sorting these problems out. She herself thrived on these challenges.

Toward the end of my time in Yemen our friendship grew, but it did not develop into any form of courtship. That would happen a year later, and by some strange method of remote control. While we did not seem to have any designs upon each other during my time working with CARE Yemen, we were the best of friends and did realise that we needed to be careful. I needed to be careful in terms of the essential criteria for good staff management. Samira needed to be very careful from the perspective of what was socially acceptable, and in this society there was no margin for error.

My attraction to Samira and the basis for my serious approaches to her in later years grew out of a professional and personal respect for her integrity and strength of character, as well as in response to her beauty and charm. I was invited to her home to meet her extraordinary family, and on a number of Saturdays we had long lunches of chicken, rice and date dishes called 'buria', enjoyable affairs where we sat cross-legged on the floor around the mat. We would dig in to grab handfuls of lamb and rice. Then she would retire to the couch with her remarkable father Ahmed to watch CNN off the satellite. He would smoke his hubble bubble without pause, knees up on the ample couch, reaching down for the long bubble hose. He was an engineer and was recognised Arabia-wide as a writer of music. The other women were banished from the room, and groups of two or three of Samira's nine brothers at a time entered the room to participate in conversation. They talked and inquired of me all manner of things, as only Yemenis can — they are the most curious people in the world, I think. Also the boys engaged in banter with their father, occasionally negotiating serious business, family or other matters with him. Samira was invited into the living room, but only because she was a work colleague. I was impressed to see that at least one family in Yemen did not engage in qat chewing.

One weekend I travelled with Samira, her father and Labani, who was to drive us, to visit the magnificent Wadi Duwan in the Hadrumat region of eastern Yemen. For me it would be both a welcome weekend break and a useful field trip through I would be able to orient myself to the nature of humanitarian needs in the back country. We flew to Makalla on the coast, linked up with Labani, and drove up into the mountains, climbing 3000 metres into the most incredible mountain desert country. We were on top of the world, freezing wind cutting though us, and at the end of the day we plunged down into the great Wadi Duwan, a grand canyon-like feature with sheer cliffs and sandstone buttresses towering 1000 metres. We wound our way to the bottom of the canyon.

Samira's father had invited me to his ancestral home: El Grain, a village of two thousand people, and one of five villages in a cluster stretching over about 5 kilometres, El Grain the dominant one.

Down the entire length of this great wadi, stretching from the high country that is Shabwa, there were scores of villages and small towns clinging to the sustenance and life-giving qualities of the wadi. The wadi is the only shelter for thousands of kilometres in all directions, a crack in the expanse of the stony high plateau desert country. They claim their ancestral line back over a thousand years in this place. Ahmed is still by blood the Sultan of this area, his father the last practising 'Grand Sultan' of Wadi Duwan. They no longer have the expansive lands they once owned up and down this wadi, the socialist government having confiscated the lot in the 1960s during their wholesale socialisation of the country. Ahmed had been left only a couple of houses in El Grain. We stay in one of these, a 300-year-old four-storey red clay house. A remarkable structure, beautifully plastered and ornately decorated inside, its doorways are now too narrow and low, reflecting the size of the people of the 1600s.

Ahmed, who is a respected and much-liked presence in the place still, even though he lives in faraway Aden, showed me two large dams, built high up in the mountains over the villages, which need some work done on them to alleviate leaking. The work would be substantial, and clearly trucks and trucks of concrete would be needed to be poured into the place. Indeed, not so much trucks but droves of donkeys would be requried, as you would never get trucks down those massive cliffs.

When inside the house I am confined to one room, forbidden to go wandering and also forbidden to look outside the window. From a discreet peephole I can gaze down along the wadi to observe the slow-paced life of the place. The wadi is about a kilometre wide and bracketed by sheer walls of sandstone. The floor is a jungle of date palms, sundry other trees and bushy shrubs. The central creek is a jumble of water-smoothed boulders and occasional water pools.

The women are strictly dressed and totally covered by their black abayas; unlike Aden, where a fair percentage of women are unveiled, here all women's faces are covered. A significant number of negro slave descendants are to be seen around this place, their ancestors having arrived ten to twenty generations ago to work as slaves on the date palm plantations and on general wadi maintenance tasks. They are now free, but this is their home, and they have no desire to see Africa.

The backbone of transport in the place is the donkey and very few four-wheel drives or any other type of vehicle are to be seen. The foothills of the great escarpments of all villages on both sides are dotted by four-storey clay houses, grouped in clusters. Like miniature Sydney city skyscraper blocks. Time has stood still in this place — but for a handful of Landcruisers and a couple of mechanical pumps servicing wells this could be the 12th century.

I take notes to discuss with Ahmed and later Samira the type of infrastructure and social programs CARE could undertake in places like Wadi Duwan, and other isolated communities scattered across the mountains of Yemen clinging to precious but limited water resources. (I later thumbnail sketch a number of project outline concepts for presentation to CARE as a series of development projects aimed at enhancing basic water systems for a number of areas along the Wadi Duwan.)

Samira and I discuss a broad range of ideas aimed at meeting very basic needs and addressing the social neglect that affects women and families. Getting community support here for the running of social programs will be no easy thing; it will need the clever persistence and charm of a determined Samira, and the perhaps grudging support of her father. But how will we overcome the obstacles in other areas of the mountains, outside their influence, I wonder?

During the 1995 Shabwa floods, Dutch government funding and general emergency assistance was to be gratefully received. CARE Yemen was to run a frantic emergency response program to assist displaced people. On this occasion Samira was deployed to Shabwa as the senior Yemeni staff member. A project officer now, she carried responsibility for implementation, pending the arrival of new international staff, who had to be urgently recruited from overseas. Samira was to find herself the only female supervising an organisation and operation of any description in that whole region. This attracted a great deal of attention from the local population, some positive, some negative. But after two months of debilitating work, according to her international staff colleagues, she was to win over many of her conservative Shabwa male critics. The program was successful, and significant relief was brought to the area, allowing families to eat while they restored their devastated farms, planted new crops and, with assistance, restocked their flocks.

In infrastructure, economy and politics, Yemen is something of a basket case, but CARE was still unable to raise the funding needed from international donors to help the place lift itself out of its 12th century rut. The programs we had designed were to go nowhere, and to this day CARE struggles to attract funding to the country. Sadly, in international terms, the backwater that is Yemen does not rate as a place of interest.

CHAPTER FOUR

An African Trial

I had arrived in East Africa at a time when CARE International members were widely involved across central and east Africa. The Rwanda massacre of 1994 had caused massive problems across the whole region. The deployment of many CARE International member teams into the maelstrom of this horrific emergency had, unfortunately, caused some tension. What I immediately noticed on arrive was that the 'creative tensions' amongst CARE International members in the Great Lakes region had not abated, but there was an atmosphere of co-operation and a wide spread desire to learn the lessons, to improve co-operation and co-ordination. This problem was not confined to CARE International, and was very much a part of the NGO landscape in the Great Lakes region, particularly in the hot spot of eastern Zaire. CARE Australia had accidentally exacerbated the co-ordination issue with its CARE International member partners. Very large sums of money had been raised by CARE Australia, with the best of intentions. It then decided the most effective way to discharge its donor responsibility was to actually deploy its own emergency teams alongside existing CARE International member country offices. CARE Australia had deployed robustly and had perhaps trodden on a few of its partners' toes.

Care International in the Great Lakes quickly set about streamlining its systems and procedures for shared member operations. Meanwhile, the greater problem — that is, of UN agencies and NGOs all rushing into complex emergency situations — had still to be addressed at that time. Progress was made in the Great Lakes over 1995–96 in this UN/NGO co-ordination problem. The need for better co-ordination was well known and something understood by all. Often, with the demonstration of strong leadership by the UN, good co-ordination would occur, as it eventually did in Goma, Zaire due to the flexibility and optimism of UNHCR.

The needy are often the casualties of these types of misunderstandings between NGOs. It was my experience in Africa that disagreements, competition, duplication of effort, not to mention inadvertent misunderstandings between UN agencies, between NGOs and within federations such as the CARE International federation, were a regular feature of humanitarian operations. These usually resulted in significant failures in humanitarian emergency responses, or significant waste. Such outcomes are rarely intended, but follow from the desire by many organisations to rush in and establish significant presences.

I attended a CARE International Great Lakes Region workshop in Kigali in February 1995, sponsored and co-ordinated by CARE USA through their CARE Rwanda office. The country director was a Briton, seconded from CARE UK. The Canadians and the Americans were there in force, but I was the only CARE Australia representative. There was tension initially, but due to the goodwill evident we were able progress contingency planning for the region and to have CARE Australia included as a contingency partner. It seemed that by this point the other CAREs generally accepted CARE Australia's presence in the region. Though maybe a little renegade in those terrible days of late 1994, I believe CARE Australia was generally recognised as possessing a 'can do' attitude and a no nonsense practicality in the field, qualities perhaps not abundantly available in some of the other CARE members. My two years in the Great Lakes were to be dogged by this need to tread carefully with our CARE partners. My diplomacy skills were to become well honed.

AN AFRICAN TRIAL

Over these two years of my African experience we were to see a positive rebuilding of co-operation amongst the CARE members in terms of developing an effective approach to tackling the Great Lakes regional crisis. Programs were co-ordinated and there was an attempt to take a 'global' view of regional planning. For example, what would the impact of certain programs in the Zaire refugee camps be on the running of CARE programs in Rwanda and on eventually settling matters there? Importantly, CARE International in 1995 and 1996 was trying to put together a co-ordinated position, based on the experience and pooled thoughts of its experienced African country missions, to contribute to the international community's Great Lakes region conflict and emergency crisis resolution. It was not perfect harmony but it was a damn good attempt to harness the efforts and talents of the CARE federation, the three operational CAREs (USA, Canada and Australia) and the major supporting CARE members, namely CARE UK, CARE Deutschland (Germany) and CARE Osterreich (Austria). To me, operating in the middle of all this, it was heartening to see. It represented CARE International at its best.

In Rwanda, CARE Australia continued to run its small but effective programs: operating medical services in Kibeho Camp (for Hutu refugees), about 200 kilometres south-west of Kigali, and running Hutu and Tutsi displaced children centres (separated from their parents because of their parents' deaths or geographical displacement) in Kigali and 150 kilometres south of Kigali in the provincial capital of Butare. CARE USA was happy to see these programs continue for the time being, and the agreement was that when CARE Australia's funds were exhausted, CARE Australia would pack up and depart the country, or perhaps, if more practical, do this sooner by transferring the programs and the available funds to CARE Rwanda. I had negotiated with the country director of CARE Rwanda a memorandum of understanding to this effect.

The CARE Australia office, with five Australians and about 200 Rwandan staff, sat on a very picturesque hillside with a pretty view down the valley — it defied the imagination to think that this very place had been the scene of such macabre behaviour and massive brutality — and housed both office and accommodation in a large modern two-storey brick bungalow. Our team leader, who had originally been deployed here during the last days of the troubles, worked this CARE operation through the CARE Rwanda office, and he in fact reported directly to the British country director for the day-to-day operations of his team. That was the arrangement between the CAREs. The team leader, a craggy and robust French Australian who was a skilled and experienced Africa hand, reported to me for his team's administration and for the sorting out and implementation of general CARE Australia policy matters.

From my office in Nairobi, our regional headquarters, I also supported our Rwanda team logistically. Using our own chartered aircraft we would fly in medical supplies for distribution into the refugee camp at Kibeho each week. I was generally happy with the arrangement for CARE co-operation in Rwanda as it was sorted out in early 1995. Our Australian staff made it work, through the application of characteristically good humour and the demonstration of good program capabilities. They did not initially understand the CARE International Code and what all the fuss was all about; they were just good field staff, keen to get on with responding to emergencies, and just as keen to avoid political shenanigans. Our Australian staff in the country teams, and my colleagues and I in Nairobi, were mostly successful in putting these tensions behind us and working effectively with our CARE partners, although we still had our moments.

On 22 April I was urgently contacted by our acting Rwandan team leader, in the absence of the Frenchman, who was on leave. He advised that the Rwandan Army — the ex-Rwanda Patriotic Front (RPF) — had suddenly placed a cordon around the refugee camp at Kibeho. It was anticipated that the Rwandan Government was going to force the closure of this camp, which they considered a thorn in the side of peace and security in the country. There was no doubt that this camp housed Hutu extremists, as did all the Hutu refugee camps throughout the Great Lakes region, and that these people were running hit-and-run guerrilla raids against the Rwanda Patriotic Front, its army and Tutsi civilians. Their aims were to destabilise the regime and embarrass it. The dream of a Hutu counter-revolution burned on. Regrettably, the Hutu camps were becoming a safe haven for these guerrilla groups. We, the international non-government organisations, were caught in the middle again.

The Kibeho refugee camp carried further political baggage. It had initially been established by the French Army at the end of the 1994 war as a safe haven for a particular Hutu group, about 185 000 (including their families), who were thought to be among the Hutu political elite. As the Tutsi army had swept across the country from the north, the French Army coming in from the south had intervened to throw a protective cordon around this particular group. With UN intervention and the consequent withdrawal of the French expeditionary force, the UN had taken over the Kibeho haven and a refugee camp was born. CARE Australia, CARE USA and a number of other international NGOs were implementing partners with the UN in the management of the camp and/or the running of refugee support programs within the camp.

CARE Australia ran a number of field aid posts in the Kibeho camp, these being our primary responsibility there. Australian and Hutu medical staff would travel daily from the small provincial town of Butare, about two hours north on the road to Kigali, and there was always a permanent Hutu staff presence. Butare was the CARE Australia team base — that is, it was the CARE International outpost in the south of the country. The sub-team leader there was a young British Australian and he reported to our Frenchman in Kigali. CARE Rwanda, a CARE USA-led mission, supervised, through the Frenchman, the day-to-day running of our Butare and Kibeho camp operations.

I would visit Kigali, Butare and Kibeho as much as I could, as was my habit. I would attempt to see where we could do more to support their operations and to satisfy myself that the operational aspects of the program were in line with CARE Australia's regional policy and regional humanitarian strategy. I had a good understanding with the CARE Rwanda British country director, and could come and go as much as I liked, providing I gave him advance notice and paid him a courtesy visit. These lines of communication across the two CAREs and within country entities probably looked pretty cumbersome and a little confusing, but the whole arrangement worked well enough.

We were satisfied, and after the initial difficulties, which could have seen CARE Australia 'sanctioned' in the region by the CARE International board, it was important to make these arrangements work for the good of humanitarian operations in the region.

Meanwhile, in Kibeho the situation deteriorated rapidly. The RPK was attempting to set up a cordon and then go into the camp to seek out and arrest extremists. The Interehamwe (Hutu) extremists did what they do second best (after wholesale killing of innocents): they intimidated their own population and forced the civilian masses in the camp to demonstrate against the Rwanda Tutsi authorities. This was the extremists' only hope of survival. They did not care if their own people struggled or died. It was even better if they died in front of the international community (the UN, CARE, et al). By forcing their own people to demonstrate and stay in place, the Interehamwe could maintain a protective wall behind which they could remain hidden.

Our Butare sub-team leader and Tony, the acting Kigali team leader, called me to warn me that up to two Rwandan battalions were thought, by the UN and UNAMIR (the UN peacekeepers), to have been deployed to seal the camp and were already conducting internal operations. Consequently, refugees were fleeing the camp. This is what the Tutsi authorities wanted, the idea being to force the Hutus back to their villages, where they could be better controlled, and more easily arrested for past atrocities.

The camp was disintegrating and the CARE program had ceased to exist; Hutu staff had gone. Already, newly displaced children had been picked up by all sorts of people — UN staff, UNAMIR troops and even the RPF. They were being brought to Butare, the nearest UN/NGO base after Kibeho. The CARE team ran the biggest and most effective displaced children centre in Butare, indeed one of the best in all of Rwanda. Our centre was being overwhelmed by new children, from newborn to 5-year-olds.

Why were these children displaced? One of the more bizarre and saddest sights in African emergencies, but perhaps one also demonstrating a quest for hope and continuation of life, is that of fleeing African mothers throwing their children to one side, out of harm's way, away from their pursuers. CARE's biggest program in

Rwanda was caring for displaced children. Initially we had in the region of 1500. Following reunification, but more likely because of the successful arrangement of foster family care, CARE had reduced that number to somewhere nearer 500. Now hundreds more were being dumped on CARE's doorstep, and we did not have the medical staff, the trained child care staff, the medicines nor the resources to take up the extra challenge. Hundreds more were anticipated, and we could not turn them away.

CARE Rwanda had decided that the CARE Australia team could take care of all this, and fully delegated the responsibility to us. They were unable to lend resources or manpower at all, and it was left entirely to CARE Australia to decide how to react. I spoke to and got CARE USA's approval to unilaterally expand the existing CARE presence in Butare.

I had sent an emergency situation report (SITREP) to Canberra that Saturday afternoon, as a wake-up call. On my way to the Australian High Commissioner's residence for a function I had pulled out and was fast at it on the phones, updating myself on the situation in Kibeho, and in Butare, on the safety and security situation in southern Rwanda, and on whether our team was likely to be in any jeopardy. I was on the phone to Canberra, reinforcing my SITREP recommending that we quickly double and then quadruple our international staff presence in Butare. Our humanitarian assessment was that displaced children and general medical cases among the fleeing refugees were the potential major need, children in the first instance. In the SITREP I had stated my intention to redeploy a medical team of five Australian staff from our Goma, Zaire base immediately to Butare. Did CARE Australia have a problem with that? I asked in the SITREP.

I had spoken urgently by phone (and backed it up with a fax) to the French head of mission for the UN in Goma, the head of the UNHCR office there, seeking his support for redeploying this medical team. In asking for the removal of that medical team I needed to reassure him that our UN-partnered medical operation (we were their implementing partners) in the Goma refugee camps would not be diminished. He was happy enough, he said, but sternly warned me that the doctor and her four medical staff had to be back within the week. Meanwhile, our Goma team leader was reassuring me that he could carry this gap, make it up with staff doubling up. He also went off to smooth the feathers of our prickly but effective French UNHCR colleague.

CARE Australia's national director rang me mid-afternoon. This was the first time I had heard the exalted voice of Ian Harris, our flamboyant and robust national director, in my life. 'Pratt! Harris! Listen, I've got a great idea, you listening? Want you to grab about five medical staff out of Goma and immediately send them over to Rwanda. Got it! Don't stuff around! Do it! Call me back if need be!' Click. Righto. We were already onto it anyway. I had spoken to the CARE Australia overseas director in Canberra. He was a thorough operator and a good planner, always able to take a phone call any time of the day or night, which was important for me given the eight-hour time difference. Col said he would find the funding out of the existing contingency funds for the Great Lakes to allow immediate recruitment and sending to Rwanda of five to ten medical staff and an additional logistics officer. The logistics officer would take on the increased administrative, logistics and general support role.

The new team from Australia would be essentially child health staff, although we agreed to throw in an impressive ambulance officer who had been on CARE's emergency staff books now for some months. This fellow had contacted CARE, some days earlier coincidentally, to state that he was looking for an immediate three-month contract and detachment. He sounded to me like somebody generally useful, even if not a specialist in child health, and, importantly, he could travel within twenty-four hours. He could be immediately released by his employer, his inoculations were up to date and he had a current passport, not something people always have at their fingertips. His immediate arrival, ahead of the others, would help lessen the burden on an already tired and overworked team in Butare. These are the typical challenges of country directors and regional managers in trying to quickly put emergency teams together. So Garry, the paramedic, was accepted and on the way.

The overseas director and I agreed we would recruit and deploy one medical team of five personnel as soon as possible. We would then, with more time, recruit a more substantial team to follow one week later, and it was my intention that they would replace the Goma medical team, who were only on temporary loan to us. The overseas director, with whom I had not worked closely before, I found to be effective and very experienced. He let me call the shots as I saw them on the ground (and I in turn relied on the advice and assessments of our Rwanda team leader), and he backed up with the resources, personnel and funds, as long as it was within budget. He moved quickly and got the Canberra human resources staff cracking. Qantas provided priority seating and donated the flight seats for these new teams, as it has always done for CARE. A great relief for a funds-strapped CARE. We had them contracted for three months, the anticipated life of the emergency (pulled out of the ether). This would be extendable, if necessary.

I received the teams in Nairobi, some days apart, had them quickly oriented and administratively inducted (no time for operational induction here) and then travelled with them by charter plane into Kigali, where I handed them over to the Rwanda acting team leader. At this juncture the Butare team — now increased to ten with the addition of the Goma five — were exhausted. The hours were punishing and the meagre housing available in Butare was overcrowded; people were, understandably, getting on each other's nerves. We moved as quickly as we could, within the constraints of the local corruption and extortion environment, to set up an additional house in the same street and close to our current housing. Proximity was needed for security reasons and also for better program communications. Things were working, in the toughest and the most difficult conditions possible, in the time-honoured CARE way, but nevertheless, working well. Our displaced children's centre had bulked out, and we had established a tented, temporary centre in Butare, alongside and in concert with a British NGO called 'Feed the Children' (FTC). Which our dry-witted Butare team leader, in his clipped English accent underlaid with ever-broadening Aussie tones, renamed 'Feed the Chooks'.

The displaced children were being brought in rapidly, many in poor health, some close to death. Dr Cathy, who was deputy to CARE's Goma team leader, and her nurses had flung themselves into the fray. Cathy was an excellent doctor. Initially I thought her a little young for the head position of our team from Goma, but as I got to know her I soon changed my mind. Dr Cathy had the total confidence and respect of everyone, she was a shrewd and effective ambassador for us in our dealings with the UN, and she also called a spade a spade. She was a good team leader too. During the hectic days of the Butare/Kibeho response she made a big difference to the atmosphere of the place with her calmness and 'get stuck in and problem solve' manner. The team had taken over and converted an old school into a new centre. The few buildings in the place became clinics and surgery rooms.

I had flown down again from Nairobi to see how things were going. It was my practice to come in weekly for a couple of days at a time, to have a look, talk to everybody in the teams and see what else I and the Nairobi base could do assist the team leaders and their teams. A range of canvas tents were erected outside in the courtyard for the children's accommodation. Many of the smallest children were on drips, exhausted, suffering from malnutrition and dehydrated — these were accommodated inside the clinics as special cases.

It is quite a distressing sight when I stick my head into a tent and see a row of ten children all lined up on their crude palliasses, the best we could do, along the back of the tent. Babies, most of them. All gazing back wide-eyed in amazement at the white fellow, the 'Muzungu', observing them. No fuss whatsoever, no fighting amongst the kids, poor little mites probably instinctively wondering what fate this visitor is bringing them. They seem quite content to sit there and await the next instructions from the Muzungu nurses, but then what choice do they have?

I have seen this same sight so often in this business in Africa — small, lonely children quietly and obediently awaiting their fate. Our nurses and social workers, some of them by now seasoned campaigners on their second tour with CARE in central Africa, are finding incredible reserves of energy and compassion to deal with these overwhelming numbers of little kids. Running noses everywhere, haunted eyes expressing silent gratitude. Our Australian staff, mainly women, getting around amongst the tents in the mud, against a constant drizzle of rain and mist in the treetops of this high plateau country. The blokes, Garry the paramedic and the logistics officers seconded from Kigali, in and out of the hastily erected tents, improving structures, patching rain leaks. All over the buildings, working to improve the sanitation, the water supplies and implement running repairs to the run-down buildings. These blokes respond without a second thought to help FTC with its logistical and infrastructure problems, as only Australian 'can do' workers can — they are famous for this throughout the region and in the aid business. Always visible they are too, in their Australian trademark boots and shorts, even the odd battered Akubra. Good-humouredly taking the rinse out of the Brits and the French, the people they are helping. I reflect on all this as I move around taking in the scene and getting real satisfaction out of measuring and anticipating the outcomes. I hope the kids are feeling safer, too.

The Butare team leader and Dr Cathy have to wrestle with the attrition rate and the toll being taken on the workers; they have been hard at it now for seven or more days, and even with the new second team arriving there appears to be little respite possible. They are both organising day and night rosters for staff to rotate through the monitoring duties in the medical area and supervisory activities in the kids' tented dormitories. Moving staff back and forth the kilometre or so between the team accommodation and the two centres, particularly in the wee hours of the morning, is tricky work. There is a lot of strange movement on the streets of this little provincial town at night, including the RPF, who are aggressive and intrusive. We do not feel comfortable with them or trust them. The odd shot can be heard during the night, and there are security incidents aplenty around the town.

The Butare team leader is looking done in; red-eyed, hoarse voice, he seems to have caught the inevitable aid workers' cold, as have a number of the other team members. The conditions, together with a combination of general exhaustion and being exposed to the colds and respiratory conditions among the children, have laid them low. He is holding up well enough under the circumstances. Eight days ago, I reflect, we entered his peaceful and sedate little world in the highland country of Butare, where a great little program seemed to be almost running itself. Now I have tripled his little team and given him responsibilities far greater than he has had before, but he has reacted well to the challenge. It is always messy trying to get these emergency team balances right, finding the right mix of skills, a good blend of personalities, and establishing a leader — always difficult, as most people do not really want to carry that mantle. Nor is everybody capable of leadership; in fact in my experience the majority are not, it is not an acquired skill. But our Butare leader is holding it together well, backed up by Dr Cathy and some pretty experienced and sensible people. This operation is making progress, I assess.

I won from the UN chief in Goma a respite of a few more days, which allowed me to leave Dr Cathy and her team in Butare. A few more days would mean we could create a meaningful overlap between Cathy's team and the new one on its way from Australia, but that would be the extent of it.

We continued to be swamped with the displaced children as well as the general medical needs of aimlessly wandering Kibeho camp inmates. The situation in Kibeho camp was very dramatic — thousands of refugees were milling around in the very centre of the camp, refusing to move out. The Rwandan Army was gradually redeploying itself to tighten the cordon, its soldiers poised up on the ridges around the perimeter of the camp. We were in touch with UNAMIR Australian troops, and I had visited the Australian troop contingent HQ in Kigali to get an update on what was happening. What new humanitarian crises could we anticipate? Importantly, what safety and security situations could we predict and plan for regarding the safety of our people and programs in Butare? These were the questions that were my job to consider and determine as a regional manager. They filled my mind when I visit the UNAMIR offices.

The UN and UNAMIR warnings were grim, and they soon became reality. On the seventh day of the Kibeho crisis the RPF started firing random shots over the heads of the crowd. But it seemed that Interehamwe extremists had fired shots from the central building inside the camp too, although it was not clear where those shots were travelling. Refugees were found dead, some shot, some hacked with machetes — which leads UN and UNAMIR to conclude that these are probably Interehamwe killings of their own moderate

Hutu civilians, who perhaps were no longer co-operating with the demonstration of disobedience.

The random RPF shooting was in the direction of the UN troops stationed at the camp. There was a Tanzanian infantry battalion in a compound on a dominating hill. Alongside them was an Australian infantry platoon, which was there providing security for an Australian UNAMIR medical detachment, working overtime in very harrowing circumstances to treat wounded and sick refugees. The CARE medical teams had occasionally visited and worked with this Australian medical team, to assist them in CARE's previous area of responsibility, but had had to get back to Butare to face the overwhelming odds there.

The CARE team was not in the camp on the day when the violence built to a crescendo and erupted into disaster. On this day the troops had their heads down while the firing over their heads continued to increase. Under strict UN orders, UN troops are not permitted to return fire. Emboldened by that fact, the RPF were encouraged to continue firing shots sufficient to keep UNAMIR pinned while they prepared for their final act in this unfolding drama. Such was the lot of the brave but powerless UN troop field commanders in that situation.

Something had snapped among the Hutus, and on this fateful day they moved massively, swarming towards the perimeter of the now wrecked and devastated Kibeho refugee camp. It would seem that the Hutu civilians — facing extreme hostility and danger from the RPF in front and extraordinary pressure and terror from the Interehamwe behind — realised that their only choice was to break out. They panicked. Perhaps the Interehamwe reckoned that before the witnessing eyes of the international community the RPF would have little choice but to allow the masses, with the Interehamwe hidden in their ranks, to escape the cordon and make their way to safety, perhaps to a new UN cordon-sanitaire. A combination of forces caused the breakout move.

The RPF opened fire, due, it seems from all accounts, to panic and overreaction among young soldiers. Certainly, as the killing went on, Australian troops were to observe some RPF officers running up and down their troops' lines hitting their own soldiers with sticks to try to stop them shooting. But once the firing started it had its own momentum, and refugees were mowed down in the grassy fields and on the undulating slopes of the now destroyed camp. The firing went on unabated for quite a while, until RPF officers were able to get their soldiers back under control. Meanwhile, the suppressing fire delivered onto the UN military compound had intensified, and still the troops were ordered by higher command to hold their own fire.

There was sheer devastation at the end of it all. In the middle of the camp, for hundreds of metres around the remains of the bullet-riddled central camp administrative buildings, there was a carpet of bodies. CARE Australia workers from Butare were there the following day, to see what could be done in the wake of the carnage. They witnessed some of the body count conducted by the Australian troop contingent, who had to use their (infantry navigation) sheep counters. The troops at first, we understood, did not realise they were walking on bodies, such was the state of the debris strewn around. The mud hid many bodies which had been trampled in panic. CARE workers were convinced that the number of bodies far exceeded the UN official figure. Other credible reports available to me at the time talked of a total dead from gunshot, machete and trampling to be between 2000 and 4000. The condition of the tangled mass of trampled bodies made it difficult to count accurately.

Our CARE workers stumbled around the shattered camp. They were stunned and shocked. For all of them this was their first glimpse of man's inhumanity to man. They must have wondered whether they could stand working another day in this place. Why not just get on the plane and get out of it? Were we making any difference? In the end the UN was to diplomatically proclaim 'up to 350 refugees killed'. We were to question the massive disparity in estimates; it seemed to me that the UN found it necessary, in terms of realpolitik and the quest for developing some sort of political stability, to downplay the gravity of the incident. As it would turn out, the Kibeho incident would be infinitesimal compared with the fate that CARE would witness falling upon the Hutu refugees some eighteen months later, or to the horrific massacres that had been committed against the Tutsis in 1994. Nevertheless, this was yet another inexcusable massacre.

CHAPTER FIVE
Zaire

My first visit to Zaire was in late February 1995, when I flew there for an orientation visit. I went down on the CARE-contracted air company 'Commuter Air', in their small twin-engined seven-seater. The pilot was their chief, a Kenyan Sikh by the name of Ramish, who was to become a very good and supportive friend of CARE. We flew into Goma airport — the view on first entry was spellbinding, and would be the same each time thereafter.

Goma sits on the border with Rwanda and on the northern shore of Lake Kivu. The lake is a magnificent affair. It is 150 kilometres long, about seventy wide and you cannot see the distant shores. It is a deep lake, and one of some mystery. Clouds of volcanic gas are known to rise to the surface, and fishing from canoes can prove deadly. Thunderhead storm clouds are always drifting around, and as you approach Goma these are vividly reflected in the deep blue waters of the lake. The country along the east of the lake is in effect Rwanda. From the starboard side, as your aircraft bobs and weaves in the updraft eddies caused by changing temperatures, you see the vivid green and steeply rolling hills of Rwanda dominating the lake and the sprawling town of Goma.

This scene, completed as it was by the tidy little farms dotting the landscape, always looked so peaceful to me. Again, I could not imagine that one of the most horrific massacres of modern times had occurred there. Looking north over the lake one could see Goma, a magnificent sight on the lake shore with its attractive and grandly built homes, hangovers from Belgian colonial times, sprawling amidst lovely lawns and gardens. The rest of the town — that is, north from the administrative centre — is an ugly, sprawling shanty town, as ugly as you will see anywhere in Africa. The plane drops in over hundreds of acres of rusting and collapsing roofs. As you touch down, you are conscious of the towering volcanoes that dominate this country, out to the middle and distant north and north-east. At 5000 metres, the most impressive of these straddles the Zaire/ Rwanda border. These mountain ranges are thickly covered in the deepest of primary jungle growth, and are home to the famous gorillas of 'Gorillas in the Mist' fame.

Goma and the lake sit at 1500 metres altitude. The climate is always pleasant, similar to that of the rest of central and east Africa. Fifty or so kilometres west of Goma the rot begins to appear. The country starts to fall away to lower altitudes, down to the steamy and disease-infested river and swamp country of central Zaire, classically described as 'deepest, darkest Africa'. Many of the refugees we were caring for were to eventually be driven into this country and hunted down in the closing revenge-filled chapter of the Hutu refugee saga.

The broad valley sweeping away to the north from Goma, winding its way between the three major volcanoes dominating the area, leads eventually into refugee camp country. In this area, encompassing Goma and the 80-odd kilometres of country to the north of Goma, called North Kivu, there were 750 000 Hutu refugees, people who had fled from expected retribution immediately after the Rwandan massacre and the civil war of 1994. There were five camps in this region. Mugunga camp was immediately west of Goma, Kahindo camp was about 40 kilometres north of Goma and sat east of the main highway and almost backed up to the Rwanda border. There were two more camps on the western side, about 50 and 60 kilometres north of Goma, and finally Katale camp at 80 kilometres north of Goma, also on the western side. Katale camp housed 250 000 refugees, one-third of the total North Kivu refugee caseload. It was a huge camp, about 3 kilometres by 5 kilometres. Small hovels of local bush materials and blue plastic sheets were packed wall to wall. The camp was sprawled over rough volcanic rock, a totally inhospitable place.

CARE Australia was directly responsible for providing medical support, socio/medical programs, displaced children centres, camp administration and sanitation to Katale camp. This was the centre of CARE's presence; it was one of the largest NGO programs in Zaire, about the second largest in the country and one of the most impressive in Africa. CARE was once again UNHCR's implementing partner for refugee support. In 1996, CARE expanded its programming and would take on a significant food distribution program in Mugunga camp, supporting 185 000 refugees. CARE would also eventually run a major warehouse established in Mugunga camp. Additionally, CARE was to take on a transportation operation in support of the UN World Food Program (UNWFP) and UNHCR, servicing all refugee camps in North Kivu.

Before I joined the mission, the CARE Goma team had established an impressive operation and had even won the grudging admiration of the French staff, who seemed to dominate the UN in Goma. With the likes of Clive, Jim (who is later to be involved in Yugoslavia), Craig and a number of other resourceful and creative Australian staff, significant infrastructure unparalled in any other camp had been built in Katale, and was later replicated on a smaller scale in Mugunga. As well as medical aid posts, medical centres, social centres, school rooms and displaced children centres, a number of food distribution points, warehouses, vehicle workshops, bakeries, and even cafes, were built, primarily out of roughly hewn timber and other bush materials.

CARE Australia staff were based in Goma, and the Katale camp sub-team motored daily to work, then returned to Goma, for security reasons, before last light. The road, which was the major highway running north, wound its way up the valley along the foothills of the volcano and border mountain ranges. The Australian staff, with Zairean drivers and some Zairean field staff, would travel with much caution in CARE Land Rovers up what was little more than a track. Severely pot-holed, it had been cut to pieces by the massively increased trucking attracted to the area after the refugee influx. In 1996 these potholes would take on far more significance; they would be used to hide landmines.

The Australian staff operated their programs through hundreds of Hutu staff, employed from within the camps. There were at the height of the program approximately 2000 Hutu staff on the CARE payroll, not including short-term labourers. Office complexes were established in both Katale and Mugunga camps, from which our staff would conduct their daily business. Both office complexes had radio rooms in which were located Very High Frequency (VHF) and High Frequency (HF) radio systems. We were always on our guard with respect to security and maintained strict radio procedures, with individual radio contact to each staff member, each vehicle and each office/program complex. Staff all carried hand-held VHF radios, as staff in northern Iraq also had. What with the many acts of lawlessness, sometimes poverty-driven desperate thievery, incidents with intimidating Zaire soldiers who roamed the whole place generally looking for opportunities and trouble, and the threat of Hutu extremists, who seemed to be everywhere in the camps like a cancer, we were, yet again, very mindful of security concerns. Yet again, as in northern Iraq and Yemen, we had strict security procedures in place. Much to the chagrin of some of my Australian colleagues, I was to very much tighten those procedures and accompanying operational restrictions in Zaire, something I would be obliged to do again in Rwanda.

Dr Cathy, now CARE's doctor and program manager for the family of medical and socio/medical programs in Katale camp, had on her team about three nurses and two social workers, the number varying as the year progressed.

Some nine Australians made up the Katale camp sub-team at the height of the program. The Australian Land Rovers — white Defender 110s all of which had been very kindly donated to CARE by Land Rover Australia Pty Ltd — would roll out of Goma daily, carrying the team to Katale. This was a bit of a talking point in the international community. The CARE Australia team in Goma had a good reputation for its dedicated presence in the camps. At the height of the CARE Australia program there were seventeen Australians in Goma.

Through late 1995 and early 1996 the security environment began to noticeably deteriorate. Hutu Interehamwe guerillas had stepped up their attacks across the border into Rwanda, and in a sad irony began launching these from the apparently safe havens of the refugee camps. The Interehamwe were becoming such a menace in the camps that our staff had to be careful to avoid them. Occasionally staff would stumble upon Interehamwe activities; on two occasions in late 1995 Australian staff drove into remote corners of the camps and happened upon groups of armed men. In late 1995 Tutsi fighters living in Zaire, most probably from South Kivu, a known Banyumelenge stronghold, were raiding the camps, although these were light incidents. The Banyumelenge were an ethnic Tutsi tribe living in the South Kivu district of Gaston Zaire and persecuted by the Zaire government. In early 1996 these counter-raids were stepped up in intensity and scope, and it seemed more and more were joined by Rwandan Tutsi soldiers dressed as rebels and fighting alongside Banyumelenge. Adding fuel to this fire were the Mobutu guards; seconded and contracted from the Zairean Army to the UNHCR to protect the camps and keep the peace in them, they were proving to be more trouble than they were worth. There were 1500 of them, and they were very soon up to their armpits in rackets, corruption and intimidation. They were supposed to be the elite of the Zairean Army, but they were nothing better than brigands.

It became clear to me at the time that if this was the yardstick by which one judged the capabilities of the Zairean Army, it was a dead loss. Through 1996, the Zairean Army had deployed in some strength to the Kivu region to combat the growing Banyumelenge insurgency — up to 4500 troops (in addition to Mobutu's 1500 camp refugee guards). Not only were they to demonstrate a total inability to even marginally combat the threat, they proved to be a great burden on the region. They intimidated the local Zaireans, and attacked the Hutus, although not the Hutu extremists or ruling elite. They turned their hand to wheeling and dealing in the region. They extorted their own people. The Zairean Army swaggered and bullied their way around the region, and we began to see them everywhere. By mid-1996 they were intimidating and harassing international UN and NGO personnel, so we had to put security measures in place to protect our staff from these so-called protectors. It was by then a regular weekly occurrence to see NGO vehicles hijacked, something CARE did not suffer until war actually broke out in October 1996.

UNHCR was forced to bring in a liaison unit, made up of ex-military and ex-policemen, whose job it was to work with the Mobutu guards, to receive requests and complaints from NGOs and represent these to the Mobutu guards. Some progress was made and the harassments began to decline in later 1996.

In mid-1996 we scaled down CARE Australia's presence in Africa. The Rwandan team had been disbanded late the previous year. CARE Australia's funding had essentially run out, but more importantly, our organisation had achieved most of its objectives and settled the vast majority of the displaced children. The last group of thirty-eight children that CARE was unable to find homes for or reunite with families was transferred to a displaced children's home run by the Irish NGO 'Concern'. CARE also transferred most of the residual funds (which had been raised by the Johnny Farnham concert in 1995) to Concern, which in effect provided them with operating costs for the thirty-eight children for a further three months. I drew up and signed with Concern a memorandum of understanding to put the agreement in place. For Cecile, our French colleague working in the CARE Rwanda team, parting with the children was a very sad moment.

CARE Australia's then overseas operations director, Col Carling, visited and attended to the reorganisation. The CARE Goma team leader, the director and I examined and discussed the options. CARE Australia then arrived at a plan to rationalise its presence, part of the plan involving the transfer of the regional manager position from Nairobi to Goma. This was a key decision, and made eminent sense; the major program action for CARE Australia in the Great Lakes was now focused there. Additionally, this was where security and safety were tough issues, so I thought, despite my growing fondness for lovely old Nairobi, that that was where I should be located. All

CARE regional policy matters were to be handled by me down in Goma, where I also performed the task of Goma team leader.

By now, I had decided for Samira's sake — and to her joy — to go through the full Muslim marriage. We had commenced the first phase of this on 6 November 1995, in Aden. I had returned to complete the courting process, which had till now only involved a couple of visits while on leave to Yemen through 1995. Samira and I had completed the second and confirming phase of the marriage process in April 1996 with the ceremonial phase, which was very similar to a Christian wedding — all white gowns and black tie. Only problem was I missed the ceremony due to a cancelled flight, while Samira was obliged to proceed. Four hundred guests had been invited and the tide was irreversible. Taking desperate measures, I arrived in the nick of time for the second day of the ceremony, but Samira was terribly disappointed. Nevertheless we had a marvellous and most memorable time — even the Aden weather was kind to us, and when we celebrated at the beach the shimmering blue of the Aden Gulf gave us solace.

Now that we were married, Samira was to join me in Nairobi, and our days there before I left for Goma were sunny, carefree and happy — at least when I was not working, which wasn't much of the time. In June 1996 my son Haydon joined me and Samira in Nairobi for about six weeks. At this time he was living in Rome with his mum and stepfather. With the northern hemisphere school holidays he was able to visit for a good break. Unfortunately, and as has happened too much in my life, the young fellow had to cool his heels in Nairobi waiting for me to return from Goma, where the exigencies of the service had me well tied down. It was also his first meeting with Samira.

Eventually we were able to take two weeks' leave, and have a good look at Kenya. It was a tremendous and once-in-a-lifetime experience for my son, who accompanied me on a couple of (photographic) safari trips in northern and western Kenya (Masai Mara). Samira was wide-eyed through this time, I felt — it was, after all, her first actual experience of living outside Yemen, indeed, her first ever living away from her house, where she had lived for some thirty-two years. She enjoyed the multicultural and multireligious life that is

Nairobi and Kenya and adapted quickly, with the lovely schoolgirl bright-eyed delight that is so typical of her. These were good and precious days, squeezed between the sobering and soon to be crushing days of mine and CARE's Zaire experience.

By late 1996 CARE Australia in Zaire was facing a great dilemma, as were a number of NGOs. The Hutu refugees were not going home, not volunteering to return. The vast majority, it was assumed, should have had nothing to worry about by way of any official Rwandan retribution. It was thought that the hard-core element of 100 000 Hutus — extremists, ex-military, ex-politicians and their families, closely identified with the 1994 massacre — would need continued UNHCR protection, but that the rest ought to be returning. (Of course this also begged the question of what the UN's and our obligations were. Did we continue to look after the 'rump' hard core while the rest of the refugees went home? What about justice for the 1994 massacres?) In terms of the desire that refugees return to Rwanda, all UNHCR efforts had failed. Rwandan politicians brought by UNHCR to the camps had failed to convince the Hutus to return. There was a growing debate within the international community, even between UNHCR and CARE, as to whether the international community should cut back the food and other support services dramatically in order to 'encourage' refugee return.

Two things were obvious. The international community simply could not go on and on paying millions of dollars annually to keep the refugee support program floating. Secondly, the continuation of the camps was clearly provocative and a major impediment to peace in the Great Lakes region. The security of Rwanda, Burundi, even Uganda (feeling the heat of the overspill of troubles, as Hutu guerillas crossed its borders to avoid RPF patrols), Zaire and Tanzania were deeply affected by the continuation of the camps, which were always hotbeds for trouble. The accompanying question was why should we continue to feed camps rife with Interehamwe and other notable troublemakers? Among them were a number who had participated in attempted genocide. Surely we had to ask whether a substantial amount of the food and medicines we provided was being stockpiled for Hutu military supplies? My answer, CARE's answer, was that the vast majority of the refugees were not killers, nor were they in control of events. There were many elderly and there were many children. It was surely our humanitarian obligation to assist these powerless and weak people, many of them innocent, regardless of the presence of the criminals hiding in their ranks. There were murderers intimidating the refugees, just as there had been at Kibeho camp, with such terrible results. How much of the culpability is shared? Where do NGOs make value judgments on these issues and where do you draw the line regarding those who qualify and those who do not qualify for help? If UNHCR has registered these people as deserving refugees, then is that good enough for an NGO to follow?

My view is, you aid such refugees until such time as UNHCR decides who among them are required to answer to charges, and who are therefore removed by UNHCR from the program. It is a judgment call in the field. I believe we are required to be broadminded, but we are also obliged to keep up to date with proceedings and to act on any verifiable information. The subject of the Hutu refugees was to be revisited during a CARE International human rights workshop I attended in the UK in January 1999. We vigorously debated the rights and wrongs of CARE's involvement with this particular caseload, without reaching a satisfactory conclusion.

In late 1996 landmine incidents were also beginning to occur. An American NGO worker had her legs blown off, and was very close to dying from the ordeal. NGO African staff were killed in a number of organisations. The pot-holes were now used for laying mines. Ambushes begun to be a feature. The Zairean Army was deployed to combat the sharply escalating rebellion. An Italian NGO had three international staff killed in an ambush not far from Katale camp. Who was responsible for the laying of landmines and the launching of ambushes was very difficult to be sure of — I thought the Hutu extremists were the more likely candidates. Interehamwe raids in Rwanda had increased dramatically, in number, scope and boldness. We had been getting UN Rwanda reports confirming that many of the raids were political, with assassinations aimed at removing Tutsi and moderate Hutu witnesses to the 1994 massacres. Wild and bizarre things had begun to happen around the region, and we prepared for the worst.

By September I had written a new security code, taking the form of 'standard operating procedures' for security and safety. These were exhaustive and strict directives to all staff across all programs on how we would conduct business in the deteriorating situation. As the number of incidents had dramatically increased and there was now a substantial guerrilla war in full blaze, more restrictions on travel were imposed. Through September we were unable to travel up that blessed road to Katale on an ever-increasing number of days. The road was often mined and had to be cleared. Government forces, arrogant and overconfident due to their superior numbers, were bumbling around the foothills chasing elusive Tutsi guerillas. Hutu and Tutsi clashes were now frequent along the road and in the vicinity of the camps. I was very concerned about hostage taking, ambush (in less accessible areas) and landmine explosions. I had no choice but to impose unpopular curfews on our international staff, which required them to be back in their houses by late evening. Most staff understood and agreed, but a few did not.

The CARE Goma team was, as usual, doing stunning work. I need not have bothered visiting the field to check on how programs were running because they were basically running themselves, well planned and executed by the Australian program managers, their officers and their dedicated African staff. However, as I very much enjoyed seeing our staff's good work, I went out as often as possible. We had the usual run of management problems with our African staff, but by and large they had continued to work effectively, even when it became obvious that war clouds were gathering. With this excellent profile, we had been looking to continue our implementing partnership with UNHCR into 1997, and preliminary discussions that I was having with UNHCR were very clearly positive. Furthermore, we had been able to convince UNHCR that CARE's new ideas for additional programming should be funded, or at least part-funded, by UNHCR. The moral dilemma as to whether we should continue the refugee operation was at the forefront of our minds, and we were considering our position on that. Against that, were we to decide we had to continue, CARE was well established as a major

NGO operator in the Great Lakes for 1997, thanks to the effectiveness of our programs and our good staff.

In October 1996 the Tutsi rebels came across and cut the highway running north from Goma. The Zairean Army had been soundly defeated by the Banyumelenge in the South Kivu region. The UN had withdrawn its South Kivu operation and the refugees were left to their own devices. The proverbial had hit the fan. Most people were surprised by the crazy turn of events: the defeat of the numerically superior Mobutu forces in the south. I decided to evacuate the majority of the international staff in mid-October 1996, retaining four with me as the rear party. As usual, the staff left very reluctantly, despite the looming danger, and we had to shepherd them onto the planes. They knew they would most likely never see their Hutu staff and possibly not even their Zairean staff again. They were pretty much right, as it turned out.

A full-blown war was underway, and large Tutsi forces were coming over the border from Rwanda and attacking the refugee camps and the Zairean Army. The Hutu extremists were now out in the open, fighting alongside Zairean troops, who at this time were cocky and confident that they would defeat the insurgency. They were numerically superior, but had no idea. It was clear to us then as we watched from Goma, attending daily security briefings at UNHCR, that Rwandan Army (RPF) battalions were committed to the fighting. UN sources also talked of Ugandan forces being involved, and indeed armoured car units had crossed the border some 200 kilometres north. The war was widening rapidly and the Zairean forces were in danger of being cut off and trapped in the south-east of Zaire. It was also becoming clear that the Rwandans were angling very strongly to cut off the refugee camps and take final action. It seemed to me at the time that the dilemma CARE had about whether or not to continue with the refugee program in 1997 was now academic. The Rwandans had brought the Great Lakes Hutu problem to a head.

We have abandoned the office and two of the houses and I have marshalled the rear party of five Australian male staff (I would not countenance risking women staff in these chaotic circumstances, as the risk of rape and murder for women is very high). Stevo, Graham, Steve, Frank and myself now occupy my house, the last bastion, only 200 metres from the UNHCR 'safe house' and international staff rendezvous. It is located on the lake's edge, so our backs are to the water as the fighting closes in from the north. The numerically superior Zairean Army and its also numerically superior Hutu Interehamwe and ex-Hutu army allies have failed spectacularly. They have been driven back down the road, the full 80 kilometres from Katale. We have no idea where our Hutu staff from Katale are. We have been out of radio contact now for some four days. All week we have heard the booming of artillery around the northern fringes of the town. Artillery is now impacting on parts of the town, fired for the most part from Rwanda, a kilometre to the east. We managed to get out to Mugunga on Sunday (26 October) and witnessed the massive movement of refugees from the north, from Katale and the other northern camps, down to Mugunga. We have joined with the International Red Cross, the American Red Cross and many other NGOs to bring emergency aid to the ever-expanding Mugunga camp. The majority of the NGOs have gone. Standing on a rocky outcrop, we gaze northwards and watch the massive movement, people ten abreast in a column as far as the eye can see stretching back up that valley plain. (Later I am to write a 2000-word story about this sight and these circumstances which the *Sydney Morning Herald* publishes.)

My nightly situation reports are sent by fax, linked to satellite telephone. I describe the catastrophe, describe the fighting, where it is heading and what that means for the CARE program and the safety of the team. The artillery booms away, and by the Wednesday and Thursday (29 and 30 October) we are able to hear the fierce battles raging at the airport. We have to find and help evacuate our CARE Canada colleagues, trapped by fighting on the other side of town; thankfully we manage to guide them out. On Friday morning, 31 October, we evacuate the house as instructed by UNHCR and join the other 130 internationals cooped up in two large neighbouring bungalows, picturesquely perched on the edge of Lake Kivu. The fighting is now very close. Rwandan patrol boats can be seen zipping around the lake and making charges into shore to fire at Zairean positions about 2 kilometres west, in the vicinity of Mt Goma, to our west. We now have Mobutu UNHCR Guards with us. They are wild and red-eyed. I notice they are, for the first time ever, very subdued, nervous, confused. This is as much a worry as anything else is, I think. I am sitting under a tree at the fence line joining the two houses with Richard Oaten, a British aid worker and mission head of Lutheran World Federation. We are quietly chatting away, trying to stay calm. He's certainly calm, having had twenty or more years experience in Africa. We have been mission heads together in Goma and I have found his experienced advice quite valuable.

Suddenly a Rwandan patrol boat makes a run for shore straight in our direction, for what reason is unclear. He fires a heavy machine gun and Richard and I watch spellbound as the plumes of water thrown up by bullet strikes march towards us, as if in slow motion. We are down into the grass and hear that bloody crack! crack! of bullets going over our heads. The lovely jacaranda tree under which we are grovelling is shedding its broken leaves upon us. The labrador dog which had come over to nestle in with us (who owns it?) is loving every bit of this and is leaping around excitedly. We get inside the house quick smart, not that that will help much. As we go in we are surprised to see a Zairean colonel coming down the stairs; I had seen him at the hotel, I remember, weeks before, all cocky and 'hail fellow well met' — now, his face is drained of colour. He is dressed smartly in combat smock, with pistol, map case and staff books, binoculars, cherry beret; he looks a little like Sean Connery's character, General Urquhart (in *A Bridge Too Far*). With him are three staff officers and two protecting soldiers. They are leaving the house. Were they seeking for neutral protection? Or were they using the upper-floor windows as observation points? Either way we see UNHCR officers trying to get them to leave, quoting the Geneva Convention and the neutrality of the UN. There is a tense moment and I wonder briefly whether they are going to take us all hostages for their own protection against the Rwandans. Because the Rwandans are on their way out and surely they know that. It shows in all their faces. They are scared, and it is clear to me on this afternoon in this lovely big house that these blokes know they have a very good chance of dying. Prisoner of war is not a well-known concept in this part of the world.

The colonel is shaking just a little, beads of perspiration on his forehead, and I feel incredibly sorry for him. He does look like a decent fellow, as do his soldiers, and I have not heard any story of killings committed by these people. Yes, they have been harassing us for months, but not killing, and not deliberately killing locals either. Not like the Interehamwe. Richard and I watch this surreal event; it is not a good time. The colonel leaves, and one of his soldiers breaks into tears. I will never forget this, because I am to hear later that there is a strong but unproven indication that this colonel, and indeed most of the senior officers of the Zairean Army in Goma, who are driven in and then trapped like rats at the port of Goma, are rounded up at last light and summarily executed. Judging by an incident I witness in the next hour, I come to believe that this could have happened.

By mid-afternoon on the Friday we are down on the floor in two houses, stray bullets from all directions flying over the top and past the house. The storm is approaching. The firing is intense. I am on the top landing of the stairway and have a narrow view (cover from fire dictates my caution). I can just see out to the front driveway gate of this house. There is a battle raging in the street. The radios are barking and somebody in UNHCR somewhere says to a UNHCR officer lying on the floor to expect fighting shortly. 'Everybody inside and down', are the instructions. It also occurs to me at that very moment that somebody in UNHCR is very well placed to know exactly what the Rwandan Army's intentions are and just what their movements turn out to be. Impeccable timing. Through the small window I can see a tall Tutsi officer in trademark knee-level leather boots — I know he is an officer because he does not carry a rifle, perhaps just a pistol and a hand-held radio. He is directing with his arms, encouraging his soldiers to move along the street. A UNHCR vehicle suddenly bursts into the driveway but disappears from my view. I am horrified to see Rwandan troops rush into the driveway and fire their Kalashnikovs in the direction of where I believe the vehicle went, but I do not see the results. The Rwandans quickly race through the front yard of the house, but I cannot see them, they are mostly out of view. Lots of firing and then they leave. They seem to be careful not to fire at the UNHCR house at all. On the landing we are the closest to the action. A Danish Red Cross worker, who turns out to be a Danish Army special forces soldier on secondment, is with me. Gingerly putting their heads through the downstairs doorway, in view of the landing, we see two Tutsi soldiers. On seeing the two of us, they silently and unsmilingly motion with two signals: a thumbs up and a flat palm motion encouraging us to stay put. They very quietly and confidently leave. The fighting roars on down the street, sweeping past us. All quiet after the storm. For the first time in five hours the desultory sound of gunfire and random bullets popping past us has abated. All the firing is rapidly moving away from us to the west. It is almost silent in their wake.

About half an hour later the Danish Red Cross man, myself and one UNHCR officer quietly venture outside, the rest of the internationals having been told to stay put. We enter the front yard. It is a bloody shambles. The UNHCR vehicle, a white, clearly marked Landcruiser, is skewed off the gravel driveway and has mounted the garden edge rocks, having knocked over a small tree. All the doors are open; they have tried to get out in a hurry. The three of us carefully approach, and what we find is carnage. The driver, a small young UNHCR Zairean staff member whom I recognise, dressed in jeans and track shoes and UNHCR polo shirt, is dead, slumped to the floor. Behind him, from the left rear seat, a soldier, one of the Mobutu guards, has fallen face first into the garden, his legs still inside the vehicle. All four of the soldiers in the vehicle are dressed in their camouflage trousers and military boots but all have put on UNHCR T-shirts. The soldier in the garden has his brain spilt into the garden and Stevo and I — Stevo has now come out to join me — recoil from the sight. All the soldiers bar one are dead, shot up to five times each. One soldier, a big strong-looking lad, is in the back seat lying forward over one of his dead mates. I think at first he too is dead, but unlike the others I can see blood slowly oozing out of three holes in his back, in spurts, in time with some sort of a heart beat. We call for the UNHCR doctor, who is coming out anyway, and pull him from the vehicle. Despite terrible wounds he is worked on right then and there in the house; he is stabilised and lives.

The following morning we come under fire again as we prepare to evacuate. All five of the CARE Land Rovers are bullet-riddled. I am able to make contact by satellite phone with Canberra and even my dear old mother. We are able to cross the border that morning (Saturday, 1 November), but fast, as we are under some random firing. We have carried with us boxes of office files, office equipment, the satellite phone and personal effects. I meet the CARE UK information officer, Liz Campbell, a remarkable lady who had been sitting on the Gisenyi (Rwanda) side of the border for the previous three days, communicating with us by satellite phone, keeping us informed and keeping our spirits up.

We arrive in Gisenyi, exhausted but mighty relieved. I am not a pretty sight. My white CARE Australia polo shirt is stained with blood and grass. We are all filthy. The boys and I have a very welcome beer at the Gisenyi hotel, the place where we are processed by the Rwandans. All four of the rear party team have done a superb job. The only mistake is that a tin trunk of vital office documents needed for financial acquittal of all our work is left behind in the house where we had specifically placed it for evacuation. I am to go back four weeks later to recover it.

After being processed by the Rwandan authorities we drive in convoy the two or more hours to Kigali that very day, tired, and perhaps with some sort of shock seeping in. We leave the vehicles, documents, office records, and office equipment in Kigali. CARE Rwanda takes charge of our vehicles and equipment. We are all ordered to fly straight out of Rwanda that night by UNHCR Hercules plane to Nairobi. The CARE Australia Goma presence is wrecked, destroyed, and we abandon that country for good. We land in Nairobi at 1 am after an eventful thirty-six hours, indeed two weeks of high drama. There I meet my loving and much relieved wife, the ever-smiling Samira.

The Hutus were driven out of the camps, the vast majority heading for Rwanda. A new emergency program was put into effect, the international community responding to assist the Rwandan government in taking back the homecoming masses. CARE Australia was to deploy a new team of ten Australians into Rwanda as part of a CARE International multimember team, co-ordinated and controlled by CARE USA through its CARE Rwanda office. This operation worked, and the outcomes for the refugees were good; sadly, however, it was to suffer in terms of outcome for effort because of the poor level of co-operation amongst the CARE members. In addition to the pressures applied by the Rwandan authorities for the scaling down of international NGOs, pressures from within the CARE fraternity gathered in Kigali took a toll.

Three experienced and effective emergency planners, one each from CAREs UK, USA and Australia (my old colleague, the ex-project manager from northern Iraq), walked out of the emergency planning activity in Kigali, which I thought at the time was a tremendous waste of talent and opportunity to bring effective aid quickly to refugees. The refugees were further disadvantaged by the unneccessarily late deployment of aid assistance programs and the misdirection of precious resources. In Nairobi, we could only sit back and shake our heads in wonder at the disharmony among the CAREs in Kigali, again. All that co-operation and carefully nurtured goodwill amongst CARE's missions in Africa was dented.

I stayed in Nairobi, where my task for the next four months was to completely shut down the old CARE Australia Great Lakes operation of 1994–1996, and particularly to acquit and close out the Zaire operation. Samira worked very hard in a de facto finance and admin manager's role in this period and her acute mind and recall of CARE's African history were very valuable.

Meanwhile, all through this period another very sad and tragic drama played out. A significant element of the Katale camp refugee population, thought to number about 180 000, did not turn to Rwanda when driven out of the destroyed camp. They turned instead westward, and fled towards central Africa — surely, some say, a demonstration of their guilt as 'genocidaires'. They were one of only two significant groups to go west. We, along with the UN, follow their plight with great interest because amongst them are some ex-CARE staff. Indeed, Majid, the CARE radio operator based at Katale camp, is able to call our Nairobi office on the CARE HF

Codan radio that he has taken with him on this great trek. But this is a mystery, one which we have not yet resolved. How did he carry the quite heavy radio and the accompanying vehicle battery and how did he recharge the battery?

We talk to Majid intermittently over three months. We pass these reports onto a briefing conference of NGOs and UN agencies coordinated by the UN Department of Humanitarian Affairs in Nairobi. These are the only reports direct from fleeing refugees. In the end, tens of thousands of refugees in this movement west are to die as a result of fighting and disease. The end of a desperate and bloody story? One couldn't be sure. Central Zaire, 'The Heart of Darkness'. Finally, I close the CARE Australia Nairobi office to end a colourful and effective chapter in CARE Australia's presence in Africa. My wife and I go off for a well-earned three-week break in Rome, before going on to Yugoslavia, my next appointment.

CHAPTER SIX
To Yugoslavia

I arrived in Yugoslavia in late May 1997, appointed as deputy country representative, without Samira, who had decided to visit her family in Yemen. I had in any case been strongly encouraged to leave Samira out of Yugoslavia until I had assessed for myself whether there would be any difficulties with her accompanying me there. The pressure for her to stay away was a little puzzling; I was not sure where the concern was coming from and thought it was a bit of an overreaction, though I agreed at the time that it was probably the smarter thing to do. On arrival, Tony McGee (the country representative), was to point out to me that Samira should not wear her abaya (black cloak) or head scarf. Amused, I told Tony that Sam disliked abayas and was not some sort of fundamentalist. I had the feeling that there may have been some expectation in Tony's mind of prejudice on the part of the Serbian staff. While I was never able to confirm whether this was so, I was to learn later that moods and prejudices within some elements of the country mission staff were capable of swinging wildly. Samira was to join me in September 1997. On the surface, she had no difficulties fitting into Belgrade life.

The first couple of months were very enjoyable ones in the field with the Serbian staff. My appointed duties included supervising

CARE's refugee centre support program, and I familiarised myself with it in some detail, guided by our Serbian field staff. The program was clearly very impressive, well put together by a succession of experienced and capable Australian program officers, most of whom had been qualified supply personnel. It covered the whole country, plus both Yugoslav states of Serbia and Montenegro. There were 650 refugee centres, in effect the joint property of the Yugoslav Government's Serbian Refugee Commission and the UN High Commissioner for Refugees (UNHCR), located across every municipality the length and breadth of Yugoslavia. CARE Serbia/Montenegro (as it was then called — it was renamed as CARE Yugoslavia in late 1998) was the implementing partner of UNHCR (as we had been in Zaire), responsible for providing heating fuel in winter, and fresh food throughout the year, to all these centres and to about a hundred more 'special institutions'. The institutions included various hospitals, old people's homes, and mental asylums where refugees had been taken in and for which it was considered necessary to supply the essentials as well. The agreement that UNHCR had with the government was that all inmates of the institutions would be supplied as well, given the severe difficulties faced by the institutions in these times of punishing sanctions.

I had found the field staff very effective, many of them quite professional in their approach to the business and others very willing to learn new practices. In terms of the practicalities of fieldwork management, the staff were eager learners, and for me these first three months of working closely with them were very rewarding and satisfying. I had noticed that the way in which the staff worked was highly centralised — it seemed that twenty-one field staff members either accessed the Australian supervisor directly or did not bother to report to anyone at all. My challenge therefore was to introduce lines of responsibility and delegations of authority down through the organisation, particularly through the field staff. I think the staff appreciated being given that type of delegated trust. The highly centralised, rambling, bazaar-like atmosphere of the Australian supervisor's office disappeared as the restructure was successfully implemented. What was also apparent was that the field workers were not used to regular visits by the Australian staff. I was to later make this a fundamental tenet of international staff behaviour in all programs, as I had done in previous missions.

The conditions of the refugee centres themselves were appalling. At the end of the Yugoslav war in 1994 the Serb refugees from Bosnia had poured across the border once the Bosnian Serb Army had inexplicably pulled back from the frontiers of fighting. Long, winding columns of refugees (numbering in total about 400 000), fearing Bosnian retribution, had crossed into Serbia and simply looked for places to drop off the road and into shelter. As the field staff explained it to me, people had found disused factories, schools, cafes, sheds and barns. Carrying only the essentials in their possession, they simply flopped to their knees. Serbian authorities marshalled many of them further south and east, away from the border, to reduce the congestion. Refugees would often spend days on the road moving down the major highways and regularly being moved on by the town police. Then the authorities got their act together and identified useful places such as agricultural institution barracks, ex-military barracks, disused gymnasiums and the like to which refugee groups could be guided. They attempted and generally succeeded in spreading the refugees across the country and into these strange places.

As I travelled to as many of these centres as possible and talked to the refugees, I was satisfied that by and large these people had not been involved in the fighting. To one degree or another many were complicit, but often without choice, due to the pressures applied by the fighting elements. It became apparent to me over the year, too, that these refugees were no more to blame for the troubles than were refugees of other ethnic backgrounds in other places throughout the former Yugoslavia. All of them were unwitting pawns.

Many of those in the refugee centres were old people, or widowed mothers and kids. Related refugees, more intact as families, had generally been able to move out of the centres into either shared accommodation with relatives or some sort of rented flat. These families would stay in contact with UNHCR for food ration issues via the Yugoslav Red Cross. Conditions were pitiful. Old women could do little else than sit on their bunks, or on their grubby cardboard boxes. There was nothing to do. The older men played a little chess, but also drank too early in the day, if they could afford to. Plum brandy was readily available around the place. A Swiss NGO was responsible as a UNHCR implementing partner for repairing or rebuilding sanitation and bathing facilities and had continued to do a good job, within its limited budget. As in Yemen, UNHCR and Yugoslav Red Cross staff were responsible for regularly visiting the centres for routine personal administrative issues, but did not.

Again CARE staff found themselves picking up too many of these issues for either on the spot fixing or passing back to UNHCR for action. CARE field workers were very dissatisfied with the role played by the Yugoslav Red Cross across the country, although in a number of municipalities they were clearly doing a good job and demonstrating considerable dedication. It was often a matter of individual personalities. Corruption was rife in the country and this permeated the aid business. We needed to be very careful of corrupt officials at the municipal level interfering in refugee centre affairs and siphoning off the supplies, fuel and food that we delivered. In my experience, though, most municipal offices and their staff appointed as refugee centre managers were pretty genuine. Nevertheless, the responsibility was heavily on the Australian staff to broker all the disagreements and to officiate in activities where corrupt behaviour could conceivably be expected.

In June 1997 I was appointed country representative to replace Tony McGee, who had spent two years in the job. He departed reluctantly and emotionally. He had done an outstanding job streamlining the country program. He was meticulous in his detail, to the point of distraction, and had systematised the program. It was now my job to make the mission grow, and this was to be one of my life's greatest challenges to date. If I succeeded it was due to an excellent country team. There was so much that could be done in this impoverished country and, most importantly, so much more that could be done to improve the refugee program. It had occurred to me as I went around in mid-1997 that we could do much more to help the refugees help themselves. For five years, as far as I could determine, all CARE Australia had done in Yugoslavia was carry out very important but very unimaginitive 'truck and chuck' operations.

Luckily for me I had a regional director based in Amman — he was responsible for CARE's Middle East operations and, for the sake of geographic simplicity, for CARE Serbia/Montenegro as well. The regional director had been the project manager in northern Iraq. I had been his deputy there and we were pretty good mates. As he had a fair amount of experience in the aid business, far more than me, he was able to advise me on the things that might be done. I then engaged in two exercises. The first was well overdue — namely, developing a country aid strategy, an identification of the most pressing humanitarian needs in the country, prioritised and quantified in terms of what was immediately achievable, what was immediately affordable and what was most pressing regardless of qualifications. Limitations to achieving such programming goals — social, economic and political — were also listed. The second exercise was the develoment of a new 'refugee self-reliance' program, one of the goals in our country strategy. The regional director sent one of his program development officers out to Belgrade — Yvonne, a young Brit on loan from CARE UK — to assist me in the concept planning for the self-reliance program. She was dedicated and clever and we soon had some good program project proposals sorted out.

The refugee self-reliance program was to run successfully. The planning and implementation of this had been a real tonic for the staff. They had been doing a good job but had been very much stuck in the 'truck and chuck' rut and needed a challenge to help them grow professionally. With the exception of a few lazy fellows, the field staff threw themselves into it, talked to the people in their refugee centres, came up with ideas; we were then able to develop livestock and protected garden activities, aimed at encouraging and helping the refugees produce their own fresh food. Those centres that could participate in the program did so, and seemed to relish the business. It gave them something constructive to do, and I thought it helped them regain some pride. Some of the centres with more enterprising ideas even produced surpluses and made some cash. Furthermore, a few refugee centres were even entering into agreements with local communities, assisted by the better, more humane and more enthusiastic municipality authorities. While the war a year later was to interrupt everything, it seemed then that the CARE program was looking to grow into larger and even more productive activities, as well as to produce follow-on dividends. UNHCR was impressed enough to support and encourage CARE and provide substantial funding for the program. What was never proved, due to the interruption of war, was whether this refugee self-reliance program could have been developed to such a level as to replace part or all of the traditional food delivery program.

In late 1997, as part of the country strategic plan, I was keen to explore programming opportunities in Kosovo, the suppressed and severely disadvantaged Serbian province. We were moving in this direction in early 1998 when the new emergency erupted there. This was also when I began to encounter resistance to country program planning among significant elements of the local staff. Not all staff were to be difficult, certainly not the more educated and mature among them. I did not, however, appreciate some of our local staff trying to adversely affect country program strategic decisions along political or ethnic lines. To plan and progress properly when a significant number of your staff will not back you is difficult enough, but when the attitude is political, you must question whether the mission can continue as a true, viable, neutral humanitarian mission. These issues were to play on my mind regularly in late 1998/early 1999, when the pressures for broader NGO commitments mounted.

I was also to revisit an old CARE bogeyman — the sometimes prickly relations between CARE members. CARE Australia was the temporary lead member for CARE International in Yugoslavia, and in November 1998 was due to be considered for permanent lead membership. Meanwhile, in Bosnia the lead member was CARE Canada. The two 'new world' nation CAREs were in these positions because they were 'operational' CAREs (only CAREs USA, Canada and Australia were in this category, the other thirteen or so members being 'supporting' members for fundraising and technical and sometimes staff assistance). However, we had found ourselves under ridiculously close scrutiny and constant criticism by CAREs Deutschland and Osterreich. One could understand, I reflected at the time, why the two central European CARE members had a vital and close interest in matters Balkan, but I believe we bent over backwards to accommodate their involvement. For both myself and my CARE Canada country director counterpart in Bosnia, relations with our central European CARE partners were extremely difficult, to say the least. The last thing two overworked country directors in the volatile Balkans needed was to have to contend with harrying CARE partners. CARE International needed to move quickly to resolve these matters; I thought progress was slow and to the detriment of delivering effective and timely aid.

Meanwhile, in Kosovo the political situation was fast deteriorating. Inspired by the massive and inspirational democratic street demonstrations of winter 1997, the Albanian Kosovars had begun civil disobedience campaigns and held political street demonstrations, protesting against the ongoing political sanctions which had been imposed by the Belgrade regime on the province. Albanian Kosovars, numbering about one and a half million, were forbidden to run their own educational and other cultural institutions. Kosovars refused to use government institutions and went to the extent of establishing their own hospitals and later 'parallel' educational systems. In November the authorities began to react with a heavy hand, and riot police robustly removed demonstrators, which did stop demonstrations recurring.

In late 1997 the Kosovo Liberation Army (KLA), or to use the Albanian term, the Uchuka or UCK was born. This organisation, it seemed to us at the time, had its genesis in the wide range of Albanian mafia bands and other smuggling brigands and clans. It was not recognised by the international media back then nor, I thought, by the naive US Government some time later, that the KLA was far from a romantic freedom fighter organisation. It seemed to me at the time that the loose bands running around proclaiming themselves as UCK were nothing but murderers and smugglers, still fighting each other and of course the Serbian mafia, while vying for the lucrative smuggling trade. It was put to me by sound diplomatic sources that the genesis of the KLA in late 1997 had as much to do with the increased stakes and tensions between Albanian and Serbian mafias, and the need for the Albanian mafias to combat them and their Serbian police allies, as with any idealistic notions of fighting for freedom. Political backing by the West had the effect of cementing the KLA into a position of some sort of political responsibility they would not otherwise have been capable of. The KLA did then develop far beyond the initial tight groups of mafia gangs, and grew into a more broadly representative freedom fighter organisation.

The KLA's first hits on the board, however, were rather inauspicious and cowardly. Albanian Kosovar postmen, electricity workers and then policemen were the first assassination targets, over November and Christmas 1997. Then civilian Albanians, including women and children, followed by the sniper shooting of an elderly Serbian couple — entirely harmless people according to reliable diplomatic and UN sources — killed in their backyard. At this point in proceedings it was apparent that the Serbian authorities were able to successfully argue in diplomatic circles that a 'terrorist problem' loomed in Kosovo. The KLA had been operating in a cowardly fashion, and their actions were unjustified. There appeared at that time little support for them from the wider Albanian Kosovar community.

It was clear to us that the Serb authorities would soon retaliate, which they did in early 1998, striking at a number of well-known clans and families. The wholesale killing of the Jariah family was a watershed incident in the escalation of the crisis and in the gradual loss by the Serbian authorities of any moral high ground they may have held in late 1997. It was the typical 'thumb your nose at world opinion and sensibilities' overreaction for which the Serbian regime was famous. And just as the Western bombing of Yugoslavia was to unify Serbs behind Milosevic a year later, the drastic Serbian reaction in March 1998 united the Albanian Kosovars behind the KLA. The Serbs were to conduct a counterinsurgency operation, but one which was to spiral out of control into mayhem and brutality.

The KLA and the political elite were to cleverly hook the interests and sympathy of the USA; the USA was perhaps responding to pressures from the Islamic world after previous Bosnian failures, and to imperatives associated with the ongoing Middle East peace talks. For CARE Serbia/Montenegro, March 1998 was a time of dramatic changes in the mission's programming and in its operational security. CARE field teams operating in Kosovo were now under immense pressure, and CARE's security and safety measures and associated concerns would absorb much of our time and energy.

Through May 1998 CARE was to commence a series of new programs targetting vulnerable people in Kosovo, in addition to the Serbian refugee caseload we were then handling in Kosovo. Once the humanitarian need arose I had no hesitation in seeking the funding and resources, albeit modest at first, to conduct such a program. It was our first program aimed at anyone other than Serb ethnic groups in the country, and the humanitarian need aside, I considered it very important for CARE to do this. There was a subtle but significant amount of resistance within the local staff at first; while much was overcome, the problem would never be eradicated. The southern Serbia field team already responsible for running supplies into Kosovo to Serbian refugee centres there would pick up the brunt of this program until much later in the year, when CARE was able to open its Kosovo office and recruit new Albanian Kosovar staff.

The sector co-ordinator for the south, which CARE called its 'Sector C', was Branko Jelen, who, along with his team, unflinchingly (and to his credit) assisted in the Albanian Kosovar medical program. The program supported displaced Albanian Kosovars who had been pushed out of their villages by the fighting and no longer had access to their own medical facilities. CARE ran medical supplies to seven selected government medical clinics around the province. CARE hired nine Albanian and two Serbian doctors to distribute and administer these medicines to Albanian Kosovar communities, which were known to be overloaded by influxes of displaced families. My German colleague Horst (an officer loaned by CARE Deutschland) was the program manager responsible for this program, and he ran it in with efficiency. The funding for this program was provided by the German Government; this was the beginning of a long relationship with the Germans. CARE Deutschland had had an influence in gaining this funding support, for which I was most grateful, and therefore they were 'stakeholders' in that program. CARE Australia had made the decision to fund and carry these missions because of the urgency and hopelessness of the humanitarian need.

CARE Serbia/Montenegro had grown to be CARE Australia's second-largest overseas mission, and by November 1998 one of CARE International's most significant missions. By the end of the year we had created 30 per cent growth in dollar terms and just about doubled the number of beneficiaries we were able to help. I had travelled back to Canberra for a country directors/head office conference in which we had reviewed CARE Australia's position. Donor sources were drying up and funding was difficult. Some country missions had been running on red for years, heavily subsidised by head office, but along rational lines. Other country directors were raising funds through bilateral donor sources and were able to fund themselves, entirely independently of head office. CARE Australia wisely decided it was time for a global rationalisation, although I was surprised to find that CARE Serbia/Montenegro was one of the missions considered for possible disbandment — apparently because of its unique and difficult geographical position. Understandably, rationalisation for CARE Australia could have meant cutting missions back to simply those located in Africa or Asia, along with a tight Middle East presence. So it was ultimately with great delight that I was able to argue for and win the retention of CARE Serbia/Montenegro. I thought at the time that retention of this mission should have been an obvious priority.

In August 1998 Robert Yallop, as overseas operational programs director, visited the mission. He came to see for himself how we worked (or didn't) and to assist and guide me in upgrading the country needs assessment, particularly with respect to the growing Kosovo crisis. He travelled widely in the country and was not shy to venture into some of the more difficult Kosovo backwoods areas. On one trip through the Malisevo Valley in central southern Kosovo he amused the driver, Zelko, a ponytailed, seven-foot-tall church choir member (deep bass). Robert was in the second vehicle as we were crossing this difficult area, which I suspected was a KLA sniper zone. I had not said as much to Robert. Zelko followed the lead of my driver and was driving very fast, headlights on and CARE flags flying, as we twisted and plunged down the hillside of the heavily wooded valley. I can still see Robert puffing on his pipe (one day somebody will surgically remove it), eyes bulging and knuckles on

dashboard grip rail white, muttering, 'Bloody Pratt, I'll kill him ...'
We had just traversed the most difficult terrain in the area, though, and I had been able to show Robert the extent of the damage to farms and housing as a result of four months' fighting.

Robert and I were also to travel to the high mountain country of Montenegro, amid the snowdrifts, where we were to find an unknown and hidden group of displaced Albanian Kosovars. These people had, amazingly, climbed the 2000 metres from Pec in Kosovo through the mountain passes on foot and with donkeys. We were to sometimes discover but mainly hear of other such pockets of people along the mountain ranges, and subsequently prepared food and medical distribution programs for them. Robert went back to Canberra and planned and mobilised CARE Australia's 'Winter Relief' Appeal, aimed at raising some funds in Australia but mainly targeted at its CARE partners and international government donor agencies. Two and a half million dollars (US) was eventually raised and used to assist 100 000 displaced Albanian Kosovars over the winter of 1998/99. The program was eventually destroyed by war.

It was in this time of shifting emphases in the mission that I was faced with another significant challenge. The staff needed to have their attitudes broadened, and after five years of simply running distributions to Serbian refugee centres I thought it appropriate to inculcate new values. We were becoming more mindful of human rights. Pursuing human rights issues is very difficult and very politically sensitive, and you have to be very careful of not treading on the host government's toes and perhaps destroying your ability to continue delivering existing aid programs. CARE Yugoslavia did not, and nor did I intend to, radically change this position. We were not a 'human rights' NGO, and had determined to maintain a strict humanitarian aid profile. But an NGO must be aware of, if not take a position on, human rights, and staff need to be sympathetic and supportive, if not overtly demonstrative. We also needed to broaden our programming to cater for people of other ethnicities: Albanians with whom we had started, Serbian Bosniaks (Muslims living in the Sanjak area of central western Serbia), gypsies, who were a very sorry lot and who suffered severe prejudices, and some Hungarian Catholic communities in the northern province of Vojvidina.

Many of our staff did not need conversion, particularly the senior more experienced women in the team and the better and more socially educated staff, who were quite sympathetic to these ideals. Such individuals in the Belgrade office were unhesitant in their roles relevant to our Albanian Kosovar programs, and to them I was very grateful.

However, there was some resistance and scepticism among the staff to the broad concept of neutrality, and certainly, as I had already found, resistance to the Kosovo program changes involving Albanians. This area was a primary challenge which I was never able to bring to a resolution, as time was insufficient and war intervened. In my estimation our Serbian staff were among the brightest and most capable working for CARE Australia anywhere in the world, but I suspect they were probably the least flexible in taking on these new values. Some had their reasons, of course — in Belgrade neutrality was going to be very difficult, with the staff themselves intimidated by their environment.

It was at this time that I received a timely reminder about my own performance as a country director. Robert, after watching the mission closely for a week, 'braced me up' on an important aspect of my work. He told me I was doing too much, to the point of exhaustion, and that I needed to delegate more. He was right; sometimes I was not seeing the wood for the trees. I think Samira, ever watchful, had got into his ear. He patted me on the shoulder as he was leaving at the airport and said through clenched teeth gripping his pipe, 'Delegate! Delegate, Pratty!'

Through late 1998 our field teams, providing assistance both to Serbian refugee centres and to the medical centres supporting Albanians, were running the gauntlet of fighting. Serbian Police Milicja units, that is ministry of interior police (MUP), with by late August increasing support from the Yugoslav Army (VJ), were conducting operations against clusters of villages across the region. By now ten Serbian refugee centres were cut off and inaccessible to Branko Jelen and his team. The field staff, as directed by me, were passing back information about the situation with the refugee centres, as well as information about Albanian displaced people movements. They were also directed to immediately pass on to me reports of incidents involving them and incidents involving disruptions to their work. For example, if the road had been cut by fighting and they were unable to get to a Serbian refugee centre or to a government medical post to deliver medicines, or to carry out their monitoring duties relevant to these program deliveries and distributions. It was my duty to do whatever I could to safeguard the staff, and it was my duty to report full details of incidents and program disruptions to my superiors in Canberra and to the donors supporting such programs, sometimes via sister CARE organisations who might have acted as go-betweens with certain foreign government donors. This I did by regular situation reports. As the situation in Kosovo deteriorated through the late northern summer and autumn, these SITREPs became more regular. It was necessary to describe the situation objectively as it developed, and to keep all interested parties up to date.

I prepared new and strict security procedures, much along the lines of those I had introduced earlier in northern Iraq, Zaire and Rwanda. These involved curfews, and strict rules to staff to keep out of areas where fighting was occurring, or was suspected to occur. On the landmine front, they included staying in constant contact with UNHCR Kosovo office and later the organisation for security and co-operation in Europe (OSCE) ceasefire monitoring force, so that staff could update themselves on possible 'no go' areas. We were not travelling with guards, so there were no weapons procedures. But the procedures and rules for vehicle travel were exactly the same as they had been in the more difficult emergency missions. Our Yugoslav and, from October 1998, our Albanian field staff adhered to these procedures without argument. I only had difficulty with one international staff member who either questioned or flirted with these (and other operational) procedures.

In September 1998 we were putting the final planning touches on the 'winterisation' program, a large program that was aimed at supporting up to 50 000 displaced people. We had a CARE US program planner, Godfrey, attached to the mission to help with the thirteen project proposals that had to be completed for submission to various targeted donors. Melissa, my program manager for the Serbian refugee program, took time out to work with Godfrey and me on this planning. She proved to be a dab hand at program planning. Melissa had also assisted me closely in the preparation of the new, beefed-up Kosovo presence. It was simply too much for one person to do, especially as I had found myself pulled to every part of the country and attending a number of CARE International meetings in Europe. Horst (my German colleague and program manager for the family of medical programs), Melissa and I were commuting regularly back and forth to Kosovo these days; I probably did the most travelling, as I took the responsibility to personally closely monitor the most difficult part of the country mission. The new office was established by late September, and a handful of key Albanian and some Serbian staff were recruited (I had insisted on a minimum quota of 25 per cent Serbian staff in the Kosovo team).

The guerrilla war was now raging right across the province. In attempting to bring emergency relief to about 136 Serbian refugee centres across the province and deliver medical supplies to the medical centres in the central north and along the western fringes of Kosovo, CARE was running into trouble everywhere. Our staff were becoming involved in numerous incidents, as they bounced off MUP roadblocks or were warned away from areas thought to contain KLA checkpoints. On a number of occasions the field teams had to turn around after being confronted by artillery or machine gun fire which, while not directed at them and some distance away, still succeeded in blocking their progress. Or else they would blunder into a column of MUP or VJ troops blocking a road. On one celebrated occasion the field teams came across an activity reportedly involving 'Arkan's Tigers', the infamous and sinister militia group run by Zelko Raznatovic, better known as 'Arkan'. During our later interrogations and the so-called 'trial', reports of these incidents sent to me, along with related relevant telephone conversations and meetings between Branko Jelen and me, are used to nail us with false charges and convictions. The situation was becoming very tense and very dangerous, but in October 1998, as we opened the new CARE office in Pristina (the capital of Kosovo province), which was to supervise our Kosovo operation, CARE was certainly committed to continuing and indeed building its operation.

Meanwhile, a number of serious landmine incidents involving NGO staffs and diplomatic observers had occurred. An International Red Cross Committee vehicle had, by eyewitness accounts, been blown metres into the air, killing an Albanian doctor and seriously wounding two others. The driver, a New Zealander, escaped serious injury. The Canadian Defence Attaché and his team had escaped serious injury by some miracle, given that their vehicle had ignited an anti-tank mine. UNHCR staff had been ambushed by the KLA and their Serbian staff were lucky to escape capture, mainly due to desperate pleas by the international staff present. Many NGOs were being increasingly harassed by both KLA and MUP as they tried to enter areas to deliver aid.

CARE Serbia/Montenegro teams were never harassed at roadblocks or checkpoints, either by the MUP or the KLA, and were consistently successful (by other people's measures, notably UNHCR Pristina's) in their endeavours to deliver aid to the most difficult areas. The most sensational of the NGO harassments was that of the medical NGO Médecins Sans Frontières (MSF), one of the organisations CARE worked with in the delivery of medical assistance. MSF, thought by many to be operating too closely to the controversial local Albanian Mother Teresa Society and therefore too closely on one side of the conflict, was stopped three times to my knowledge in the Djakovica area in south-west Kosovo by the MUP. The MUP and the authorities generally accused MSF of running guns and ammunition for the KLA. On each of these occasions MSF had their vehicles searched, had supplies confiscated and were turned back. For this reason, in late 1998 they often failed to deliver aid.

We often found during our field visits that MSF had not visited their designated visitor medical centres and aid posts. We did not think that MSF were carrying weapons and considered the MUP allegations to be arrant nonsense; however, we, UNHCR and other NGOs were critical of MSF for their unhealthy closeness to MTS. It was with much grim irony, on my return to Australia, that I was to witness the head of MSF in Australia criticise CARE Australia for supposedly endangering the neutrality of NGOs in Kosovo — a simply inaccurate charge and from an organisation in no position to criticise.

By and large, the rolling bare hills and countryside of Kosovo were more than ever alive with combatants and moving, displaced people. Through the second half of 1998 the Western press was barking about Serbian-instigated 'ethnic cleansing', but from what we could see this was not the case. In their ham-fisted and often brutal way, MUP units would warn villagers to evacuate and then regardless of whether they had or hadn't, would attack that village if confronted by KLA. After the smoke of battle cleared, villagers did not seem to be prohibited from returning to those villages. This seemed to be the pattern of events across most of the province.

Also, crucially, our assessment of the numbers, movement and location of displaced people did not support the sensationalist notion that any form of state-orchestrated 'ethnic cleansing' was under way. I had personally seen villages burning, on one occasion witnessing two armoured VJ vehicles leaving the scene. The three villages that I saw in the Vucitern municipality in late September were by and large totally on fire. These were ruthless and brutal actions. But to put it in some sort of stark context, of the villages we came across in late 1998 which had obviously seen fighting, about one in six had been burnt or had been flattened, the remainder sometimes damaged but intact. We looked out on a terrible, almost Dark Ages environment, but I was learning fast that this was the Balkans through and through. We went about our business, but couldn't help wonder what hope there was for the place.

In October 1998 we were able to breathe a temporary sigh of relief. The Rambouillet talks had concluded, an American-concocted affair which I and others thought was pretty unfair to the Serbs and would back them right into a corner — which is precisely what it did. Islamic world pressure, Middle East peace talks issues (tied to other strategic and US oil interests), and guilt over Bosnia (a 'too late' mission to rescue Muslims) combined to commit the Americans to a course of action they otherwise may not have pursued. It was soon to become apparent that the lopsided Rambouillet peace agreement would lead to war. There was, however, some respite. The shooting and burning had stopped and we were able to move rapidly and freely to get our winter program mobilised, before the worst of winter set in. CARE Yugoslavia (as the country mission was now to be known) had selected the upper Drenica region as its area of concentration for the delivery of aid. I had determined that this region was the one with the highest degree of need, and one where we would not be duplicating other NGO activity. We had established a working relationship with Oxfam, the British NGO, to co-ordinate our activities and to complement each other's programs. The Oxfam Balkans regional head was an Australian, Jane, whom I would often meet when she visited Yugoslavia for the purpose of co-ordination.

Our work soon slowed down, though, as it became apparent that landmine sightings were increasing. The hitherto tight landmine zones, confined to two relatively small areas in the southern Drenica district and the district of Malisevo, were now being added to. More and more often we were seeing previously evacuated MUP 'front line' posts in the Drenica now occupied by the KLA. This was a most direct and provocative contravention of the ceasefire rules. The OSCE peace monitors were simply not strong enough to police these types of breaches, and by all accounts it was mainly the KLA, in the earlier days of the ceasefire, who were doing the breaching — certainly in Drenica, as we were to witness. Despite some weeks of ceasefire, it was clear to me that the KLA was emboldened — they were clearly confident, and believed that they had a licence (ie, Western backing) to do as they pleased. These thoughts were spinning in my mind as I raced across the windy — and now cold — barren fields, checking the finalisation of our winter program preparations and the settling in of our new Kosovo office. It seemed to me, a chilling thought, that war could come after all.

CHAPTER SEVEN

Kosovo — Crisis and Response

It had been 'all hands to the pump' in establishing CARE's expanded presence in Kosovo. Just in time too, as the Kosovo crisis was escalating. Melissa had been a central player in this implementation effort. This was her opportunity to prove herself more than just a routine program officer. Her Serbian refugee centre program, covering the whole country, virtually ran itself — we had good Serbian field staff of high calibre (Branko, later imprisoned, was perhaps the best of these men) and they knew the program inside out. Still, Melissa's presence and supervision of them were essential.

During October 1998, as we were in the process of developing our new presence in Kosovo, the National Director of CARE Canada paid the country mission a visit. At this time I was settling Peter Wallace and Jim, the two new Australian staff, into our country mission. They were to be the mainstay of our Kosovo presence. The new sub-office was in Pristina. It was late October, and heavy snow had fallen, frustrating our preparations for the new series of winter relief programs we were planning. I had sought monetary and general resource assistance through our CARE federated partners around the world. After his staff visit to Kosovo in early October, Robert Yallop, our director of overseas operations from Canberra, had put a very effective fundraising program into place — we called it CARE Australia's Kosovo emergency appeal. Robert is a great strategist and very experienced at planning and quickly responding to emergencies. We knew that we didn't have in CARE Australia the funds or the resources and nor did we have the financial backing of the Australian Government to bankroll the US$2 million that we would need to implement the type of winter programs we thought essential in Kosovo. The Australian Government's interest, after all, lay more in Asia.

A large part of the necessary fund seeking was undertaken through our federated CARE partners around the world, and as a matter of course involved their own country governments and corporations. It was my job to invite senior programming and emergency officers from our sister CAREs to the country. This would assist Robert in the selling of our appeal. I had been continually annoyed by people in our CARE partner organisations who wanted to visit for the sake of visiting — middle-ranking officers who had little meaningful to contribute, but were inclined to meddle or to 'check' that CARE Yugoslavia was 'doing it right'. This kind of irrelevant interest was, as I have said before, the bane of my existence as a country director.

In contrast, I welcomed a proposed visit by John Watson, CARE Canada's national director and, from CARE USA, Ted Robertson, their roving emergencies manager. John Watson was a learned and dignified-looking man, with a quick temper lurking near the surface. He was single-minded and had something of a reputation for stubbornness around the international CARE brotherhood, and particularly at CARE International. Frankly, I thought CARE needed his type of no nonsense approach.

John had been responsible for CARE Australia's presence and for its continuing role as CARE International's lead member in Yugoslavia. Meanwhile, to one degree or another, both CARE Deutschland and CARE Osterreich had questioned the appropriateness of CARE Australia continuing as the lead member in what they both considered to be 'their backyard'. Watson had been very direct in his criticism of these and other CARE members during the two previous CARE International board meetings. It was clearly in his interest to be so — after all, CARE Canada's presence as lead member in Bosnia–Croatia had also been under intermittent pressure by the Germanic CAREs, more so from CARE Deutschland, with whom CARE Canada had a vitriolic relationship.

Ted was a like-minded fellow. He was very effective, and always got to the nub of the crisis. He had a direct approach to his work. He could not stand the CARE International in-fighting, having seen this insidious phenomenon severely affect CARE International operations in Rwanda in late 1996. Like John Watson, he too had a good deal of faith in CARE Australia's ability to get on with it in Yugoslavia. And he backed me and my colleagues all the way. These fellows were friends in court, and with their support we were going to make something of this country mission expansion in Kosovo. We were going to thereby effectively increase our assistance to these wretched, displaced Kosovars, whose numbers grew daily.

During their visit, the two North Americans underscored the importance they placed on the programming and funding support that would be coming to CARE Yugoslavia from the North American CAREs. They were happy with what they saw of our operation and with the way in which we intended to utilise the resources donated by them to CARE Yugoslavia. And they didn't interfere in how we intended to deploy those donated resources. At the same time, they brought some good ideas to our country-wide planning. John Watson was a very experienced and wily emergency mission planner — he had done this for years, steering CARE Canada effectively into emergency deployments around the Americas and Africa. CARE Canada emergency deployments were well regarded, and their reputation was pretty sound.

As we were to trudge around the ever-deepening snowdrifts through the next week, scanning the heavens and asking God to hold the snow falls off for awhile, John would quietly suggest how we might best concentrate our dwindling resources and meagre donations to bring about the most benefit. Ted agreed on the need for dealing with landmines, which were having the typical destructive and disruptive effect on community life throughout the Kosovo countryside. Ted had had experience with them, and between Ted and myself,

I felt we could usefully fight this insidious community threat. He proposed planning and mobilising a Landmine Awareness program, aimed essentially at children in schools, but also with a wider community application. While I was keen to get straight into 'Landmine Clearance', or 'De-mining', as it is often called, Ted convinced me that the way ahead was to start with 'Awareness', then gradually build the program and CARE's reputation in the field. From there, it would be a matter of moving slowly and carefully into 'Clearance'.

Many of the ideas and conceptual planning for effective CARE International operations in the Balkans came out of the Balkan experience shared by CARE Australia and CARE Canada. It was against this background that, in correspondence before his visit, I was uncomfortably niggled by a request from John that we arrange a visit by him to the OSCE Kosovo Verification Mission HQ in Kosovo. His visit, I had thought, was primarily for the purpose of inspecting the country mission and assessing how CARE Canada could input funding to that.

The Watson/Robertson visit coincided with the new Australian staff arrivals. For Melissa and me this was a hell of a busy time. Melissa had been most helpful to me in the development of our Kosovo presence. Between us we had shuttled to and from Pristina during the intense planning period of September and October, ably assisted by Horst, who had regularly done his share of Kosovo visits later in the year. This had been a year in which the Kosovo problem had grown inexorably, and consequently so had our involvement. I had been to a two-week planning conference in Australia and rushed back when war looked possible in September 1998, subsequently missing out again on an overdue leave. I was beginning to get very tired.

Steve and Jim, our new arrivals, had to go through a country mission orientation and induction, which meant a couple of days briefing in Belgrade. Familiarity with the country head office and familiarity with the country-wide program was important, and would allow them a sense of where they fitted into the scheme of things. I would then give them their Kosovo briefs and my instructions on what their missions were — and then it would be down to Kosovo for on-the-ground familiarity and orientation. This second phase marked the taking over of the Kosovo operation by Peter from Melissa, to whom I had previously given the planning responsibility.

In this week there was a round of meetings, visits and briefings, settling in Peter and Jim and escorting Ted and John around our Kosovo operation. I needed to impress upon John and Ted the extent of the destruction and the misery wreaked upon the place. It was essential that they learned the extent of the displaced people problem and that they understood the numbers were real, not inflated media figures. To access US and Canadian Government funding to bolster our program this was critical — these individuals had to go away with a fire within if they were ever to be able to assist us. This is the strength of the CARE International federation.

I decided to kill two birds with one stone and escorted Peter, Jim, John and Ted out to the northern Drenica region where Melissa, Horst and I had been gradually laying the foundations for our Kosovo program. I knew this place backwards, having assessed its needs and then frequently gone back to deliver aid and to plan and then finetune the plan. The day we set out from our newly established Pristina office was bitterly cold and miserable. Winter was coming early, and this worried us deeply. We really needed to mobilise and get our winter relief programs onto the ground before the worst of the winter settled in.

Fighting had broken out along the Pristina–Kosovska Mitrovica road, the main arterial road that bisected the province from east to west. By the time our convoy of two Land Rovers had reached the area of conflict the fighting had dissipated. There were ongoing and increasing guerilla raids against MUP police checkpoints and strongpoints. Everything was blanketed in snow; there was no person or animal to be seen in the vicious, horizontal snow-flurried winds. It was a truly godforsaken landscape. Winter, the Balkan version, was well on its way and being particularly vicious, sucking in the bitter winds and general winter patterns from the Russian plains. The region seems far more exposed to these bleak conditions than its European neighbours. I have sometimes wondered whether this climate is a factor in the miserable social and political atmosphere and general disposition of the Balkans compared with its quieter and more relaxed neighbour regions.

I drove the front vehicle. We dared not bring our Serbian staff out to the Kosovo field these days, hence no driver. In the back, huddled in their huge parkas, were two of our best and most senior Albanian Kosovar field staff. We had often travelled together to the field, and as we motored north to the Drenica region they remained very quiet, studying the two new Australian staff, Peter and Jim. John Watson was with me in the front and Ted was in the next car. We turned off the road from Kosovska Mitrovica and headed west into the Drenica, along that now never-used road, twisting and winding through deep gullies, surrounded by bare hills with intermittent clumps of low scrub.

Our tiny convoy was watched from the ridgelines, and by those huddled inside isolated and mostly shattered farmhouses, or in sandbagged strongpoints. All now blanketed by snow, we passed one after another miserable little hovel from which the smoke of small fires rose — if the occupants were lucky. The eyes of the KLA and the MUP on their respective ridge tops were upon us as they held their ceasefire lines (or slowly breached them, as the KLA was now doing). We were hurriedly waved past the checkpoint by frozen and frightened MUP policemen in their quickly icing-up blue camouflage uniforms — hopeless uniforms in these conditions. They recognised us, with our green CARE signage on the doors and the blue CARE flag flying aloft at the rear of the vehicle. They also recognised me, a regular traveller in these parts. Serbian policemen waved us through, no time wasted in checking papers, not coming round from behind the sandbagged strongpoint wall and staying out of that horizontal, biting wind. The Serbian policemen, scanning the ridgelines, thinking 'those cursed KLA snipers up on those ridgelines, the wily little shupta bastards hide back inside those dark, deep shadows with their old hunting rifles ... and they can shoot straight, too'.

We eventually arrived at the town of Srbica, the capital of the Drenica district and headquarters for our programs. This town also headquartered the major MUP presence in the Drenica. We drove through and turned south, continuing about 4 kilometres out of the town.

● ● ●

Wind and snow are becoming blizzard-like. As we top the dominating ridgeline south of the town visibility is down to half a kilometre. Snowdrifts are mounting on the fringes of the road, which is now running south through the Drenica Valley. Difficult to make out the old familiar turn-off that I need to wind our way south-east up into the foothills of the Cicavica mountain range, where the two villages of Poljuvec and Cirez straddle bare ridgelines. These are the two major community centres for our current medical programs and where I intend we focus our new programs, hopefully with US and Canadian support. As we trundle through the wretched blizzard I am hopeful of the support of Watson and Robertson.

At the top of the ridge we are overtaken by an international media crew, ploughing through the lousy conditions in their armoured Land Rover. All the press teams now drive around in these things. I would give my back teeth for a fleet of those. Measurably better protection for our field teams. We stop and get out because it is polite to do so in these barren places. It turns out we are the only fool NGO people out in the field today and these desperate media souls need a story, need a quote from some NGO people about the sharply deteriorating security situation and sudden onslaught of winter. Good television — here we have a driving blizzard, rapidly approaching winter and what is the international community doing to help these poor Albanians as winter falls upon them?

Standing next to the vehicle, my little bush hat ineffectively tilted against the wind, ice quickly matting my beard, I am speaking into this ridiculously ostrich-feathered microphone boom, whose feathers are icing up. The journo is a short woman, a girl really, wrapped in parkas and shivering but determinedly doing her job, asking intelligent questions. I reckon she deserves a story for having made the effort to come all the way out here. And importantly, it's a good opportunity for us to continue highlighting the developing disaster picture and keep building on CARE's winter appeal. That done, we carefully drive off the main road, guided by a local farmer who points out the track.

As we cross the windswept ridgeline and descend into the valley, the track now becomes more evident. We plough through the half-metre deep snow, winding our way slowly down through the gully, past a couple of farmhouses, one of these with a partly destroyed roof. There is damage everywhere — here a burnt-out barn, there a perfectly good-looking cottage but with a metre-diameter tank shell hole in its red brick front wall. I imagine what this deceptively cute-looking little cottage looks like inside — a blackened mess, probably missing its back wall. It will soon fill with snow.

We have now definitely travelled beyond the MUP's front line; in fact, I notice the normally heavily fortified and well-manned strongpoint located up on the top of the ridge, where we had been coralled by the media crew, is now abandoned. The MUP would seem to have pulled all the way back to Srbica. Again we see eyes, now peering at us from dark windows. I am mindful of the landmine threat in these parts but am confident about this track. Plenty of tractor tyre marks in the snow now, a good sign that the road is safe. We see the odd Lada sedan ploughing along the track and at the bottom of the gully, through the muddy creek crossing. Makes me feel a little sheepish as I tenderly drive our Land Rover Discovery. We climb back up onto the next ridgeline, again exposed to that cursed wind and sleet. Despite the appalling conditions, old farmers somehow manage to get their cars through the muck.

As we travel further up into the foothills we begin to see signs of the KLA. Mainly dressed in civilian clothes at first, farmers really, but the odd one armed, usually with an old shotgun or hunting rifle. They wave pleasantly, don't attempt to stop and question us. They look to me like typical, friendly European farmers, not like fighters. We politely but curtly nod in return, careful not to demonstrate any overfriendliness. You have to wonder about these men though, huddled up here on the ridgeline today outside Poljuvec, ever vigilant. I used to think on these occasions that if the Serbian military ever rolled out of Srbica and came on over these barren ridgelines and farmlands, they would roll straight over the top of these blokes. They wouldn't stand a chance — they are too lightly armed, and while they probably have the numbers, they would only hold these ridgelines and villages for a couple of days at best. Every time I drive out here and see these farmer fighters and their KLA professional colleagues, these thoughts flood upon me. I feel like screaming at them — you stupid idealistic bastards, give it away, for the sake of your lives and those of your poor families. But I never do. It is not our place to engage in such dialogue, nor can we be seen talking to fighters, even out here.

We drive past the Poljuvec mosque. Like all village mosques it sits behind a high brick wall, its minaret tower reaching about 13 metres high, a beacon in these barren farmlands. Through a broken gate I can see into the little mosque courtyard. Curiously, the little gate is the only part of the mosque which has been damaged; like the mosque at Cirez, 10 kilometres further west, this has also largely escaped the fighting. These villages have up to now remained largely intact, with only the odd artillery shell having been lobbed in to damage the place. No tank or infantry attacks or general police security sweeps have occurred in this region yet. But it must come. The war clouds are gathering, and finally the Drenica region too must suffer what many other areas have already suffered.

Through the battered gate I see the more professional-looking KLA fighters lining up for some parade on this bitter day. They are all dressed in uniform, more professionally equipped than their informal KLA farmer colleagues. Some of them saunter out casually, oblivious to the biting winds and snow flurries, to check us out — but of course they had been told half an hour earlier who we were, when the CARE International Land Rover was seen approaching. Sentries would have passed on the information quickly — this is their only defence, along with vigilance, flexibility and the ability to move lightly and quickly.

You can see these are a tougher and more seasoned bunch than their KLA farmer mates. To me they do not look as if they belong here in this village. They are ex-Yugoslav soldiers — seasoned and well trained, as so many of the KLA are — and Albanians from south of the border. The odd one or two in the region will be Mujaheddin, blown in from the Middle East, probably of Saudi, Afghan, Iranian or even Yemeni origin. Hard to tell, peering at them in this cursed snow, just who they are. They eye us carefully; they are on their guard but remain relaxed and friendly.

I have had some trouble with KLA interfering with my Albanian Kosovar staff in the past. I wait for the same to happen again. Will they demand that the Albanian staff get out of the vehicle and produce their papers? If they do, I am ready to tell these people to go and multiply somewhere. I have sent word back through the senior Albanian community heads in Pristina to let the KLA know that CARE will not tolerate such interference. Melissa and I have been very concerned, and have reaffirmed this position whenever meeting community heads. Such is life in the hurly-burly of humanitarian politics.

Peter and Jim watch this scene in silence. This is their orientation, a rough introduction to CARE's business in Kosovo. They are calm, if frozen. However, I feel sure that both of them will take the various aspects in their stride: the weather, the extent of the assistance needed in these villages, and of course the prickly issue of the presence of the KLA. Particularly Jim, who is appointed to run, hands on, the winter relief blanket/clothing and household goods distribution programs. Sitting as we are at the moment, in Poljuvec, we are in the centre of his program area.

Jim will report to Peter, assigned to head up and run our Kosovo office. Peter and Jim quietly ask questions and I keep up a running commentary as we slosh on through Poljuvec. John Watson observes all without comment. The village was built to house about 2000 people, perhaps 250 families, 250 houses. The houses are typically Albanian Kosovar: red brick or cement bungalows, with red tiled roofs, the same materials that most houses throughout Yugoslavia are made of. But in accordance with Albanian Muslim tradition they are designed quite differently from Serbian houses. They are at most double storeyed, many single, and all have a little barn leaning against one side. They are all surrounded by walls, up to 3 metres high.

The women are not in sight on any of the occasions we drive through, regardless of the weather. Unlike their sisters in the larger towns, country women live in more restrictive and conservative environments, being confined indoors or to the house courtyard. On better days kids can be seen playing in the muddy streets (tracks really). Red tractors and trailers dominate the place — the tractor is the livelihood of every Kosovar village family. There are not too many cars out here, and those that do exist are virtually village community cars. At this point the villages are largely intact, but there is enough damage evident around the place to require substantial work on many houses.

As we jolt and slide our way up the village track I explain to Peter, Jim, John and Ted my intentions, repeating my Belgrade office briefing of some days earlier. It is CARE's plan to conduct two major programs in the Drenica region. Firstly, a clothing, blankets, household goods distribution program to displaced families who have fled other villages and who are now doubled up with other families. Secondly, a very rudimentary house repair program, designed to patch moderately damaged houses, that is, houses that have had less than say roughly 30 per cent structural damage, and need roof patching and holes in walls plugged. Those houses selected would be occupied ones, and ones where the owner family has taken in or is prepared to take in another family. That is, we would be rushing to repair these places in time for winter, something much on my mind as I scan the grey, snow-clad skies, hoping this is only a pre-winter freak weather occurrence. We have little time to prepare.

As I am waving my arms around and yelling over the roar of the engine and the hiss of the heating system I stop, decide to abandon any further progress towards Cirez and try to turn around. I expertly back the Land Rover into the gutter on the side of the track, which was deeply concealed by the snowdrift, and bog us firmly. My face goes very red — here, surrounded by all these rough-and-ready colleagues I manage to bog the bloody car. I reflect that if my old Mechanised Infantry mates could see me now they would be hissing derision. John Watson gallantly gets out of the vehicle with the others to push — I notice he is wearing a pair of nice business shoes which soon get buried in the snow and the mud. As is often the case in these circumstances, the chap responsible for bogging remains warm and dry behind the steering wheel. How embarrassing! We get out fairly quickly, turn, and manage to get both vehicles back down through the village.

On the way out we stop at a number of houses, speak to the families, build on our knowledge about their and the community's condition, concerns, shortfalls. I can see John Watson becoming more impressed with what CARE Yugoslavia is planning to conduct in the way of assistance programming. I think I am winning him over to the cause — we want about US$200 000 out of our Canadian partners. I sense that he is impressed with our professionalism, or what I like to think of as our professionalism. We examine a couple of houses to check for the type of repair work required. This is down to the business for Peter and Jim; a realisation of the scope of the social and humanitarian problem is dawning upon them.

We discuss the difficulties of selecting the type of houses which will be salvageable within the meagre budget limitations of our program. We discuss among ourselves the politics and realities of how we will select the beneficiary families and houses. How do we work through the village committees in an objective way? Can we trust the committees to lead us to the most deserving families, or will they select their own extended and politically loyal families? These are the issues that Melissa, the Albanian staff and I have been wrestling with for weeks.

This is a good opportunity for me to impress upon Peter and Jim these essential planning and implementation issues. I wearily think to myself, thank God for the arrival of the cavalry, in the form of Peter and Jim. It pleases me greatly that they are here; my back feels bent, and while the indomitable Melissa would never admit it, I reckon she too is beginning to stagger under the weight of this fast-growing country mission. These two blokes are switching on to the challenges, asking good questions, already testing theories on their first day in the field. Melissa and I have got to let go of this Kosovo programming asap; we need Peter and Jim to grasp it and get running, to take the delegation. I know Jim will, he loves the field. Ted has some good ideas on how we might best monitor — as far as is possible — the actions of the village communities. Someone debates with us vigorously the notion that perhaps we should dispense with the village committees and simply run our own field teams to make all beneficiary selection decisions, but we shake our heads to this.

Jim quickly demonstrates a practical understanding of how we might best develop a working relationship with the village communities, and empower and delegate them to do much of the selection and distribution work, monitored by our field teams and Jim himself. Jim does not seem to have lost the field co-ordinating talents he displayed in the ZAIRE-based refugee camps a couple of years ago, working with CARE Australia. As we stand there, heads bent, in the snow, he shouts his feelings and ideas. I am relieved, and confident that he will be able to run an effective hands-on program. I like that. I have always expected our Australian staff to spend a lot of their time at the coalface supervising and encouraging our national staff, talking to the locals, and I know Jim believes in that concept of programming.

Now we slide and shove our way back to the valley main road, without further incident. Glad to get out onto the tar-sealed road, we breathe sighs of relief. Happy too that Peter and Jim have begun to see the realities of CARE's program area, to get an idea of our programming objectives. Too often in CARE we take our staff and hurl them into the deep end, with little or no orientation, no clear guidelines and no clear job description. In 1998 this fundamental principle in organisational matters is improving. Peter and Jim have come to this mission better prepared administratively than many before them. CARE Australia Canberra staff have done a good job with their preparation. The performance of Canberra human resources has dramatically improved since 1996, and I have found their support to me, as a country director, consistently effective.

I am doing my best to conduct a useful orientation for the new team members. I have always taken pride in at least trying to organise and conduct effective induction processes for my new field staff; I made it a practice in Africa and attempt to improve and refine the process here in Yugoslavia. It doesn't always work properly, and it is typically the overwhelming, competing priorities in the job that make it difficult. In these first few days after Peter's and Jim's arrival in the country, I try to devote most of my time to their settling in and encouraging a clear understanding of what their duties and mission are.

Escorting our visitors has also been an important part of this Kosovo trip, as we strive to build our winterisation project, for which their support is vital. I feel they are happy with our approach to identifying and prioritising the humanitarian needs. The harnessing and channelling of CARE partner support into the CARE lead member office is the essence of the CARE fraternity as I see it, not the fighting and interference I had experienced this past year. It has been a busy and taxing trip, I think as we carefully make our way out of the Drenica Valley and back down to Pristina, with darkness advancing. I go as fast as I safely can to get back to Pristina before darkness hits.

John Watson, Ted and I discussed over these couple of days the types of additional programs we could add to the winterisation programs. Ted and I talked at some length about the feasibility of a de-mining program. He was not so much in favour of cranking one up in the immediate term. We argued about this, and I proposed that we should introduce it as a concept proposal to the donors. CARE Australia and CARE USA do run sub-contracted de-mining programs in Cambodia and Africa and I suggested that CARE establish its own de-mining unit. The argument against, though, was that there are sufficient de-mining NGOs. It is an ongoing debate. Ted went off to talk to UNHCR, UNICEF and USAID (the US Government aid agency) people in Pristina about the less challenging concept of 'landmine awareness'. I finally accepted this position and was glad to leave it to Ted to do the research.

Ted was to be with us for about ten days, busy trying to put the concept analysis together. We talked regularly. I liked his concept, he was realistic and practical. I could trust Ted to do the hard and detailed planning; meticulous and experienced, it seemed to be a cakewalk for him. Before departing he got the nod from UNICEF and USAID that the proposal was agreed to in principle, pending the country mission putting together the formal project proposal. Ted would complete it at CARE USA head office when he returned to Atlanta. That was one less proposal that Melissa and I would have to do, overwhelmed as we were by the number of proposals needed for the winterisation package. Ted would prepare his draft and then e-mail it to me here in Belgrade for Melissa and me to go through and adjust or sign off on.

We agreed that the project would only be modest to begin with and, much like our first shelter project up in Poljuvec, a kind of trial. If we were happy that the thing is workable, is achieving something and is supported by the Kosovo community, then we would expand the program to include more schools. Schools in Kosovo is where it would start, appealing to children to learn to recognise dangerous areas and know how to get out of trouble. We would be relying on those kids to go home and pass on this knowledge and their new alertness to their parents and others in the community.

The day after our field trip, John Watson went to visit the Organisation for Security and Co-operation Europe (OSCE) Headquarters and asked me to accompany him. We arrived at a complex of buildings about 10 kilometres west of Pristina. Serbian and Albanian security guards were posted outside. They radio checked to the people John wanted to see. These big American GMC four-wheel drive long-wheelbased vehicles are all over the place. The orange Kosovo Verification Mission (KVM) vehicles at this point are thin on the ground, and are still being imported as KVM now proceeds into its supposedly rapid expansion. KVM is to replace the small but very effective KDOM (the old Kosovo diplomatic observer mission), but the international community will still rely on the KDOM group — about fifty embassy staff personnel and ten-odd vehicles — for weeks to come as KVM very slowly arrives and builds.

The slow pace of this changeover will turn out to be fatal. Ceasefire breaches will continue unabated, allowing the KLA to not only breach the ceasefire line continually but to become more emboldened. They will eventually move into and occupy ex-Yugoslav MUP and military positions. But as we went to John's meeting we were yet to know any of this. At this time, we thought the build-up would be rapid, and we held great hopes for this magic peace panacea. More fool us! However, the OSCE KVM did provide a very valuable, timely and accurate source of safety information to all fifty-five NGOs, UN agencies and government agencies in Yugoslavia, sending detailed brief daily to all parties.

Having never visited the new KVM or the old KDOM (Kosovo Diplomatic Observer Mission) before, I was glad for the opportunity to gather some vital information about the Drenica Valley district, the place in which we intended to establish the bulk of our winter program. I was growing extremely concerned about the suddenly escalating landmine problem in the south of the valley, just outside our intended program area.

Up until now the problem seemed to be low key and sporadic, although there had been a couple of nasty mine incidents involving death and severe injury. But the landmines had been contained within two or three areas where there were heavy concentrations of KLA camps — they had been mining the approaches to those camps, but the radius out from the camps had generally been only a few kilometres. Now the area was growing insidiously. I also needed to know what the OSCE assessment was of the potential for fighting in the Drenica. I wanted to know what the OSCE KVM assessment of KLA positions, strengths and intentions in the Drenica Valley was. Were we going to be safe, and would it be worth the investment of US$2 million plus in this area? I needed to know what somebody, anybody, thought about the current behaviour and intentions of the Yugoslav Army and the Serbian police in the Drenica Valley — how were they likely to react to whatever strength of KLA threat existed, or was building, in the valley district? It was my business as country director to know and assess these things, and I owed it to my colleagues and to CARE International to have the best answers possible. I did not intend to send my staff into a death trap. My visit that day was brief. I was to meet some useful people, and get the information and assessment updates.

I left John Watson after an hour or so, satisfied that I had got some information about the Drenica; not much, no magic panacea, no magic crystal ball. I simply had to plan for our Drenica program as we had previously. The Drenica was thought to be a potential hot spot, but no worse than many other Kosovo districts, which didn't say much for the rest of the province. Anyway, on the basis of that assessment, and given the serious level of humanitarian concern in the Drenica, I felt we had no choice but to get on with the plan.

John Watson went back a number of times to see the KVM during the next couple of days to discuss his proposed project. I let him go alone; I did not have the time to wait around, as I had to head back to Belgrade. The CARE Canada project proposal was an administrative support activity, where Canadian civilians needed for the OSCE peace-monitoring organisation would be recruited, transported and administratively inducted into Kosovo by CARE Canada. They would then be handed across to the OSCE KVM, at which time they would become the 'property' and responsibility of KVM. CARE Canada would look after some of these people's personal administrative requirements and pick up full administrative responsibility for them again when it was time to ship them home. I had no problem with the proposed program in terms of its appropriateness or its morality. The KVM operation was a laudable and honourable operation, one run under extraordinarily difficult circumstances, and which provided the only hope as far as I could see for both the Yugoslav Government (in terms of its tight political predicament) and for the salvation of the people of Kosovo. The CARE Canada support activity was a straightforward and very simple affair.

In Berlin, however, I had not supported the proposal for a variety of reasons: firstly, I had enough on my plate putting together a set of essential programs for Yugoslavia, north and south. This extra activity was not essential, and we could do without the distraction. Secondly, it was not a humanitarian activity and might confuse people as to CARE's actual Yugoslavia charter. Thirdly, while we desperately needed a good working association with OSCE KVM, as with other agencies in the area, we did want to maintain a healthy gap, operationally and for appearance's sake, between ourselves and all other agencies. Finally, we had resisted other CARE member partners establishing stand-alone programs, and so allowing the CARE Canada activity would have been unfair to our other CARE partners. In the event, CARE Australia agreed that CARE Canada could proceed with the support program. (It was with great irony that later in Australia I would see an SBS 'Dateline' program suggesting that the CARE Canada program had something to do with my arrest and my and Peter Wallace's ordeals. This was categorically not the case. The interrogators and the military prosecutors did not raise the issue with me at any time, nor did they refer to the CARE Canada program in the 'indictment', nor did they raise the issue once in court.)

I was desperately concerned that we stay on top of the growing landmine problem, and be able to better monitor the pattern of ever-growing conflict. We were running blind in Kosovo. Our field teams were now taking increasing risks with their field trips. It was going to get much worse. The fighting was on the increase, despite the so-called ceasefire which had been in place now for some weeks. With the ambitious array of assistance programs we were now beginning to put in place, our spread of field teams would quadruple. The number of CARE subcontracted resupply convoys going out into the Drenica and other areas would dramatically increase.

All of this weighed on my mind these days, as I took much pride in maintaining the security of our operations. I directed all our information staff and field team leaders to update their situation maps daily, a vital component of safe operations. As things were now, I had directed that Peter and his staff call in each morning without fail to the UNHCR briefing room to check for landmine information. This was the minimum requirement, although I was not entirely confident that the UNHCR office was up to date, despite their very good and effective UN security officer. The security team at UNHCR was too small. While they were diligent and very co-operative, the deteriorating security situation at that time was getting beyond them.

I wanted all bases covered in terms of keeping up with safety information. No CARE field teams and their vehicles were going to be catapulted, burnt, twisted and broken, into the sky by bloody anti-tank mines if I could help it. Through November and December 1998 we rushed to get the programs implemented. The weather had turned totally foul, and the snow had really settled in. And still we struggled to get our funding from the European Union's emergency agency, ECHO. We were severely frustrated and annoyed with ECHO. Their staff had essentially disappeared for the Christmas break! So as we attempted to finetune the project proposals for the shelter program we had to wait days and weeks for responses to our project proposal adjustments, and the flow of funding was impeded in the process. No signed agreement, no money, no activity.

Jim and Peter were understandably frustrated that I would not allow them to commit to expenditure on the shelter program. They already had the local subcontractors lined up. But I could not. It is the perennial battle that country directors have with their field colleagues. The latter just wanted to get on with it (having an agreement in principle with ECHO, as we had in this case), while Pratt and Canberra were holding them up! We were all just bureaucrats! Fundamentally, even if emotionally, these workers were right. It was very, very hard and very disappointing not to be able to start work on essential winter housing projects when the snow was bucketing down, and with so many displaced Albanian Kosovar families doubled and tripled up in these snowbound villages, up in the Drenica. Thankfully, at least our winter clothing distributions were off to a good start and progressing.

Meanwhile, with the ECHO program agreement in principle available, at least referred to in writing, I was able to commence a new recruitment for another Australian field staff member. Peter and Jim were doing it tough on their own in our new Kosovo operation. The third worker I had planned for (as essential) some months ago was needed yesterday. As soon as the ECHO authority letter arrived I telephoned CARE in Canberra to ask them to quickly activate the recruitment process for the position. Partly because it was Christmas and partly because the new position was highly specialised (a construction engineer), we had difficulty getting the position filled quickly. This was embarrassing, because ECHO expected to see the talent on the ground in order to be confident that CARE could and would do the job properly. They were in a position to pull the funding from us and give it to somebody else — there were plenty of new NGOs sniffing around looking for the lucrative type of ECHO contract that was being offered to CARE Yugoslavia.

Our experience, as I recall, was ever one of high competition, almost a dog eat dog game. It is difficult always to have the talent on the ground when you do not have the funding, and I needed the flow of this project money to be able to pay the new appointee. On this program, CARE UK was our implementing partner; it was in fact CARE UK which helped us prepare and submit the project proposal to ECHO in Brussels, a good example of how, when it is working, the CARE International network works wonderfully. So we pressed on through the ever-deepening winter, trying in the face of every frustration known to man and beast to get these winter programs fully established — a good start, but not good enough. When I went off to the UK in January 1999 to attend a human rights workshop, the new shelter engineer position was still not filled.

CHAPTER EIGHT
Grim Expectations

CARE YUGOSLAVIA continued its operations in Kosovo, despite the looming threat of war. The OSCE-brokered ceasefire had rapidly deteriorated through January and February 1999. In the northern Drenica region we were only too aware of how fragile the ceasefire was. In the villages of Cirez and Podjuvec we were constantly running into the KLA. It had always been my intention that CARE would carry out the bulk of its operations there — no other NGO cared to operate there, because it was a tough area, and in my assessment the needs of this Kosovo district were significantly higher than others. The infrasrucutre in this part of Kosovo was the poorest I had seen anywhere. People were traditionally poorer, and the destruction from the October 1998 'security problems' was more significant here than in many other areas. There was a risk for us in that the KLA were well entrenched in the Drenica, but again there was that old debate — how did we stack up the KLA threat/presence against the pressing needs of thousands of innocent people, older men, women and children?

For me this brought to the surface the old dilemmas of Zaire, where our refugee camp operations were in close proximity to the Rwandan borders and the murderous Interehamwe. These were the

Hutu militias responsible for the 1994 Rwandan massacres. Like the Interehamwe, the KLA hid within the community and relied on it to provide their sustenance. Like the Hutu refugees, the Albanian Kosovars did not have any say over the presence of fighters; they certainly feared them, but in some paradoxical way were also glad of their presence.

The Albanian Kosovars were a stoic lot. Particularly those in the villages well away from Pristina. They were far more conservative, significantly more religious, and well organised in the traditional Muslim rural way — strong patriarchal hierarchies, strong village committee structures, exceedingly high spirited and to be admired for their endless generosity and compassion to one another and to families of like mind. However, the men and the KLA in these rural communities took a ruthless stance towards any dissension. Reprisal killings had been a regular feature of rural life in Kosovo. The KLA was a loose organisation which had arisen in the late 1990s from a basis of mainly village committees, and family clans which felt a desperate compulsion to defend their lands. But there was also, as mentioned earlier, some widely dispersed brigand and mafia elements in the early KLA structure. Many a revolutionary group in the Balkans has started this way.

I had often wondered whether the outbreak of hostilities in early 1998 in Kosovo was also a result of the tensions arising from the competition between Serb and Albanian mafias in these lucrative smuggling route crossroads. That had to be a cause, it seemed to me, alongside the political repression visited by a clumsy and ruthless regime, and the KLA terrorist activity visited by bandits on the innocent of all ethnic backgrounds. This was the atmosphere within which our country mission operated, and the atmosphere was becoming increasingly charged.

I was now running back and forth between Kosovo and Belgrade. My habits of 1998 were revisited. Four to six hour drives on appalling roads in lousy weather to get from Belgrade to Kosovo. Trips took the form of a quick visit out in the field and a few hours in the CARE Pristina office talking to Peter Wallace and his staff. Then it would be back into the Land Rover for a hurried return to Belgrade, where there was always plenty to do in terms of the rest of the country's operations. Inevitably my driver would be irritable because as I usually didn't leave Pristina until late afternoon, there would be a tiresome drive in lousy, sleety weather through the dark of night. Back in Belgrade there would be a worried Samira, always relieved to get me on the mobile phone with its terribly restrictive network. Samira was always encouraging me to get out of Kosovo and back on the highway before last light to avoid the ambush threat. Just get home, Pratt.

My regular, hectic visits to Kosovo reflected my worry about the field operations, the development of new programs (despite the looming war clouds it was important to keep the eye on the ball with respect to our growing operations), and, above all, the safety of CARE staff. I have long held this perhaps romantic view that one should 'lead from the front when the chips are down, be there for the troops'. Hence, with the deteriorating Kosovo situation I was back on the road again, probably to the detriment of some of the rest of my country director responsibilities. Still, that was my call on priorities. It always came back to this poor country mission capacity problem. Insufficient staff, for instance — where the hell was the admin/finance manager I had been trying to get since May 1998? I appreciated that head office were doing their best to recruit, but the matter was critical. We were all tired, and I was lucky that the three experienced professional internationals I had in the team hadn't burnt out and gone home. Who could have blamed them if they had?

Two dedicated Australians — Jim and Edward were constantly out in the field in Kosovo, and this meant they were regularly in and out of the Drenica. I needed to maintain a pulse check on the growing security threat in that region, and I relied on these blokes to keep me informed through Peter Wallace. I needed his ongoing assessments as the clouds continued to darken on the horizon. I often found it necessary and more comforting to go direct to the field with Jim and Edward, travelling with them around the villages to view the progress of our programs, speaking with local farmers, Kosovar Albanian and Kosovar Serb alike, and getting a feel for the security temperature while we were at it. Jim and Edward were quiet achievers, good field leaders, well respected by their Albanian and Serb staffs, typical of the good Australian hands we had around the country missions.

Toward the middle of March these two men were warning of a catastrophe in Drenica. Clearly the Yugoslav Army was building its forces for what could only be an all-out attack on KLA strongholds in the Drenica region. New field units of armoured and mounted infantry units were deploying into the Drenica north of Kosovo, concentrating heavily in the town of Srbica. We could not help but see them, as our field teams moved daily back and forth through Srbica to the villages involved in our programs. New mine incidents had occurred. The KLA had broken their part of the deal in the ceasefire and had begun mining the roads closer in towards Srbica and again further south. Our field teams were very wary, and I had issued strict security procedures to deal with both the mine threat and the generally growing threat of ambush. There would likely be war in Drenica (we did not anticipate a province-wide conflagration at that point), a disaster for an already fragile and dislocated Albanian community. My regular situation reports to CARE Australia head office in Canberra painted the picture of this continually deteriorating situation affecting both the country and CARE's presence in that place.

My regular fortnightly situation reports through January and February 1999 were now added to by bi-weekly updates, and as we fell into a deteriorating March the frequency increased until right up into the war, when they became daily reports. By February these reports were also going out to those sister CARE International organisations around the world who were involved in supporting our Kosovo programs: CARE USA, CARE UK, CARE Deutschland, CARE Osterreich, CARE Norway and CARE Canada. I deemed it necessary to keep our partner organisations with international donor backers informed of the deteriorating situation through regular country mission reports, because we did not know whether we were going to have to upgrade our emergency programs there, in which case I would be seeking their program funding support — perhaps even emergency staff support from their own national staff — and I would need rapid responses from them; or conversely, whether we would need to cease all Kosovo operations, in which case CARE offices needed to be informed so that they could inform their supporting donors why we had just lost hundreds of thousands of

GRIM EXPECTATIONS

dollars of programming down the drain. Such was the purpose of my country mission situation reports. My situation reports were to feature largely in my capture and 'spy' trial later.

I had issued security and safety instructions in February governing our operations both in Kosovo and across the country generally. The threat of NATO air strikes had by now dramatically increased, as had that of a general war in Kosovo. The international organisations and embassies were scaling down. I had called Peter Wallace and the other two country mission program managers in to Belgrade to issue these instructions and to check our preparedness for trouble. Firstly, in the event that war broke but was of a restricted nature, and operations could continue, we needed to and did develop contingency plans for increased or new refugee emergencies. Secondly, in the event that operations became untenable in Kosovo, we needed shut-down procedures and emergency plans to evacuate all our staff from there back up to Belgrade. Albanian staff, of course, could not come to Belgrade but would have to retire home, or out to the country with relatives, depending on the ferocity of the troubles. Thirdly, in the event of wide-scale NATO bombing, we needed and did put into place contingencies for wholesale evacuation of the mission team from the country, as well as for the cessation of operations country-wide. As is often the case in these circumstances, we had our sceptics, who wondered whether I was wasting their time discussing and planning such measures, but most just got on with it.

The Serbs had agreed, albeit reluctantly and obstinately, to the deployment of 2000 OSCE monitors onto sovereign Yugoslav territory. They had finally, after much chain dragging, agreed to pull back their army and police militia forces from conflict areas. Despite the increasing evidence of heavy-handed militia operations, the much-heralded 'massacres of hundreds to thousands' of Albanian Kosovars were never confirmed, despite the presence of OSCE monitoring teams. Thirty-three Albanian bodies had been found in the village of Racak; this was probably the work of renegade Serbian militia forces, although the jury was still out regarding exactly who was responsible (until recently at least). The findings of a Finnish inquiry were kept secret. In the five months leading up to the start of the war, about four massacres of up to this magnitude were discovered. The tension in the country in March was at breaking point. Against this background I had to make judgments as to where the country mission was headed.

Meanwhile the battle of wits between the Yugoslav Government and the majority of other governments around the world continued. The number of incidents, clashes between government troops and the KLA, was increasing dramatically. As far as I could determine, both sides in the old conflict, which had been brokered to ceasefire status the previous October, were at fault. The Serbs had felt bitterly betrayed by the outcome of the Rambouillet talks. It seemed to me, and to a lot of diplomatic and UN/NGO people in Yugoslavia, that as pig-headed as the Yugoslavs may be, they had got the rough end of the deal — very much a case of simplistic and knee-jerk politicking on the part of Madeleine Albright. Desperately trying to keep a handle on what was developing in the country, I was keeping in touch with the embassies. Good friends in some major Western embassies, people who had a close understanding of the diplomacy surrounding Rambouillet and the events unfolding in the country since, were fairly scathing of their government's handling of the Kosovo problem. I agreed. Clearly, ignorance and diplomatic laziness underpinned the approaches of some governments. Any armchair diplomat could see that the Serbs were going to be impossible to handle diplomatically — they were being driven by an impossible situation to accept a pretty much one-sided ceasefire arrangement, one which breached their sovereignty.

This was a very challenging and difficult period for me. To find the right balance between restricting operations to a safe level and still maintaining essential life-saving activities was paramount. I had a belief, one shared by the best of CARE Australia's and CARE International's country directors and emergency directors and managers, that providing you had a good and viable relationship with the host government of the country you were operating in, you strove to continue operations in the face of war. After all, what was the good of an emergency NGO if it was not prepared to commit to operations when the going got tough? This ethic drove me heavily in my deliberations about the war that was rushing towards us. The question, of course, was whether we had in CARE generally and in my country mission particularly the capacity to swing into emergency action, to sustain such operations under difficult and challenging cirumstances. Was I fooling myself that we did? Was I asking too much of my staff and did CARE Australia in turn expect too much of the mission?

I continued to follow events and kept an eye on the deteriorating security situation in Kosovo. All mission heads in Belgrade were now, that is by mid-March, meeting daily at the UNHCR Belgrade office. We swapped information with UNHCR and each other. One mission head might recall an incident the day before in Kosovo where one of their field teams had encountered a landmine, or had noted increased military activity. Margaret O'Keefe, UNHCR head of mission, would quite diligently and firmly pass on information — often in the form of written UNHCR reports, or else verbally on more sensitive issues — about developments or potential for trouble as assessed by her Kosovo office and team. Sometimes she would also be in possession of some embassy-sourced information. Generally the mood in these meetings was of impending war, frustration, weariness and a pox on both their houses, Albanian Kosovar militants and the Yugoslav militia.

We did not generally trust the KLA. The KLA was thought to be provoking the trouble, and perhaps goading their people into a war which we reckoned was bound to lead to massive suffering in the immediate term. The Yugoslavs had been humbled diplomatically and were absolutely itching for a fight. Given the smallest of excuses they would launch a bloody, revenge-seeking operation — of this we in the UN/NGO community were sure. Milosevic was surely prepared to gamble with NATO and the West generally. He was a champion at brinkmanship and desperate to ensure his own survival and that of his praetorian guard and close ruling elite. The maintenance of his grip on power was absolutely essential in Slobodan's mind. It was becoming increasingly obvious to us during these days that a NATO-led operation would consolidate people behind Milosevic, people who for the most part, in the misery of their lives, disliked him and his regime. It could be predicted that Serbs would defend their national honour, regardless of how archaic an idea that might be. We on the ground in Belgrade at that time could feel it, could read it in local papers, and were being constantly told by our Serbian staff that the collective psyche was developing just this way. Even the Serbian middle class, passionate in their political opposition and every bit as informed and as sharp as any other middle class in southern Europe, would stand by indifferently as their government marched into a Kosovo war. This was all becoming increasingly clear to me at this time, even if I found it hard to comprehend.

My colleagues, my wife Samira and I would discuss these issues in the depressing days through early to mid-March. Melissa and Horst would gingerly and quietly check out their staff's attitudes on these issues. Not only were we increasingly uncomfortable about the mood in the country, the feelings of our staff were on our minds. We did not want to embarrass our staff, who were clearly wrestling with their own devils. Our staff seemed to us to be at once angry, frustrated, fearful of what their country would get it itself into, and of a NATO war, and also afraid that their poverty-stricken nation would continue to drift even further away from the rest of the civilised world. Melissa, young and idealistic, and Horst, older and more experienced in the ways of the world, came to the same conclusions.

The days were still bitterly cold and dark; winter was not yet over. We were working long and stupid hours, as usual. The lights in the office burned well into the evening, and we would drag ourselves out about 7 to 8 pm on many nights, work Saturday afternoons, work at home Sundays. We were flat out these days working on the final preparations and planning for new programs in Yugoslavia generally and in Kosovo in particular. It seemed to me a classic case of push/pull. Working hard to launch either new or expanded humanitarian programs while concurrently planning hard to cease operations, as a contingency for the worst case. This work situation was taking its toll on all of us. The irrepressible Melissa was months overdue to take her rest and recreation leave and I was keen to bundle her out of the country. The same with Horst. They were good people, with a strong sense of responsibility and concern for their staffs. Like me, they were becoming trapped by this place — too focused on the job, understandably close to and worried about our workers and not well placed to look after their own best personal interests. Samira was onto me as well. Cannily aware and worried about the situation the country mission was facing in terms of the looming war clouds, she was constantly at me about taking my leave, which was overdue by many months. Stubbornly I didn't listen, and went on with the work, just getting more and more tired.

So it was against this background that we were preparing for all sorts of contingencies. Horst, Melissa, Samira and I would wearily drag our way up to the pizza place in Banavo Brdo for dinner. We would ponder these issues, the mood of the country, whether the government would go to the wire, the mood of our staff, who we could rely on to be strong enough to carry on under difficult and emotional circumstances. Quietly we would discuss the contingency plans for international staff evacuation, a subject we felt uncomfortable discussing in the presence of our Yugoslav staff. Preparation for evacuation included earmarking vehicles for evacuation, setting aside the essential files and office equipment that we would need to take out of the country. Prepacking essential personal effects that could be carried in a limited number of vehicles and storing other personal effects and office records that could not be removed. Preparing to pay the staff one to two months' salary in advance, whatever the mission budget and the program budgets could afford. Not a time for emotional, irrational and unaccountable decisions.

My poor wife Sam had been helping out in the office most days, mainly without pay and always faithfully working back on these bitterly cold evenings. She felt more secure, I think, with us — there was nothing else to do anyway around the place, despite her quite extensive diplomatic and international network of good mates. She was very concerned for me, and getting more and more frustrated with my one-track determination to work. In this she was closely supported by Melissa. Why don't you go on leave, you silly old bastard? What about a break for your poor wife? She was of course right. She was right, Samira was right, so I solved the problem — I sent them both on leave together. I kept my counsel that the balloon would go up in the next few weeks and that they were better out of it. In any case it was clear to me that I would have to evacuate all or most international staff within weeks, and having Melissa and Sam out of the country was a comforting start. I also knew that I had Buckley's chance of getting my wonderful, faithful and fearless wife to evacuate without me once the emergency was in full swing. I had had that experience in October 1998 when I had ordered a partial staff evacuation out to Budapest. Samira had to be almost carried out of the place, a bitter and worrying experience for both of us. My wife was famous for her determination and strength — a characteristic that worked famously for all of us on many occasions but just occasionally drove me to distraction. It was to work incredibly in our favour later on when I was jailed.

Samira and Melissa went across to Egypt at the beginning of the second week in March. This was a good rest and recreation destination for the Australian staff. It was within the six-monthly travel entitlement in terms of travel costs and, being a world away from Yugoslavia culturally, was therefore a worthy break. Going into the third week of March it was now apparent that a severely curtailed country operation and at least majority evacuation of international staff was likely, so I asked (ordered actually, in my inimical, sometimes not so popular style) Melissa and Samira to extend their leave and remain on standby in Egypt until I had a better understanding of what was going to break. As it turned out, I was to direct Melissa to fly to Macedonia. Typically, Melissa wanted to hurry back and we had a couple of disagreements over the phone and via e-mail, but cool heads prevailed. Melissa was professionally determined, and well intentioned, and of course hated to be left out of the action — a good team member who didn't like being away from the team. I was very worried about Horst, my CARE Deutschland staff member. As he had been under quiet and subtle investigation earlier by the secret police, I decided to get him out of the country now. It was very difficult for me to do this, because he was the one staff member I would have liked to have kept with me to the end. He was experienced and very sensible, and had previously experienced adversity. So he went too, on his now due R and R. Meanwhile the war clouds rolled ever closer, dark and menacing. The more radical Yugoslav elements were calling for war. They wanted to mobilise the country against the NATO threat, to attack and secure Kosovo once and for all, to defy and overrun the OSCE ceasefire (all but lost in any case), to rid Kosovo of the OSCE monitors and all UN and 'meddling' NGO organisations. It was looking very grim. The staff were very nervous, unusually quiet, the noisy environment of the office dramatically changed.

Through the third week of March the Yugoslav troop build-up in Kosovo and around its provincial borders suddenly escalated. The war of words between Yugoslavia and the West intensified. The West was accused of creating the conditions for destabilisation of the province. This, to a degree, was true. Since January OSCE monitors had undoubtedly failed to stop the KLA filling the vacuums around Kosovo left by the previously withdrawn Serb troops and militia. Certainly in Drenica we had calculated strong movements and strong concentrations of KLA fighters. They had crossed 2 to 3 kilometres inside the ceasefire lines in the vicinity of Srbica, tightening the noose on this strategic town. We passed their patrols in these areas. On the other hand, I thought it was sheer hypocrisy for the Serbs to be complaining about their sovereignty being eroded in Kosovo. The Serbian Government had by now frittered away its political chances to bring some sort of parity to Kosovo's situation by getting the West to lift the punishing sanctions against the country. They missed the boat through misplaced pride and pig-headedness.

The OSCE Kosovo Verification Mission and its allied diplomatic observer missions had probably done their best to keep the peace in Kosovo. However, it was my view then that Western governments, having forced Rambouillet, were to be severely criticised for not having put in place more effective methods for maintaining the ceasefire. Firmer methods may have encouraged some rapprochement between the KLA and the Serbian administration and, more importantly, given the moderate Albanian political elite a stronger hand in influencing events. The Serbian administration may then have been more effectively forced into quickly and effectively implementing the political initiatives needed to create a better atmosphere and some form of acceptable autonomy. By March, though, this was no longer possible. The place was a disaster about to happen, we could see that. Civilian Kosovars were severely disadvantaged. Serbian police were being killed at roadblocks — domestic police, not the sort who had been involved in the brutish field operations conducted over the previous year. We were witnessing another Western initiative at peacemaking that was too weak, toothless and perhaps more trouble than it may have been worth. Perhaps the kindest thing to be said about the initiative is that somebody was trying to do something, to beat an impasse; it was well intenioned, and perhaps it brought the problem to a head. A bloody head, as it was to turn out.

Towards the end of the third week the Yugoslav Army placed large tank and mechanised infantry units in Srbica, the base town for our humanitarian programs in the Drenica region. We were tripping over them. Strangely, the military did not stop our CARE staff moving into and through Srbica on their way to the villages dotted throughout the region. They did not care if we observed them or saw their strength. Jim reported the build-up, and his concern for the safety of his and Edward's programs in the Drenica to me. I was reading the routine OSCE information bulletins now coming to the office daily by e-mail. One of these e-mails detailed the presence of armed forces in Drenica. I checked these as well as the UNHCR information bulletins, both of which explicitly detailed security incidents and troop movements. We grasped at this information in a vain attempt to keep on top of the situation and so that I could warn CARE field teams to keep out of certain areas. My concern for the safety of our field teams, not only in Kosovo but across the whole country, was now paramount. Information, information, information was what was needed. My diplomatic friends and contacts were a precious source of information, especially the British, who were cool and professional, probably the most experienced diplomatic observers on the Kosovo situation. We would regularly compare notes, and I would receive warnings on areas my CARE field teams must avoid — landmine sites, areas of military and police activity. This allowed me to measure the deterioration of programs in our area and pass this information on to head office and our CARE International partners. Our field teams and our subcontractor truck convoys could be warned to avoid trouble spots. My situation reports were becoming far more dramatic these days. But they were laborious to write. They often had to be written late at night, after I had collected all the information from my field teams, key staff and the external sources. With Samira away I worked till the early hours of the morning, sending increasingly worrying reports and honing our security, safety and contingency plans. Then it became obvious that the Western embassies were planning to evacuate and close their embassies. The OSCE observers were clearly planning to pull out of Kosovo and Yugoslavia entirely. I placed Peter Wallace and his entire team on 24 hours' notice to move. He must be ready to pay his staff, send them safely home, have all essential files packed and all vehicles prepared to depart Belgrade within 24 hours of the order to do so.

The OSCE e-mail reports spoke of a large tank force — thirty or more tanks — moving into Srbica. I directed Peter to check and confirm this. He prepared and sent his situation report, detailing the sighting of 38 large battle tanks parked along the main streets of Srbica, to the Belgrade office. This meant that our Drenica presence was now untenable. I reported the fact of this military presence to Canberra. I also informed our CARE International partners in the Drenica region aid program of the very grave situation. It was time to abandon the program, time to get out of Kosovo.

CHAPTER NINE
Closing Down Kosovo

On 20 March it was quite clear that I would be forced to evacuate our Kosovo team. The situation in Kosovo was now untenable. I had received notice from UNHCR and from the OSCE KVM that they would be withdrawing their full teams by about 11.30 am on that day. Having assessed that the situation had deteriorated badly, to the point where it was now futile to continue operations in Kosovo, I rang Peter Wallace and directed him to pack all his essential files, stand down all his national staff, and send them home.

There was little else we could do for the staff. What was upon us now was something I dreaded, something I had gone through in Zaire and really had hoped never to experience again. We would be unable to evacuate them out of the country. Certainly the Kosovo Albanian staff would not wish to withdraw to Belgrade with Peter and the international staff; that was simply out of the question. Peter had had plenty of warning already (per our standby plan and schedule of preliminary actions) and had pretty much packed and was ready to go. When he and the others departed Pristina late in the morning, the town was almost deserted. As Peter was to advise me later, he found the town very tense — the only people moving around were the MUP and the army. Moving east, he and his crew encountered MUP troops who, he related later, questioned them fairly closely and treated them with suspicion.

With an understandably heavy heart the Pristina crew continued east in the direction of Nis. The team found the road to Podujevo blocked by fighting, and they scanned for alternative routes; however, it took quite some time before they were able to find a good escape route from Kosovo province. In hindsight they were lucky, and I believe their escape from Pristina was fairly timely. They had taken a little-known road, very rough and useless to large vehicles, which twisted through the heavily wooded hills that dominated the south-west of the province. The only foreigners left in Pristina were members of the International Committee of the Red Cross and the French organisation Médecins Sans Frontières, who were operating closely with the Red Cross. Most organisations had departed with the OSCE and UN convoy travelling out to Macedonia, but a fair number had, like CARE, chosen to turn north and evacuate to Belgrade for an onward journey to Hungary. When finally, some two and a half hours later, Peter called me on the mobile phone and told me they had got across the border, I was very, very relieved.

Meanwhile, in Belgrade, I called in all of our local national staff teams and stood them down from their duties. The air was thick with tension. People were very pessimistic, and there was a hush ahead of the imminent bombing. Our local staff teams operating in Belgrade and the immediate countryside were in danger from groups who were conducting anti-war protests. It was pretty clear to me that they were really relieved to be given this direction — now they were free to concentrate on looking after their families. These guys were quite frightened of what local people might do to them if they drove around in UNHCR vehicles.

It was now time to park all the vehicles in the office car park, out of harm's way and out of sight. The car park was an underground concrete structure about half a kilometre from the office. By the end of the day the vehicles were secured, and the staff had been paid some additional months' pay, everything we could possibly pay them. I did not know whether I would ever see them again. This had been a very tough and emotional day. There was a serious question as to where our Serbian staff were to go. They were not allowed to leave the country — in any case, young men (the majority of our staff) would be stopped on the roads at police roadblocks and cashiered straight into the army, something they desperately feared. Sending them home to their families was the only comfortable and humane thing I could do with them — while praying that in the days to come none of them or their families would be subject to bombing.

Definitely a bizarre feeling, to be anticipating the worst. Being in the middle of a war zone was not new for me, but being in the middle of a range of potential strategic NATO targets was a new experience, one I did not relish. This was likely to be a zone of general war, as against the comparatively 'limited war' scenarios I had previously experienced.

Some four hours later the Pristina team arrived in Belgrade. They were elated to be away from the fighting and in Belgrade where they felt quite a deal safer. I then gave instructions for everybody in the team, with the exception of Peter Wallace, to pack anything they had left in Belgrade and be ready to move at two hours' notice — to Budapest. I would stay and attempt to continue the essential Serbian refugee programs in those parts of the country which might still be accessible during the bombing. It seemed to me that Peter Wallace was the best person to assist me. Peter was hired to be program manager responsible for Pristina and therefore, if by some chance we were able to continue operations in Kosovo, it made sense that he would be the man who would return immediately to continue operations there.

Nevertheless, I didn't think we had much chance of resuming operations in the immediate future. As dusk rushed in, we said farewell to our colleagues. I distinctly remember Jim and Horst looking deeply worried as they got ready to leave. Jim, in his normal laconic fashion, just looked at me with a smile on his face, and said, 'Pratty, keep your head down.' Horst gave me a big hug. Typically, he had a deep frown and looked quite worried, and I hugged him back. This business brings the emotion out in you, as there is always somebody you know going somewhere dangerous, and heightened greetings and farewells become commonplace. But these were very tense times, and I drew strength from the feelings being shared. I had a deep sense of loneliness, and mixed emotions crowded in. I actually wanted to get on the road with them. I would miss them all, especially Edward giving me his very quietly spoken advice, telling me to be careful. As we talked quietly at the back of the vehicle in the car park we both shivered involuntarily. I was torn. One half said get on with the job — while UNHCR remains in town CARE does too, meaning Steve Pratt stays and ought to be the last to leave. The obligation to stay was strong. The other half said this was going to get nasty and I should be out.

And then there was Samira. I missed her terribly, but was very comforted by the fact that she was out of it. Our CARE USA and CARE Canada colleagues were pleased to be going, but at the same time were quite worried to be leaving Peter and me behind. I remember that it was a bitterly cold evening, and while there was a very clear sky, there was no breeze whatsoever. As the two vehicles departed the suburb of Banavo Brdo in that still cold evening, it suddenly became deathly quiet and very lonely indeed. Looking around the area I could see a few civilians scurrying here and there to get out of the cold. The tension and some feeling of foreboding increased.

Peter and I went back to my house at the top of the Barnava Brdo hill and found ourselves turning to the international television news, striving to keep abreast of the deteriorating situation. We had become television junkies, flicking between BBC and CNN. It was too soon to know then that despite this diet of international news we would still not be getting the whole picture; however incomplete, though, it was going to be a hell of a lot more balanced than what we were getting from local Serbian television. It felt more than a little strange to be relying on pictures from outside the country to keep up to date with what was going on. I felt very much as if I was flying blind, while the challenge of judging quickly what was going on was weighing on my shoulders.

There were difficult questions: the safety of our staff and operations; which way to direct emergency programming without putting staff where refugees were in any form of jeopardy; the judgment I had to make as to when Peter and I should leave the country if it became necessary to do so quickly; and if we did, what kind of balanced operation could we feasibly leave behind us? And of course the vexed question of keeping up our staff's morale, and doing everything we possibly could to prepare for their welfare and safety.

On this issue of safety of our staff I had a cold hard rock in my guts, because I could not anticipate what the hell was going to happen or what position our people were going to find themselves in. Would they be arrested, would they be press-ganged into the army, would they become casualties of NATO bombing, could they get out of the country if they wanted to? These fears dogged me and were constantly on my mind.

On the evening of Saturday, 21 March, Don Foley, the acting Australian ambassador, called me again on the mobile phone, as I sat over a relieving beer. He spoke to me quietly, as he always did, in that reserved, clipped and quietly professional manner of his. He again encouraged me to pack up and leave with the Australian embassy's staff, who were due to leave the following day. I told Don I would consider his advice, but also that I had made a decision, as had CARE Australia, that we probably had to continue operations. We were confident that we could stay quietly and safely. Don said he would call me again in the morning (Sunday, 22 March), a couple of hours before they were due to leave, to check whether we would be joining them.

I was in constant turmoil about this — as I worried about the effects of our staying on Samira and her pregnancy, I knew that she would be worried about me in turn, and this added to the pressure. There was also clearly a fear that we could be in danger from NATO bombing — another unpredictable factor that confronted me in my planning for the immediate future. I spoke to Peter a number of times through the evening about these issues and wondered whether I was sounding sufficiently decisive to him. Thinking clearly and acting strongly are always prerequisites for instilling confidence in your subordinates.

That telephone call came from Don Foley the following morning. I had made up my mind. I was sticking to my guns on the decision I had made some three or four days earlier about what my intentions as country director would be. It went back to the heart of the issue, an issue I had discussed often with my old CARE Australia emergency colleagues — namely the ethos of the emergency mission and what your moral obligations are during a time of a crisis.

I consulted regularly on the telephone with Charles Tapp (CARE Australia national director/CEO) and Brian Doolan (CARE Australia human resources director). The obligation to stay was strong; as well, Charles had talked the issue through with me — my impression was that he leaned to a stay decision, for as long as UNHCR continued, if I was comfortable. While feeling a little uncomfortable and burdened by the decision, I felt that it was the correct one under the circumstances. Once made, I believed I was obliged to stick with it.

So with Don Foley's comments ringing in my ears, the Australian embassy's staff, along with the British embassy's staff and other international groups, drove out of Belgrade at about 1 pm on 22 March. While Don did not formally warn me to leave Belgrade, he had given me, in his own quiet way, clear advice that we should leave. He also made it clear that he understood and respected my decision and that of CARE Australia to continue. I was to remember Don Foley's words very clearly months later when I saw him again during his first consular visit to me in prison.

With the departure of the last of the embassy and foreign groups from Belgrade there would be were very, very few foreigners left. Over the next couple of days I was to count some six to seven international UN and NGO staff, who were of European origin and now located in Belgrade, and it became increasingly difficult for foreigners to drive around Belgrade. We were soon holding daily situation briefings at UNHCR which Margaret O'Keefe, UNHCR head of mission, would conduct, and I began to move around town in one of my staff member's own cars — a decidedly safer way to move around Belgrade during those tense and emotional days. I was very concerned that I or my Serbian staff in our CARE Land Rovers would be stoned or blockaded, or even run off the road.

Getting on with our normal duties was becoming increasingly difficult; there was the constant distraction of watching the news to try to get some sense of how events were playing out. Would Milosevic blink? At the eleventh hour would he bend to the requirements of Rambouillet? I question to this day whether he thought the West would have the courage or will to start the war. He may have gambled on it not starting, or perhaps on his ability to weather a short war effort, with a nervous West backing off after perhaps two to three weeks of bombing. He would then reap the outcomes he desired from the West.

The office was very tense and the staff absolutely confused in their reactions and emotions. They did not really want to stay home. They did not know what to do at home, and seemed to be more comfortable in Peter's and my company. They perhaps thought we had up-to-date news of what was going to happen. And while our staff clung to us like insecure children, they were also a little critical of us for the tough talking coming out of the West against Yugoslavia. It was a very strange situation as Peter and I would huddle over the TV set, a mixture of excitement about how the West was reacting to the Kosovo problem and deep concern that this might involve general bombing of the country. The political issue may have been coming to a head, but our staff were in danger, and our programs would be in disarray.

I had selected a team of about eight national staff to comprise, along with Peter and me, the crisis 'rear party' team located in the Belgrade country office, all other staff in the mission having now been stood down. The Kosovo office team had scattered to the four winds, and as we tried to remain in some sort of contact with them it became apparent that many had fled with their families for the borders, to Macedonia and to Albania. The general exodus of the population had begun in earnest as soon as the OSCE had been seen departing. Our occasional contact with one of our Albanian staff members by satellite phone worked for only about forty-eight hours, then this line of communication dried up. He understandably fled the office, which he had bravely attempted to man. The office became a target for snooping MUP policemen and wandering civilians, Serb and Albanian alike.

The atmosphere in Pristina, I was told, was quickly taking on an air of anarchy; with the dreadful emptiness in the streets came the darkening of the skies. The Serbian staff from the Pristina office generally headed north into Serbia proper, though a number with connections in Macedonia went there. The lucky few who had papers crossed borders to family on the other side. Especially lucky among those getting out were the young men who wished to avoid the general mobilisation fast occurring throughout the country. There was no love for this war, and my distinct feeling talking to our staff was that, while very angry with the West and bitterly aggressive towards the Albanians, they did not support going to war over Kosovo.

So on Sunday, 21 March, about the time the Australian Embassy staff are finally evacuating, I am on my way again up to the UNHCR office in the south of the central city zone. I am anxious to get as much information as possible about what is developing and to talk also to Margaret O'Keefe about the continuation of the refugee centre program. I have had constant meetings with Margaret over the last week. This daily grind through Belgrade's hopeless city traffic from Banavo Brdo across the city to UNHCR I would normally avoid, but these days I strive to keep in touch, to keep up to date with the ever-changing and deteriorating situation. Ploughing our way through the traffic, my driver calmly and skilfully gets past slaving Yugos, the most common small sedan here, belching and lumbering buses, homicidal drivers and suicidal pedestrians. The atmosphere is surreal. People go about their business, and on the surface it seems nothing is really happening. But when you look more closely, that air of indifference is cracking at the edges. Look closely into their faces and you can see the confusion and uncertainty.

The UNHCR Serbian security staff at the front door treat me with respect, as friendly as they have always been these last twenty-odd months; but I can see the deep uncertainty in their eyes and even perhaps a touch of fear, greater than I see in people on the streets. The UNHCR local staff have a much better understanding of the gravity of the situation and a more realistic feel for how genuine the Western alliance's threats to Yugoslavia are. They can see that their international staff seniors are preparing for the worst. The old security guard Borvan, as usual resplendent in his wide-lapelled 1970s purple suit, greets me with relief — at least this foreigner appears to have stayed in the country. They are clinging to us, these more enlightened Serbs; perhaps they think our presence in their country will allow sanity to prevail? Somehow I don't believe that will happen. What the immediate future holds for this country I do not know, but I dread it. This, along with our intentions in the humanitarian community, is to be the subject of today's meeting.

The meeting hall is down the stairs. As I go through the lovely halls of this ornate pre-World War II house, rather grand in the old Austrian style, as so many of the old places are here at this southern end of the city, I experience an uncanny, chilling reminder of that terrible European war. Here, I am far from Australia of the 1990s. Looking out through the tall picture windows at the stark silhouettes of bare trees against the steely grey skies of late winter, the tension of war all about us, I feel as if I have been transported back to Eastern Europe during World War II. The images of war I had as a student of history collide with the realities here, and I think humanity hasn't advanced a centimetre since day 1, really! To be personally experiencing the build-up and commencement of a war in Europe is at once awe-inspiring and frightening — I feel the pit of my stomach tighten — and saddening. But we have a job to do, and I need to see whether it is going to be viable to try to stay on and continue our Serbian refugee programs.

Margaret O'Keefe is hushed, drawn and pale. She has worn the burden of this office heavily on her shoulders for two years now, and it is beginning to show. She is a marvellous head of mission. Calm under pressure, she has taken a great deal of abuse from the Yugoslav Government over the years, but has not budged in her commitment to running the refugee program in this sorry country. However, today those lovely Irish characteristics of twinkle, charm and wicked dry sense of humour are absent. There are only nine of the normal thirty-odd mission heads in the room today, the rest having evacuated already. I think we all feel a little vulnerable — that phrase 'safety in numbers' rings loud and clear in my ears.

We all compare notes, and one by one the mission heads report that they have largely evacuated all their international staffs, closed their missions down. Most of them, unlike CARE, have completely shut down. That is understandable, because most of these NGOs do not conduct life-saving programs in greater Serbia, or if they do, they are on such a miniscule scale that somebody else can absorb their activity. I am keenly aware of the burden I have to bear this day, in that CARE Australia is singularly placed within the NGO fraternity in this country. CARE Australia runs a very large program delivering vital aid to 650 refugee centres throughout the country. Delivery of winter heating fuel and fresh food is life-saving, although the delivery of heating fuel will only be necessary now for another four to six weeks, through the last of winter and early spring.

The load to be placed on CARE sits heavily on me today in this UNHCR meeting.

Most of these mission heads intend to evacuate with the last of the foreigners during the coming weekend. We all pass on our reports, giving updates on incidents around the country. Those of us with substantial Kosovo presences brief on the rapidly growing refugee crisis there. I present to Margaret a copy of my latest SITREP. Information from CARE field teams about refugee numbers, the direction of refugee movement, the condition of villages in the Drenica region, and the location of fighting form the basis of these situation reports.

Margaret very solemnly underscores her warnings of the last few days that war is imminent and that the bombing of Belgrade — the threat of which had been treated very lightly and indeed scoffed at by all — is quite likely. The conference members are shocked. I am not so surprised; it makes sense to me that this must be the direction of NATO thinking, in as much as bombing would minimise their own casualties and deliver big political hits where they can be seen, in the interest of trying to put maximum pressure on Milosevic. Margaret is wan, but remains dignified. She quietly gives her advice to all NGOs to minimise their countryside activities and keep away from the obvious strategic targets — bridges, communication towers etc. There is a weird feeling in this conference room.

Sitting around this beautiful highly polished timber table, in this ornate room, all is silence. The fashionable clothes on the young 'power women' mission heads at the table (one of the perks of working in Yugoslavia is that short, cheap flights to the European capitals are within easy reach — we all shop well on these trips) now somehow look out of place in this 'cabinet of war'.

I stay behind with Margaret after the meeting and discuss CARE's and my intentions. I let her know that I will stay in country with one international staff member and attempt to continue running as much of the Serbian refugee centres program as possible. She is grateful, but fully understands that Peter and I could evacuate at any time, with the consequential shutting down of the CARE program at short notice. She certainly has no qualms whatsoever about CARE Australia workers staying in a time of war and I question her closely on this, if only to vindicate my own decision. Her own US, British and other NATO member country international staff, however, have been evacuated already, per her own orders.

I point out to Margaret the fundamental concerns of CARE Yugoslavia and CARE Australia, as described in my reports to CARE Australia head office and discussed with Robert Yallop and Charles Tapp. We are very anxious that detailed locations of the Serbian refugee centres be passed through diplomatic channels to NATO, to avoid the danger of them being bombed. This is the second time in four days that I raise this issue with UNHCR. My latest SITREPs detail this concern, illustrating the vulnerability of the centres to possible NATO bombing. The centres are scattered throughout the countryside, the vast majority of them away from large towns and too often very close to industrial targets and military bases — many of the centres are old factories, or old factory or farm workers' barracks and quite often, old disused military barracks! There is little CARE Australia can do in terms of relaying such information; it is clearly a UNHCR responsibility to do so.

Margaret assures me that she will pass on this CARE Australia concern through the emergency Belgrade diplomatic corps meeting now held daily, of which she is a key member. When I return to the office I debrief myself, as always, to the staff on the contents and the outcome of the conference. Again, as I had done on Friday, 19 March, I sombrely warn them that I believe war is imminent. They are shocked and outraged.

The crisis team of seven staff are finding it difficult to hold to their tasks, but they do so nonetheless. Our deputy finance officer, Jasna, however, comes to me and begs to be relieved of her duties. I am taken by surprise; she is such an outspoken person and so diligent in her duties that I figured she would be able to endure the pressures. I realise I am being a bit tough on her — she has four children and her home is in the middle of the city, close to Knessa Milocia Boulevard, which could be the target of NATO bombing. Knessa Milocia is one of my favourite streets in Belgrade, very picturesque, with lovely old Austrian architecture. But it also has a number of military headquarters along its length.

This crisis staff helps me work out a scaled-down program which we think we might manage during war. We develop ways of prepaying our subcontractors to deliver at least through the last of the two winter months left. If we can get the heating fuel out to the people until at least the end of April and the food through to at least the end of May, we will greatly minimise the suffering. That means that even if communications are broken, in telephone and transportation terms, these contractors may still be able to operate on 'autopilot' for a couple of months. We are hoping the war will only continue for about three months. That is the thinking — Milosevic will demonstrate his prowess, resistance and strength, and then seek a ceasefire, even possibly give in to NATO's demands over Kosovo. Through the next ten days we are to work together around the city establishing the plan.

The warning from the diplomatic community about when the bombing is to start is spot on. Milosevic is defiant, brinkmanship all the way. The rumours move wildly among the staff. He will back down, no he won't. Our staff become increasingly angry about the West and I find myself, as does Peter, in the difficult position of taking the abuse, without being able to comment at all on the faults of Milosevic or the state.

The war has been waged now on a grand scale for the last three days. On 24 March the air raid sirens start. Deep mournful sounds, the same sound exactly as those you hear in old war movies. Eerie, the noise sends a chill up my spine. There seem to be about seven sirens across the city and they all go off in sequence. The warning sound is an oscillating tone, wavering between a high-pitched scream and a deep thundering drone. The all clear siren sounds as a long, mournful, flat tone, deep and resonant, for about half a minute. I am to hear these damn things for the next five months.

On the first few occasions of the sirens going off we do not hear any bombing; they were probably triggered by NATO reconnaissance aircraft, or perhaps the bombing is well out of town. It is now clear, though, that the bombing is definitely going to occur here in the north, in and around Belgrade, not just down in Kosovo. On the Wednesday of the first week of the bombing, at about 10 am, while the key staff are in the office, there is an air strike about half a kilometre away, likely a cruise missile. It bloody well thumps in! Devastating noise thundering and echoing across the lower suburban streets of Banavo Brdo, with a shock wave that thrashes the building.

And now we hear anti-aircraft fire for the first time — the deep booming and thump! thump! of what sound like 12.7 mm heavy machine guns. At the time I think silently to myself that the fools are firing at nothing. A broad daylight strike is likely to be a cruise missile, which is what it sounded like to me. 'Don't waste your ammo' I think, with a strangely misplaced compassion for fellow soldiers! Our office is on the top floor of a six-storey building, a building which sits in an exposed position, high on a hill, with a commanding view of the Sava River. We learn later that this first explosion was a strike on the military railway yards at the bottom of the hill. Our first taste of war.

CHAPTER TEN
NATO's War

25 March 1999, and we have now entered a surreal and dangerous world. More than my fear of the bombing is my developing concern for the unpredictable. But I have felt like this many times before, in northern Iraq and Zaire, and I tell myself the unpredictability was far greater there in those hot, dusty and tribally corrupted places. You just did not know what the Arabs, Kurds or Hutus and Bantus were going to do next — we had lived with that and got on with our work, with few illusions. I kept telling myself there had to be a measure of predictability and a sense of 'fair play' among these Serbs. This assessment very much predicated my decision to stay on, at the outbreak of war, in this already godforsaken country.

Since the commencement of NATO bombing on 24 March, I've had a nagging doubt as to how long the Serbs can continue to be rational. Their behaviour towards foreigners is questionable. I am, however, Australian, not a national of a NATO country, and I have absolutely no sense that the Australian embassy will take a one-sided position and support war. I know of course that the Australian Government, like most democratic governments, is bound to side with the Western alliance, and the Serbs will know that too.

The Australian embassy does not warn me against staying. I am given no formal, nor informal, advice or order, and they have known for some time that it was our intention to stay behind. This is something I am to reflect on deeply later, in prison and back home after the ordeal. I am to assume later that the embassy had no idea that the Government was going to adopt the comparatively high-profile position of support for the American-led NATO offensive that it eventually did. Certainly CARE Australia did not anticipate such a strident position, otherwise I am sure they would have ordered our total evacuation before the war, rather than encouraging my stay.

We may be neutral Australians, but CARE Australia has been in this place now for five years — five long years helping Serbian refugees. CARE hasn't wavered in the face of some criticism from various organisations around the world that we have no place staying in Yugoslavia, given those critics' perspective on the nature of the regime and the parlous state of democracy here. CARE has faithfully stuck to its mandate to help the disadvantaged and those in danger, regardless of their creed or ethnicity.

I am very much aware, as I continue to review the viability of my situation in this place at this moment, that the Yugoslav authorities are quietly appreciative of the CARE Australia position and attitude. I am sure the UN too is confident of our capacities and worldwide experience; otherwise they would not have been supportive of us as an implementing partner to assist them in their Serbian refugee program in this country. I have personally sought and received assurances from ministers and departmental directors in humanitarian affairs of their government's attitude to our presence, war or no war. I have always prided myself on being capable of logical analysis and calm assessments, rather than merely emotional judgments. I remind myself, as I sit in my office looking down over the Sava River, to stick to my assessment and steel myself to get on with my job, which is to continue delivering assistance to these benighted refugees. Or to at least see that the mechanism for continued program delivery is working.

Nevertheless, a belated evacuation of Peter and myself is very much on my mind in the days to come. It still may be the case, I think at this time, that despite the life-saving nature of the essential Serbian refugee program, the time may arrive where there is little that Peter and I will be able to do here. In the event that I do eventually decide to evacuate, I want to know if our key local staff and our contractors can still deliver the commodities to some, if not all, refugee centres. Will the contractors still be willing to travel out daily in the face of possible bombing? My staff think they will — continued operations means continued pay for them, vital in a time of war shortages. Poor desperate bastards. I have given away entirely the idea of carrying out refugee centre distributions monitoring. We will not dispatch our field monitors — too damn dangerous — and we will minimise the number of staff in the field. UNHCR is prepared to wear this and supports my plan for scaled-down but continued operations.

My daily meetings with Margaret O'Keefe, in addition to updating us all on the security and war situation, deal essentially with the issues relative to salvaging and continuing the critical support programs. Issues include how best to scale back our joint UNHCR/CARE operations, while still bringing essential commodities to the maximum number of refugees — all without seeing our staff and subcontractors killed in the process. Additionally, Margaret and I discuss and complete an outline concept for a new war emergency program. We plan for the concentration of food stocks and make new distribution plans for an estimated 50 000 Serbian war-displaced people fleeing Kosovo. We both wrestle with our joint objectives to carry out and continue these humanitarian operations. We both feel that the bombing pattern will become predictable and that we will eventually have a very clear idea where we can continue to deliver our convoys and where we cannot. We intend to pool our resources with the International Committee Red Cross and Yugoslavia Red Cross. I feel much happier that we will work closely with Red Cross, as this will greatly increase our neutrality and safety. Will the Government allow UNHCR to transfer the refugees to safer areas and consolidate some of the refugee centres? How humanitarian will they be towards their own?

As I gaze this late afternoon beyond the Sava, winding its way south-west and glistening in the pale afternoon sun, I focus on the airport some 15 kilometres to the west, and imagine I can see the little refugee centre sitting on the southern fringe of the airport complex. Sited in an old farmers' barracks, this is one of our 650 refugee centres, a smaller centre and one, as I recall, filled mainly with old ladies. There they are, sitting on their ancient iron beds, or cardboard boxes, bored stiff after five years of just sitting and waiting. Except now they are probably scared as well as bored, but I am betting they still retain their dignity. What is to become of them, these old girls in their traditional Serb orthodox black shawls, head scarves and black dresses and black stockings? The girls in black, I call them, bearers of craggy, strong, honest faces in that lovely old Slavic, country folk way. Who will feed them and keep them warm if we piss off? These thoughts trouble me on this very calm and deathly quiet sunny afternoon.

On the still, surreal evening of 26 March I sit quietly on the little balcony outside my bedroom in the apartment, musing on our position, and again that deadly feeling of loneliness arrives upon me. As country director I am in isolation while I assess and make decisions. I look at that pale sun, still glistening brightly off the Sava River below. The south-western vista spreads out before me; the air is cold, but all is incredibly peaceful. The absence of any breeze, the brightness of the sun and its reflections all add up to the illusion of a lazy, carefree end to the day. Nothing moves — no traffic, no aircraft, nothing on the river. The world waits patiently, silently but nervously, for the next hit.

Peter and I have come from the office early to pack our belongings and be ready at a moment's notice to move out of the apartment to somewhere safer, probably one of the international hotels; at the same time, we remain ready to completely evacuate. Although Samira and I packed all our essentials some weeks ago, before she departed for her rest and recreation trip to Egypt, I figure it is time to pack the last of the important household items. Unlike the other international staffs, who belong to the country mission and who generally each have about three suitcases' worth of gear maximum, Samira and I have a considerable pile of belongings. As the only permanent staff member in the mission and the only one accompanied by a partner, I have a travelling entitlement of a third of a tonne; but of course we have exceeded that with my six years' worth of accumulated goods.

Having far too much to pack and carry in an emergency, Samira and I have packed and prioritised our personal effects, and these are stacked in priority order in the middle of the lounge room, where they have sat for some three weeks. Additionally, I have stacked in the lounge room about 40 kilograms each of the personal effects belonging to Horst and Melissa. I having turned my apartment into a rallying point. I hope and wonder whether we will ever see this stuff again.

At this juncture I feel that Peter and I will have to move out of the apartment; it is just no longer practical or safe to stay. Being the only foreigners in the street we stick out like sore thumbs, and even going down to the corner store will become more and more problematic. Peacetime was bad enough, with the storekeeper always chipping me about that 'bloody Bill Clinton', and how 'the stupid West never understands us much-persecuted Serbs'. Now it will get much, much worse, and I know in my heart of hearts that all the goodwill Samira and I have built up over the last year in this neighbourhood will amount to nought now. The quiet, peaceful evening air is again shattered by that hair-raising mournful sound of air raid sirens. In the distance I hear the sound of bombs falling, way out to the north of the city, far from us. But I now notice the bombing is increasing in frequency and the raids are beginning to get longer. Thankfully the suburbs proper continue to be spared.

On that same Saturday we resolve to move not just ourselves into the International Hotel but also the essential workings of the CARE office. It has become increasingly difficult for our key staff to travel to the office at Banavo Brdo. This little hilltop suburb sits out to the south, about fifteen minutes drive from the city centre. Fuel is becoming scarcer and our staff find it difficult to drive to the office. Although I can always get UNHCR fuel for our vehicles and we could pick our staff up daily, it is becoming increasingly apparent that our vehicles, with their 'CARE International' stickers displayed boldly on doors, are targetable. The signs of neutrality in peacetime become the targets during war. We are increasingly dealing with an unsophisticated and very unruly gaggle of people in the streets. Understandably, and rightly, they are very angry and outraged about the bombing. Not understandable or acceptable is their blind rage to all things foreign — why bite the few hands that can help them? The possibility that mobs may soon rule the streets also comes to mind. While all these things had been predicted in my planning and deliberations, it remains unnerving that they come to fruition. The Banavo Brdo office site now becomes untenable. What was not predicted is that the local army militia would set up a military defence and civil defence headquarters in the old municipality head office directly opposite my office.

Through the Thursday and Friday, as we come and go to the office, our staff and I become increasingly nervous passing the military guards, vehicles and all the military paraphernalia collecting on the footpaths on the corner of the little town square, which our office overlooks. Cheerful and boisterous guards, too loud and full of bravado, swagger around the square or lean up against the sandbagged wall they have constructed outside the municipal building, adjacent also to the post office. Their demeanour and gear reminds me chillingly of a scene out of a Cold War thriller. The classic Soviet helmets, the drab-coloured 1950s-style winter uniform, even the old-fashioned long leather boots some of the soldiers are wearing. Some of them wear the old red leather cross-over shoulder belts. And there are AK47 assault rifles, and the older SKS rifles, with bayonets attached! Are they expecting to repel boarders storming the municipal offices? It all strikes me as lot of overreactive theatre, aimed at impressing the civilians, but this is the stuff of the Serbian regime, so I should not be surprised. Still, I am unnerved by this circus performing outside my office. Now is the time to shut down for the duration. The decision is taken just in time.

On the Saturday, as we pack the essential files I decide to take with me to the hotel, we are paid a visit by a plainclothes policeman who decides to inspect the premises for any sign of bomb guidance equipment. He quite jovially and respectfully inspects the upper floor of the office, accompanied by a tense and unhappy Mikhail, my administrative officer. It is clearly appropriate to take the last of the pressures off Mikhail and the other key staff and send them home, out of immediate harm's way.

Bad news arrives. One of my staff alerts us that our vehicles have been confiscated. They had been stored about 500 metres from the office in an underground car park which services both UNHCR and CARE. As the population slips into their war routine, this car park gradually becomes an impromptu and auxilliary air raid shelter. The few people who had begun to gather there were easily accommodated; however, it is understandable that they wish the vehicles to be removed to increase space for shelter. Before we get time to act, the confiscation occurs. Ostensibly the Yugoslav Red Cross have 'transferred' the vehicles, but they have not done this with UNHCR approval, nor did they seek to notify CARE or UNHCR in advance. My staff, observing the incident, had the clear impression that the 'removers' were not Red Cross; they were more likely to be the police. The mystery continues — a genuine attempt to round up vehicles useful for humanitarian work or just another cynical confiscation? The evidence increasingly points to the latter, although some of the vehicles are eventually located in a Red Cross compound.

The day is also spent packing the one and only Land Rover we managed to get out of the CARE car park earlier, at some threat to the drivers. Another pointer to the surliness and unpredictability of local people. My drivers are accused of siding with foreigners, of operating with NATO agents. The people doing the abusing down at the car park are nondescript types; from all accounts, as I listen to my anxious drivers in the office, they are uneducated men, workers, hard-smoking and loud-talking. The car park attendants who have been so friendly to me and our people these many months apparently stand by hopelessly and are perhaps themselves a little frightened as these roughnecks hurl abuse at the drivers.

I have one more CARE vehicle, the Opel station wagon locked in my apartment garage about half a kilometre up the hill from the office. I am determined to rescue and transfer it, along with the Land Rover, to the Intercontinental Hotel, where Peter and I will base ourselves from now on. One of the younger staff members accompanies me to my house where I pick up the Opel and the last of mine, Samira's and Melissa's essential bags.

It is a windy afternoon, the usual rubbish scattering across the ground, plastic bags ubiquitous as far as the eye can see. How filthy the landscape in Belgrade is, I muse as I walk head bent against the wind down to my apartment garage. OK, there are sanctions, and little work to be had, but is there no pride amongst these citizens to at least get out and clear the garbage overspilling every street corner? Do something about the layer of garbage draped over the neighbourhood landscape? Thoughts that were often fleeting over these past twenty months oddly come to mind now during this very tense afternoon. I feel vulnerable, one of the only people moving around on this windswept afternoon. I get the car out of the garage cautiously. Will it be seen by the neighbours, will they sound the alert, tell of a foreigner on the move? My trusty — and I think quite brave — young staff member helps me remove the 'CARE' stickers from the side of the car. Under the circumstances, this has become a very necessary precaution. As well, we remove the UNHCR number plates and place them inside the car as a precaution against being attacked by Serbs seeking to vent their rage on foreigners. I do not underplay the road rage factor; it has been a bad enough problem over the last twenty months, let alone during wartime. Again I am visited by the nagging question of whether it's worth the risk, staying here to help these poor Serbian refugees, when many in the country have always been and must continue to be so hostile to our presence.

In the office I had packed all the essential files. Mikhail wonders why this is so and I have some difficulty explaining to him that if it is going to be necessary to evacuate the country, I will take the essential finance, programming and operational files with me. Though a mere portion of the filing system, such a collection of records will allow me to either continue operations 'offshore', so to speak, or, as I explain to Mikhail, to close down the mission and curtail operations, should it come to that. This is tough for Mikahil to swallow. He is of course mainly concerned for the welfare and continued employment of the staff, and cannot really understand my not returning, or not staying.

I am determined to take these files from the office with me for the obvious reasons, but I have also been strongly encouraged to do so by Canberra.

The drivers continue to work loyally, as do the finance staff, especially Gordana. One of my newer admin staff, Nicola, is tireless; and fearless too, it seems, as she comes into the hotel where I set up temporary office. Over the next week she is to brave the journey through the bombing threat, refusing to stay at home, although I insist. One of the other head office staff regularly picks me up to drive me through the city in his unmarked, but very battered Yugo. This is the only way I can discreetly get around the city during these first, tense days of war. And I must get up to the UNHCR head office daily, as it is vital to stay in touch with the reality of the situation and to continue emergency refugee planning, now the most important task.

A number of excellent staff whom I know I could depend on unfortunately cannot assist in these difficult days. I have no choice in relation to them, given where they actually live, their lack of transport, and, more importantly, their difficult family circumstances. This group of saints is to be remembered for their willingness to cheerfully go about their work despite the fears; they are true humanitarians. One of these is Branko Jelen, who, from his home in the southern city of Nis, anxiously remains in touch with me, continually updating me on the state of the refugee centres in the south, those most vulnerable to the fighting and especially vulnerable to NATO bombing. Branko is the humanitarian saint of saints.

The thoughts of the day mill around in my head as we head away from my apartment. We motor on down the steep hill from the top of Banavo Brdo towards the office. I wonder if I will ever see that pretty and comfortable little apartment and our gear again. I tell myself I will. Peter meanwhile informs me on the mobile phone that there is a large gathering of military people at the checkpoint across the road from the office; so we determine not to drive to the office but to swing about a block past it, pick up Peter and the Land Rover, already loaded with the essential office files, and move straight on to the hotel. We do this without further incident. The drive into town and then across the main highway bridge crossing the Sava is quiet and lonely for the three of us. My staff member drives his little Yugo and we move in convoy.

When we arrive at the hotel a nasty incident occurs which to this day I believe was probably a watershed in the events that unfolded. The Opel is parked outside the hotel foyer and we are unloading the essential files and records needed for office use. It is too much of a public affair but there is no choice. A little fellow with a stubble of beard, dressed casually in jeans and jacket, stops me and questions me about the car, pointing out that the number plates weren't displayed. I show them to him. He prevents me from moving anywhere and quickly proceeds to question me about who I am, what I am doing and what my actions and intentions are. He identifies himself as a policeman, and with my staff member present, we describe why we have evacuated the office and my apartment. I gladly dismiss my colleague who is increasingly nervous under the aggressive questioning and the policeman's reluctance to accept the perfectly normal and plausible explanations of what we are doing and why.

Suddenly, with my colleague still hovering close by, this policeman with a face distinctly reminiscent of a ferret, breaks into a broad grin and astounds me with his knowledge of who I am and with considerable detail about my organisation and its personalities. He is also clearly very knowledgeable, by name and habit, about the UNHCR and CARE foreign staff. Ferret is a cynical, nasty little bastard. One of the regime's finest, no doubt. He takes and tears up my residency card, saying that by evacuating my apartment I no longer qualify for the honour. I am angry but remain calm. The questioning is over and he indicates there are no difficulties.

But Ferret is to watch me closely over the next four or so days, as I move in and out of the hotel. Indeed, on two occasions I walk up to him and offer him a beer, which we quaff at the reception counter. He is quite friendly in a surface way but cocky with it. Clearly he is a creature of the regime, and a trusted one too, given that he is posted to one of only two international hotels in the city. This interplay should have been a warning to me of things to come — it did not matter how reasonable and logical were my explanations about entirely respectable affairs, the shutters had probably already come down. I debate to this day whether Ferret's intervention was the beginning of a plot by secret police and military intelligence to stitch me up, as one of few Anglo-Saxon types still in the country and a mission head at that. In my mind the jury is still out as to whether we were the victims of an active conspiracy or an opportunistic arrest, despite the strong views that some observers still hold relative to the opportunity arrest theory.

The Intercontinental Hotel is one of only two respectable hotels in the city. The 'Inter' is situated close to the Sava River and about half a kilometre from the Hyatt, which is by far the best of the hotels. I would have been pleased to camp in the Hyatt, but at US$200 daily I felt it was too much for CARE's budget (the Inter being about US$35 cheaper). The Inter was now home to many of the international media, and I felt we would be safe there. And from NATO bombing we certainly were, but retrospectively the place was very uncomfortable and full of creeps. The staff, although very kind to me, were tense, and as the days there progressed I reflect now that they were not only silently empathetic but worried for Peter's and my positions.

I awoke one morning to the sound of air raid sirens and bombing, and plenty of it — clearly NATO was concentrating on bombing in the direction of Novi Sad, between which point and Belgrade lay the military airport. I experienced a surreal moment during the bombing of that area. As the explosions could be distantly heard, I took a telephone call from my dear son Haydon. I sat looking out the window in the aftermath of the bombing, on the mobile phone, trying to explain to my boy why I was still there in the country. 'The old Serbian refugees son, they're buggered. They're crouching in their broken-down and pitiful old refugee centres, cold and hungry, 50 000 of them. Son, I am responsible for feeding them and keeping them warm. They're not in this war, have nothing to do with it; what are we to do otherwise?' My boy understood, I could hear his calm and manful reply, I could imagine him nodding his understanding.

Our conversation was being drowned out by the stream of military medical helicopters flying back and forth, their flight path straight over the top of the hotel. Obviously the air base had taken serious hits, judging by the number of medivac choppers. Haydon could hear the deep drone of these Soviet-era 'Hind' choppers plying their way back and forth — he was actually hearing at first hand the sounds of war. My 14-year-old boy, bless his heart. How I missed him at that moment. I could not wait, I reflected, to finish doing what I had to do here — and what I could reasonably expect to do — and get out of the place to be reunited with my wife and boy. A deep feeling of yearning flooded over me as I shouted into the phone to make myself heard to this wonderful boy, as the choppers beat back and forth carrying their tragic load.

In this period I make the few telephone calls I can to Samira, as she makes her way back from Egypt to Budapest, where she is to wait for me. They are poignant calls, made even more so by the atmosphere of war. My primary concern is to reassure her of my safety amidst the NATO bombing. Samira is always so sweet on the telephone, and while she always worries too much about me, and the strain of this comes through all of her calls, that lovely and engaging giggle of hers is always there too. Every telephone call I have ever had with my lovely Samira, the sound of her gentle laughter always breaks in, no matter how tense and worried she might be. Her naturally warm and charming personality is a great antidote to my worries. Calls to her are invaluable during these tense and tiring days.

I am not alone in feeling the heat at this time. Margaret O'Keefe, too, has had a bad week. Crossing the Sava her car is road raged and nearly forced into the side of the bridge. She is badly shaken, but before being able to pause for breath she is summoned to the Ministry of Foreign Affairs, where she is severely dressed down in the way that only Serbs can do a dressing down — screaming and ranting, repetitively and for a long period. She is accused of passing information to NATO, the accusations presumably based on her routine reports to the emergency council of ambassadors in Belgrade about the humanitarian situation. The pressure is being turned up. Finally, around 26 March, she receives personal death threats. Now things are really getting nasty. O'Keefe is gentle, very professional, a grand Irish lady and not deserving of this treatment. It is becoming obvious that she will not be getting much protection from the local authorities, and the tiny international community left in the place is somewhat worried for her wellbeing. I discuss the situation with her.

Margaret indicates that she may be ordered out by Geneva and suggests that the UNHCR mission will still be able to function on autopilot, perhaps with a couple of 'neutral country' international staff keeping things ticking along. I advise Margaret, during one of these weekend meetings, that I will probably leave with Peter Wallace when she does, and that I would like to accompany her in convoy. She agrees in this meeting to let me know her movements and indicates that she may depart in the next few days. I tell her that I will therefore complete my own 'autopilot' plans and be ready to move when she does.

I am now resolved to get Peter and myself out in the next few days, once I have arranged for essential bank transfers which will allow me to pay the subcontractors a further six to eight weeks' worth of funds, sufficient to allow essential deliveries at least through to the end of winter. The arrangements for the plan are completed except for the paying of funds to the subcontractors. This can be done quickly once we gain access to the bank. The Banka Kommercialja has been closed since last Thursday, but is thought to be re-opening on Monday. I hope it does, otherwise our operations are severely impeded.

CHAPTER ELEVEN

Arrest

I am exhausted. A tough, tough year is catching up with me. I think to myself that this is a mug's game, being country director in an emergency mission — as it is for any of my international colleagues in key positions.

We are forever nervously on our toes. The days have been icy, we are always cut through by a rotten wind, the food is bad, everybody smokes and the roads are atrocious. After long days in the office we are late getting home; often, of necessity, I take advantage of the time difference and spend a couple more hours preparing and sending late-night faxes and telephoning colleagues in Canberra or Atlanta.

Samira had found herself caught in the middle of this, and her last six months had not been much fun. Helping me out regularly at home in the evenings with e-mail and fax preparation, worried about her cranky and exhausted husband — there is not much fun in our lives these days. Throughout my life I have been keen on a strict regime of exercise, but I have had very little of that lately. On a few weekends in recent months I managed to do the 8 kilometre walk around the lake at the bottom of Banavo Brdo, rugged up in winter hat, scarf and overcoat. Such walks are always invigorating for me and the best stress releaser I could find, though in these last four weeks there have been precious few.

I saw myself on CNN the other night and was shocked at my appearance — gaunt, pale, deep lines in my face, all the signs of exhaustion. I have not been able to lose this bloody, hacking dry cough which seems to have been with me for months. I know I am well overdue for a break and must take it at the next opportunity. This general weariness does me no favours at this critical time when good and sensible judgment is needed as it has never been needed before. I can feel myself motoring along on pure adrenaline.

On Sunday, 28 March I determine that I will send Peter out at the very next opportunity, and I tell him so. There is no more that he can do now. It is abundantly clear that the war will continue for a significant period and there will be no quick chance for us to reactivate the Kosovo mission, the primary reason for my retaining Peter in country. Peter is also ill with the flu, has spent the last two days in bed. He has not been able to travel with me or assist me in my travels around the town. I have spoken to Eduardo Abelede, the deputy head at UNHCR, and have sought to have Peter travel with the next UNHCR vehicle leaving. Eduardo promises to contact me when this opportunity arises. Meanwhile, I determine that I should follow Peter two to three days later, once I have completed the bank and funding transfers to allow the subcontractors to continue operations. I imagine I will travel out with Margaret O'Keefe on the Tuesday or Wednesday next, all action on my part complete.

The difficult and awkward thing is not being able to be open with the national staff about my intentions to evacuate Peter and myself. I know they can guess this intention, and that they dread the thought. They would be more comfortable and feel more secure if I stayed. These days and nights the air raid sirens are more frequent. A number of quite spectacular hits have begun to impact in and around parts of the city, or so it seems to me. A couple must have been within kilometres, judging by the brightness of the flash lighting up my hotel room. God knows whether innocent civilians are getting caught up in these strikes. The local news says so but I cannot confirm or deny this.

I am now well into international media mode. The media are using me because I am one of very few international staff left in the country and, to boot, I am a director of one of the major international NGOs. Requests for interviews abound, from CNN, BBC, ABC Australia and a host of international papers and radio. I am too busy to take more than a fraction of the interviews requested and so can afford to pick those I think will best serve our purposes. The international media is also aware that since CARE Yugoslavia has been well entrenched in the country for many years, we are a good source of information and news. For my part I use the media, as does CARE Australia, to highlight the plight of both Albanian Kosovar displaced people and those Serbian refugees for whom we remain responsible.

Contentiously, CARE Australia and myself also use these media opportunities to promote our fundraising for the Albanian displaced people disaster which is unfolding. We unashamedly exploit the media for this purpose. We are keen to get CARE International and CARE Australia's names into the ether. If we are to bring world attention to this human catastrophe, what else can we do? CARE will need vast funds quickly, and the world media is a directly useful means of achieving this. It is only arguable from the sidelines whether our mission should have been engaged in such activity; when you are on the ground, there is little conscionable alternative. We are careful not to exaggerate numbers, and amidst the drama of international television reporting our proclaimed numbers of displaced people are conservative estimates.

In my daily situation reports I am able to describe the tragic events as they gather pace. I collect information from UNHCR briefings, which I continue to attend daily, still able to get past roadblocks in my trusty staff member's little Yugo — occasionally also in a battered old taxi, which I am convinced is driven by a secret police operative. I do not talk to the taxi drivers and always get out of the taxi a block or two before my destination. I am able to get the odd bit of info via mobile telephone calls received from around the country, as I am still in contact with our national staff in the provinces. Even as late as 26 March, information direct from Kosovo is available.

The rumours of ethnic cleansing are loud and frequent in the international press. There is talk of 150 000 Albanians on the move, but again it is not clear to me, one week into the war, that wholesale ethnic cleansing has commenced. It seems to me that if the Yugoslavs had been bent on full ethnic cleansing they would have had the resources marshalled at the Serbian borders to allow for a rapid cleansing operation on a massive scale commencing the minute the OSCE had departed, fully eight days ago. So I am puzzled about just what are the real Yugoslav intentions. Are they only intending to carry out 'counterinsurgency' operations, temporarily sweeping aside the civilian occupants of the villages while they get at the KLA, but with no plans to impede later civilian returns? This is exactly what I saw in Yugoslav operations undertaken throughout 1998. I was never convinced of the massive ethnic cleansing alleged by so many.

However, opportunities arise in war. Where would the turn of events take Kosovo's history, I wondered? UNHCR's role was to monitor; intervention in Kosovo was impossible. And so the numbers game was being played, the questions being where and how many people are moving? Does this ragged and spasmodic movement constitute ethnic cleansing? My SITREPs at this time, which form the basis of CARE Australia media releases highlighting the humanitarian drama, do not outline any notion of ethnic cleansing, although I am to report bluntly that '… there is much mayhem and brutality in the field'.

My feeling at this time is that the KLA have stupidly and irresponsibly provoked a hell of a fight, one I cannot see them winning but one which will unleash a terrible wrath on their own people. The Serb military will not need any excuse to push into the hills and wage war, a clumsy war that will not pay much heed to the plight of civilians. Over the months since the Rambouillet farce the Serbs have endured sniping attacks and landmine ambushes throughout Kosovo, and they will now strike back with a vengeance. Of that I am certain. That question of whether or not there was an ethnic cleansing intention continues to rattle around in my head. Surely the Yugoslavs would not be so crazy as to deliberately engage in massive ethnic cleansing, and thereby bring down upon themselves the dogs of war?

Monday, 29 March, a bright crisp and clear morning. Standing on the lower rooftop at the Intercontinental Hotel, I am wired up for an interview with Kerry O'Brien for ABC Australia's '7.30 Report'. On the northern horizon I can see the smoke billowing skyward from what may be the aftermath of an air strike. In the street below, the same sorts of numbers of people you would expect to see on a normal day mill around, catching the decrepit old Mann buses. I scan this sea of humanity, smoking, rugged up, all heads bent, going about their business as if no war existed. Life in struggling Belgrade goes on. Greg Wilesmith, ABC Australia correspondent, conducts an interview with me shortly after this one, and last night it was CBC Canada. It seems I am in high demand, and while these are time-consuming affairs I do not mind too much. We are getting the story out and I know people around the world will take some note of a country director's version of the events taking place.

I quietly tell Kerry O'Brien our conservative estimate of the numbers of people on the move in Kosovo, based on information I am getting from a variety of sources within the Belgrade diplomatic and humanitarian community. About 175 000 people are on the move from the Drenica and other northern Kosovo districts, heading in a south-westerly direction past Pristina. Reliable information is no longer available from our field staffs, who are now well and truly out of contact, for God knows what reasons. With a sinking feeling in the pit of my stomach I wonder about the whereabouts of our Albanian staff. I hope they have got away with the general movement of people; surely they would not stay in Pristina.

I see one of my major roles now being to assess and report upon the movement of displaced Albanian Kosovars, to try to determine where they are moving. CARE Australia and its CARE International partners are mobilising to establish refugee crisis reception areas in the countries and states adjacent to Kosovo. I recommend to Canberra certain courses of action regionally — an attempt by CARE to pre-empt what is likely to happen emergency-wise in areas adjacent to Kosovo — and they now put these into place. I allow Canberra to take charge of planning regionally, given Peter's and my predicament here in Yugoslavia.

Melissa cuts short her R and R in Egypt to move as quickly as possible down to Macedonia to carry out a humanitarian crisis assessment. I am miraculously in touch by mobile phone with my Yugoslav Sector Co-ordinator in Montenegro, who is now undertaking assessments of movements of Kosovars across the state border into Montenegro. This has long been anticipated, as through late 1998 just such a movement, and in significant numbers, did occur in that direction. Planning in the field sometimes just has to be like this, more a matter of educated guesswork, prediction based on the balance of probabilities. I decide, and inform Canberra, that when Wallace and I leave Serbia I will endeavour to travel around through Croatia and in through the bottom of Montenegro to take charge of Ratko's team and assess the need or otherwise for a humanitarian intervention there. Brian Doolan, in the absence of Robert Yallop is now my point of contact in Canberra. He is directing the redeployments in the Balkans right now.

Brian Doolan meanwhile has ordered Jim and Edward, still sitting in Budapest, to move from there to Macedonia and link up with Melissa, in anticipation of a significant intervention in that state, prophetically as it turns out. It will take them quite some time to get there. There is something of a myth prevalent that our CARE emergency teams and those of other UN and NGO agencies are ready and able to move swiftly to these places, but in truth this is rarely the case. Diplomatic, political and logistical niceties most of the time get in the road. These urgently needed movements of staff and equipment, be they reconnaisance assessment teams or full team emergency interventions, rarely happen at the speed the situation demands. And so Melissa, Jim and Edward, with our CARE International colleagues in tow, are clambering around seeking airline bookings, connections from dubious places to dubious places, as well as visas. Canberra head office is moving rapidly to facilitate these new deployments and already recruiting new staff for the Balkans. All the old experienced CARE hands are gathering and returning. Head office staff are all working tirelessly and effectively again.

I conduct a meeting in the house of one of my senior staff with all our remaining staff. The purpose is to finalise the collection of funds from the Banka Komercilja for payment to the subcontractors, and to finalise other operational arrangements to allow the continuation of the next round of food and fuel deliveries to the Serbian refugee centres. The air raid siren sounds yet again. We are sitting up in the eastern suburbs, not more than a few kilometres from the centre of the city. These fine people decide not to abandon the house in search of a bomb shelter, and besides, we all believe that NATO will not bomb this part of the town. I feel a deep gratitude towards these fellow workers. They have come in from the outer suburbs to what is essentially the most central point for all of us.

It is a large and comfortable apartment by Belgrade standards, an old concrete building in the typical Belgrade 1950s style, desperate and terrible-looking on the outside but warm and comfortable within. Almost everybody except the finance and admin staff and myself smoke, so I am encased, as usual, in the perennial Belgrade cloud of smoke — this does my dry hacking cough little good. I confirm my plans for Peter and I to evacuate over the next few days; whether individually or together, evacuation is imminent. We are all silent. It is not a good moment. Again the admin officer suggests we not move, but I explain the reasons why. I stress my satisfaction that some remnant of our refugee centre program at least should still be able to continue.

I appoint the admin officer as officer in charge for CARE Yugoslavia and sign an authority to that effect. I hand over to him a financial delegation that increases his spending power, but in balance with two other key staff members, who will run a check and balance role. This expenditure is strictly in line with a program that we have decided today, here in this fine, if smoky, apartment, and which I have approved. Thus the autopilot program is now in place. It is not perfect, and there are risk factors inherent in this plan, but in a time of war and desperation I am totally satisfied that I can demonstrate to my superiors and CARE International that we have enacted an emergency plan of much substance. There is also provision in this plan to supply food and shelter items to any new Serbian refugees who may flee out of Kosovo and up into Serbia.

With planning more or less complete, on Monday night, 29 March, and for the second night in a row in the hotel, I see and am greeted by the infamous 'Arkan', Zelko Raznatovic. This warlord extraordinaire, infamous for leading his 'Arkan's Tigers' on ethnic cleansing duties in Bosnia in former years, is again tonight dressed in black, quite tastefully, and is charmingly possessed. When I say he greets me, he merely nods curtly, but with a touch of a smile curling at the corner of his lips. He is again flanked by no less than six men, none of whom, like him, is under 1.8 metres in height. I am to see him in the restaurant or the bar every night for the next few nights. All together we are the flotsam of war, refugees and rats alike. Clearly he knows he is safe from NATO attack in the residential company of international journalists and NGO men like me.

Branko calls from Nis. He is deeply worried and angered. For the second time in four days he reports to me the apparent destruction of another refugee centre by NATO bombing. I am really possessed by this and we talk for some time and then two or three more times through the night, checking the details of this incident. If I am going to bring this to people's attention, which I intend to, I need facts. I call Branko back and put the pressure on him to check the facts. I ask him to get me information on the location of the centre, how many refugees were killed, whether there are any eyewitness accounts, and, God forbid and forgive me, is there a body count. The refugee centre is in the south, about 65 kilometres south-west of Nis, the provincial capital of southern Serbia. It is on the road to Pristina, about 20 kilometres on the Serbian side of the Kosovo border.

As Branko describes it to me over the mobile phone, his voice is shaking with anger and worry; he also sounds tired, having been constantly on the go for the last week. The refugee centre sits in a collection of eight old ex-military barracks buildings on top of a sparsely grassed hill, and is sited next to a factory or warehouse of some type. In my previous communication to Canberra I had reported that this centre had been 'directly hit' by NATO. At the time we could not fathom why. Now it becomes abundantly clear: a NATO air strike, clearly carried out by medium flying height aircraft, has made a direct hit on the warehouse or factory but with sufficient force to collaterally damage the collection of ex-military barracks buildings nearby. Two of the buildings are destroyed by fragmentation and fire, eight of the refugees are killed and fifteen are wounded.

I remember this place, one of the 650 centres across the country to which we supplied food and winter heating fuel. During an earlier familiarisation tour Branko had taken me there, as it was one of his 165 centres. It was the typical centre, although a little better off in that there were more substantial buildings and more space, so the people were a little more cheerful; I recall also that a better atmosphere existed among the people there, compared with other centres. Now the place would be one of terror.

Painstakingly I gather the details from Branko, who abuses all Westerners, including me. He savages NATO. Branko is one of my most loyal, innovative and capable field staff. He has sweated hard for the Serbian refugees and for CARE. I and my predecessors have tried to inculcate the Western ethic of neutral service and ideals into him. Right now he cries tears for his country and bitterly abuses the West. It is all I can do to hold him on the phone. He says that as we speak, Nis is burning not 2 kilometres from his apartment. I am astonished to hear this and wonder why NATO would bomb the outskirts of Serbian Nis.

In a sweat of anger I find the nearest respectable journalist and volunteer the news of this NATO bombing of the refugee centre. I also report on the total destruction of the centre in Pristina which had been caught up in an air strike conducted against the Police Field Force headquarters. Miraculously only one refugee has been killed, but that is one too many. Why does NATO carry out attacks that may by chance damage civilian areas? I report these incidents to UNHCR on the Monday and seek their assurances that they will pass on the facts and our concerns via diplomatic channels.

While speaking to Eduardo on Monday, 29 March, I discover that Margaret O'Keefe has been spirited out of the country. I am surprised, and wonder why she or UNHCR did not contact me to advise me. Leaving in convoy with O'Keefe would have been the surest and safest method of departure from the country for Peter and myself. I understand why she has left suddenly: clearly the threats against her had gone far enough, particularly the lies about passing on information to NATO. Eduardo had driven her down to the border in the dead of the night, where she had been picked up by another

SEPTEMBER 1998: Yugoslavia, central Serbia. CARE distribution to a Serbian refugee centre, with assistance from foreign embassy community volunteers.

OCTOBER 1998: In the field in Drenica district, northern Kosovo, as CARE country director. On the right is national director CARE Canada, John Watson; on the left is new staff member Peter Wallace.

OCTOBER 1998: With newly arrived Peter Wallace outside the CARE Pristina, Kosovo office.

OCTOBER 1998: Northern Kosovo, during the guerrilla war, just prior to the ceasefire. This photograph was taken while returning from a field visit to our Drenica program, and shows villages burning in the hills to the east of Kosovska Mitrovica.

NOVEMBER 1998: At a diplomatic and war remembrance dinner in Belgrade with a senior diplomatic attache representative with OSCE.

30 APRIL 1999: Results of NATO airstrikes in a Belgrade suburb. Serb civilians point out damaged homes. (AAPIMAGE)

UNHCR officer. I gather that in the haste to leave they could not contact me.

On Tuesday, 30 March I visit Madame Buba Morina, the Yugoslav Minister for Humanitarian Affairs. It is a luckily timed visit as she has spent most of the day in a bomb shelter. She is known to be a close ally, politically and personally, to President Milosevic and his wife Madame Marcovic, and a member of Milosevic's Serbian Socialist party (the SPS). The object of my visit is to seek assurances that the government understands why CARE has stayed to continue its programs, understands CARE's intentions. Further, I am there to ask government support for our continued work and for the security of that work. Madame Morina is a charming woman, unless one happens to be on the receiving end of her wrath, which can be very uncomfortable.

Today, curiously, I do not get a raving lecture about the shortcomings of the criminal West, something that I had steeled myself for as a necessary prelude to other discussions. I am able to explain our current programs and how these will continue, our contingency plans for operating with UNHCR and the Yugoslav Red Cross during the inevitable disasters about to befall the country; I also stress the need for protection as we go about our work. She promises all assistance. Finally, I get from her letters of safe conduct for myself and Peter to cross borders back and forth, having explained to her my intentions to go out of the country immediately and then to try to return, if possible. She hands me a letter, personally signed, in which my name and CARE's are extolled. Pointedly, she tells me that when I leave the country I should do so via the Budapest exit in the north. 'This would be better,' she says, although reassuring me that I should be safe exiting at any open border crossing. For the tenth time in as many months I sit in this grand conference room of the Serbian Refugee Commissariat, sipping the vile Turkish coffee for politeness' sake. Madame Morina impatiently and blusteringly gets to her feet, signalling that the meeting is over. But she rises tentatively, quite afraid, I am certain, that the chair with arms had become wedged to her ample bottom. She is actually quite famous for doing this, and I amuse myself on the subject as I leave.

● ● ●

Towards the end of March Samira had returned to Europe from Egpyt where she had been holidaying with Melissa, both of them on R and R. On 30 March Samira was staying in the Budapest Hyatt hotel as a guest of and with our good friends from the British embassy. Samira and I had spoken that evening and I had asked her to organise an apartment locally for us and one for Peter. This was to be our Budapest base for the 'offshore' CARE program in Yugoslavia I was planning to run. I had also asked Sam to arrange a doctor in Budapest for Peter to see on the evening of 31 March, our anticipated arrival date. As well, I had faxed to Sam, via the Hyatt Budapest, my last SITREP and asked her to forward this to CARE Canberra. Attached to that SITREP was a copy of the letter of 'safe conduct and authorities support' that I had obtained from Mrs Buba Morina, the Yugoslav Minister for Humanitarian Affairs.

I have one last meeting with the staff who are to remain and I make sure that the admin officer is clear on his instructions for continued operations. I say goodbye — a sorrowful and tense one, a mixture of emotions I am sure, as I detect a little resentment as well. We engage in the old Serb three kisses on cheeks routine, while the back slaps which follow are a little firmer than usual. Not much to say really; we are all a little frightened, I think, of the possible outcome for all of us. This is the fourth time in as many years that I have said my goodbyes to locally engaged staff who are about to disappear behind a curtain of war, and once more I wonder which ones I will never see again. Again I ask myself whether my decisions as a head of mission have benefited or will benefit these people after we are separated by war. For their part, my staff are generous in understanding that I have a pregnant wife about whom I am worried.

Peter remains in bed throughout Tuesday. On the night of Tuesday I pack and ready myself for an early morning departure. I have been up to the UNHCR office and seen Eduardo, who is also leaving — this is the deciding factor for me. I am now committed to crossing the border on Wednesday, 31 March, in convoy with Eduardo. I feel safe with this plan, with Eduardo's company, his neutral UN passport, and also because I am armed with my Morina letter.

Robert Yallop, CARE Canberra's overseas director, who has just returned to Canberra from ten-odd days away in Asia, calls me at about 5 pm on 30 March and urges me to depart at the earliest possible time. Curiously, he seems a little surprised, and concerned, that I have remained in the country after the outbreak of war. I am surprised. I write it off as just another instance of the left hand not knowing what the right hand is doing. I plan not to signal my time of departure to the hotel staff and quietly pack things away, my intention being to settle the bill just before departure. I plan that we will drive away at first light to avoid the street crowds, and I hope to minimise the number of people who know about our departure. I have not seen Ferret for a couple of days and hope we can escape his attention.

Dawn on 31 March breaks with a clear sky but with the usual blanket of smog draped along the horizon, the residue of last night's home heating with coal. A pale blue sky, streaked at the edges with orange, is overlaid with the dirty smudge of an industrial city under sanctions. Weary as hell, I have been up most of the night finishing the last SITREP for faxing to Australia, along with other reports with final written instructions for the CARE Yugoslavia office, which the indomitable admin assistant will pick up today from the hotel. I will miss the staff, and wonder about their safety. Will the men be picked up for military service and be sent to the front or sent to man the anti-aircraft guns, very dangerous missions both? My male colleagues dread this, and more than one has fled town for the hills to escape the draft. It is sobering to think that though angry with the West and inclined to rally around Milosevic, very few of the young men I know in this country are reporting for voluntary military duty.

Peter has packed the Opel and I am ready to go as Eduardo pulls in to the hotel in his UNHCR station wagon right on schedule. I am mightily relieved to see him and some of my tension dissipates. My major concern is being recognised as foreigners and run off the road. I do not feel so concerned about the border crossing itself, despite the amount of gear I am carrying. Eduardo has a woman with him, whom he introduces. I recall from yesterday's conversation that she is a Serb member of the UNHCR staff whom he is trying to evacuate out of the country as well.

We drive off and find the roads essentially deserted apart from buses. So far so good. Nobody seems to take much notice of us, and we continue along the road towards Novi Sad, the northern provincial capital, on the road to Budapest. About 15 kilometres out of the city we are stopped by police, who turn us back at a roadblock. It seems the road to Novi Sad has been bombed through the night and one of the overpass bridges has been destroyed. We continue for about half an hour trying to find bypass routes to get us back onto the Novi Sad road but give up as we approach more police roadblocks. We have no option but to turn around and head back towards Belgrade.

Upon arriving at the major freeway which runs west out of Belgrade we stop to discuss matters. Do we return to Belgrade and wait for another opportunity to leave via Novi Sad to Budapest or do we take the road west towards Croatia? Eduardo says he cannot travel to Croatia because the woman with him will not be allowed entry by the Croatians. Robert Yallop is adamant that Peter and I get out of the country today and expects me to call him hourly to advise progress. I discuss this with Peter. Like me, he is happy to go on without Eduardo's company and head towards Croatia. I heartily hug Eduardo, and bid them farewell and good luck; as he begins the drive back to Belgrade, he looks very unhappy and tense.

Peter and I drive off along the freeway heading west. I am feeling less tense now that we are outside the built-up areas and away from the crush of people; it looks like a clear 45 minute run down to the border on this quite modern four-lane freeway. The sun is out, the sky continues to be clear, and there is a light but cold breeze. It is about 12°–15°C. You would not know there was a war on. Tired as I am, I am beginning to feel a little more relaxed. Very mixed emotions about leaving the country: dread about my local staff, a feeling of deserting our Serbian refugee charges. Have I done all that is possible to keep the humanitarian mission going? These thoughts are mixed with the anticipation of soon seeing my pregnant wife, of getting out of this godforsaken sanction-ridden country, and with relief at the prospect of getting away from this Serbian intransigence and the dangers of war. I reflect on all this from my comfortable Land Rover Discovery seat, staring ahead and looking for that border post.

ARREST

This vehicle, like Peter's, is heavily packed. It contains a couple of my suitcases, one of Samira's, some of her smaller bags, Melissa's three bags and a couple of my briefcases with office files and personal papers. Regardless of whether I am able to get down to Montenegro and then return to Belgrade during the war, I have determined to leave the bulk of our personal belongings in Budapest. I have also determined to leave the bulk of the essential office files in Budapest, sufficient to set up and run the 'offshore' office. Alternatively, I can relocate to Sarajevo and set up operations in the CARE International mission headquarters there. It is my intention that through telephone contact with our Belgrade staff we can continue the essential Yugoslav refugee programs. And, perhaps, with a number of short visits to meet the staff at the border or possibly in Belgrade (bombing permitting), I can refinance and continue the mission right through the war. To do any of this, however, it will be essential to maintain the primary office files, key documents and reference material and other records. Which is why I also have two large boxes of material squeezed into the back of this vehicle, along with a couple of laptop computers, printers and a satellite telephone. This robust vehicle is basically a mobile office for deployment wherever in the Balkans I need to go for the duration of this war.

Robert Yallop calls me, his second call for the morning, and I advise him that we are some fifteen minutes from the border. He sounds mightily relieved and gives me clear instructions to call him once I have crossed over. Eventually we approach the border, with not a vehicle in sight on the roads. I quietly pull in. I am first in line. I hop out of the vehicle and present my passport to the police. Meanwhile, a customs man who is quite friendly in manner gestures me to advance to the next bay.

The border post we have come to is like any routine European post: space for about three vehicles to park in tandem and a long line of benches for inspecting possessions. Off to one side, level with the last barrier booth, there is a one-storey administration building. I voluntarily pull everything out of the vehicle and laboriously line the dozen or so suitcases, bags, briefcases and boxes up along the benches. I open the suitcases first and the initial item I pull out is the satellite telephone, something the policeman is not familiar with. It is one of these new hand-held 'Iridium' types, which I had only received a week before from CARE USA, via Yugoslav customs. The bloody thing has not worked yet. Peter, parked behind me, has fallen asleep in the front seat of his car, partly bored by the proceedings and partly worn out by the flu, which he still has not shaken. The policeman suddenly becomes excited when I describe the object as a phone, and quickly bundles it up and takes it inside the administration building. I can see that it is going to be the usual long process here at the border. I am used to this sort of delay at border crossings in Serbia — and every other country I have entered or exited in time of war, which has been often.

The policeman returns and continues his painstaking checks. He has not been pleasant in demeanour since we started, and now he grows more surly, partly because I have presented him with a major checking task and this is irritating him, and I think also because I am a foreigner. This overweight little policeman has a scar on his chin and bears two stripes on his uniform. Another taller and older policeman with the rank of sergeant joins us at the benches. He is more pleasant and quietly asks me a dozen questions — what are the files? What are these prayer mats in my wife's bag? What is the Koran doing in my wife's bag? And so forth. These Islamic religious items are taken inside for further inspection. For the first time, I become seriously concerned. Behind me in the queue is a Dutch photographer accompanied by his Serbian staff. He asks whether I need assistance and his Serbian offsiders very kindly translate for me in my discussions and explanations about the luggage with the police. The two translators are clearly perplexed with the police attitude, their silly and ignorant questions about the things I am carrying, and do their best to explain what an NGO worker does and what he carries. They are familiar with CARE's work and quite sophisticated in their views. They joke rudely about the Neanderthal policemen that I am dealing with.

The mobile telephone rings and I pick it up to find Samira calling me. This is about 11 am. My wife has the world's most wonderful and sensitive antenna and always seems to know, no matter where in the world I am, whether or not I am in trouble. She detects that now, but I do not worry her and advise that I am merely held up at the

ARREST

border. The policeman reaches over, and as he attempts to cut off the call I hurriedly say my goodbye and give Samira my love, telling her that I will see her in Budapest later that day. 'Do not worry Habibti,' I say. This is to be the last call I make to the outside world for many months. The little fat policeman with the chin scar snatches the phone and orders me to shut it down. I respond angrily and we stare coldly at each other. As it turns out, this is to be my last act of defiance in a free state for the next three months (until the trial).

On 31 March at 10.30 am Samira recalls ringing me on my mobile telephone to be met by a terse and hurried response, that I could not talk right now, but I was at the Lipovac border crossing point and would call her back within an 'hour or two'. Around noon, a little worried, and unable to raise me on the phone, Sam called Peter's mobile. Peter answered, and explained that we had re-routed ourselves to Lipovac because the road to Budapest had been closed due to bombing, that we had been stuck for hours and that I had been inside the border post building 'for quite some time' being questioned. (In fact by this time I estimated that I had already been taken away.) Samira consulted with her experienced diplomatic hosts and the man who had that day returned to Budapest to collect his wife for evacuation home. The man, himself worried, checked the details of the Lipovac border post with British consular staff in Zagreb. Samira, after discussions with the man and now worried, at about 1.30 pm quickly called Don Foley, the Australian Belgrade ambassador's first assistant, who was also temporarily based in Budapest. She alerted Don to the fact that I was hours overdue to cross the border in terms of the last telephone calls to me. Don noted my passport number and details (Sam always carries a photocopy of my passport) and promised her he would try to get in touch with the Yugoslav authorities to help with Peter's and my safe passage. Samira's hosts offer Samira their comfort and advice; the man, an old hand at adversarial tactics and also wise to the ways of the Yugoslavs, anticipated that the Yugoslavs were probably temporarily detaining me to 'give him a hard time'. The man tried to call Peter's mobile at about 2 pm, but there was silence then from both mobiles.

• • •

I have been here two hours now and I am distinctly worried. The boxes of files have been taken inside, as have my personal papers. On top of the papers found inside Samira's suitcase is a 4-year-old curriculum vitae which has excited much attention. That CV details my first two years of work with CARE Australia, and also summarises my twenty-three years of military service. At this point they are halfway through my possessions and have yet to reach my briefcases which contain the latest copies of my office correspondence, including the SITREPs of the last month.

A policeman in a blue camouflage uniform and the boots and cap of the Ministry of Interior Police directs me to follow him inside the building. Frustrated, I follow him, and looking back I see Peter still asleep and the Dutch photographer now stepping forward for his inspection. I assume I am going inside where I will explain in more detail the nature of the items they have removed. Inside the building I am seated in a small room by a pleasantly smiling MUP guard who casually sits with his AK47 assault rifle across his lap. After about fifteen minutes, a short, thin, plainclothes policeman enters the room. He forces me to strip and I am searched. I ask him indignantly whether this is a joke. I am outraged, and as he at least speaks good English, I let my feelings be known. He smiles quietly back and says this is no joke. He is very thorough and checks inside my mouth, making some supposedly humorous remarks about my gold tooth. I am not in a joking mood. Then I am handcuffed. My rage grows.

The MUP guard throws my dark winter jacket over my head and I am carefully escorted outside to the opposite side of the building. There I am bundled into a small two-door sedan, and forced to sit centrally in the back seat with my head bent between my knees. I am flanked by two policemen. The car roars off down the freeway at maximum revs and speed, in the opposite direction from which I have come this morning. A sinking sensation comes over me. Where the hell am I going, what the hell am I supposed to have done wrong and what is going to happen to me? Breathing heavily, doubled up in the back of this small car, a deep chill and the first pangs of fear begin to grip me.

CHAPTER TWELVE

The First Twenty-Four Hours

The small car comes to a dramatic halt. I cannot see a thing. They pull me carefully out of the vehicle, and seem to treat me gently enough. We have been driving for roughly twenty minutes since leaving the border post, and I judge we have headed east back down the freeway. I judged that they turned off the freeway and then headed north. By the sounds around me we seem to have arrived in a town. I am half-carried up some stairs, solid concrete stairs, arms beneath my armpits. I am brought into a room about one storey up and they pull the jacket from my head. I am roughly shoved face up against a wall, legs spreadeagled and arms outstretched upwards, hands splayed on the wall. I can see one man in the room, which seems very large and almost ornate, as far as I can tell from the corner of my eye. The ceiling is very high, the windows waist height to ceiling, almost like an executive-style office. It has that Austrian architectural grandeur about it, so it is probably one of those old Austrian empire administrative buildings which are common along the western stretches of Serbia. Deep carpet and long window drapes. Serbian officialdom loves this stuff, all hangover paraphernalia of empires past, Turkish or Austrian, both grand, simply different in style. The police in this area hold the real power and have the best of office and administrative trappings; the politicians and the mafia also have their share, but it's all part of the same state network.

Silly little observations rush in and out of my head, mixing with the emotions of fright and just plain wonderment. And fury — I am really pissed off with this. Who do these bastards think they are? When will this bloody charade be over? What a mistake! What do these fools think they are doing? I tell the policeman behind me that I am Australian, to which he replies, 'No, you are British, you are NATO.' I banter with him, unable to look around, and repeat that I am Australian, work for 'Humanitarna pomoc' (humanitarian organisation). He speaks some broken English and replies, 'Ah, so you speak Srbski, you must be a spy.' He says this without malice and with a hint of a laugh. From beneath my armpit I can see he is wearing Nike track shoes, well-cut good quality jeans and the ubiquitous sports jacket, typical of most young Serbian men. He is in his late twenties. Eventually he tells me to shut up.

Another man comes into the room. He is taller, older, heavier set, heavy breathing and gruff in voice. He grabs me roughly by the shoulders and kicks my legs to broaden the gap between them. I am pretty uncomfortable and must have been like this for over an hour. I am determined, though, not to show these bastards that I am weak and I maintain this pose without any difficulty. I simply adopt the rigid parade ground mentality of my youth, and of my life as a soldier — breathe deeply, grin to myself and bear it. I don't like it, I am deeply worried, but I bear it. The two policemen mutter quietly to one another, and the waiting continues. They chain smoke, like everybody else in this country. I have been stripped of all valuables — watch, wallet, even wedding ring.

There is movement. A number of people come into the room and set themselves up in chairs, or so I suspect. I am seated facing the wall and am only allowed to look half left to an English-speaking interpreter; when my head turns too far from this traverse they yell loudly. The young police interpreter speaks poor English, but he is pleasant. I can just make him out. He has enormous trouble with my Australian accent. The senior policeman, whom I judge, by his voice, to be in his late thirties, sits right behind me but on the opposite side of the room. He is playing with handcuffs, banging them onto a table I think. He is abrupt, speaks loudly in a baritone and gestures impatiently.

The senior policeman begins an interrogation that concentrates on my CV. This rather routine line of questioning goes on for about three hours. There are no threats, no severely raised voices, and a procession of policemen walk in and out of the room. There is no interrogation protocol here. The interpreter is patient, but he is wearing out quickly; he is not used to or good at speaking English. A lot of misunderstandings occur. He is even apologetic. Judging by sound, he too chain smokes. He wears black jeans, a rather trendy shirt more akin to night wear than police uniform, and has handcuffs plus a small pistol on his police belt.

The senior policeman seems rather satisfied with proceedings. I have simply explained my background. He has taken a great interest in my work as a country director, seems genuinely surprised that anybody has looked after Serbian refugees. I detect from one exchange between two policemen that CARE's work is known in this area of Serbia. 'Ah, huh, ah huh, ah huh, CARE! Humanitarna pomoc, ah huh, ah huh.' Revelation. My hopes climb, this bloody awful mistake must soon pass.

I think of Samira a lot now. She must be wondering where I am, she will know that something is not right because I have not called her for half a day, hours after the appointed time. Robert Yallop will be worried, I am well past schedule for calling him. I take some comfort in this fact, sure that within hours CARE Australia and CARE Yugoslavia will be calling the authorities to clear up this misunderstanding. I again patiently explain to the police my position, my work, my intentions. They seem to listen and seem to nod their understanding. My spirits soar. There is a break of about an hour. The interpreter remains to guard me but also, I am sure, to see what I may say casually to him. Silly thoughts occur to me during this hiatus. I picture that lovely old television show 'Reilly, Ace of Spies'. I picture Reilly under Soviet interrogation and imagine how he coped.

More serious thoughts now as I recall my training as a young army officer, the teachings about the communist military and police system, the methods of interrogation and the habits of these sorts of people. My thoughts too go back to the training we had in 1992 on the UN Observers course that nine officer colleagues and I went through in preparation for operations in Cambodia and Yugoslavia. While there was no great intensive stuff preparatory for the experience I now face, sufficient training over the years through a number of these activities helps me as I consider the next phase and try to prepare myself mentally for what may come. Above all, I try to maintain my composure and pride — I'll be buggered if I'll let these blokes think I am weak. I reason that if I maintain their respect without creating additional hostility, this will help me get through the ordeal. I wonder where Peter is. I hope they let him go, but cannot imagine that they have.

The interrogation resumes and this time it takes a nastier and rougher turn. More policemen have come into the room — about eight, I judge. Sometimes three policemen ask questions in succession, sometimes overlapping, confusing the interpreter. Now they concentrate more heavily on my movements of the last few months. They want to know who I have been associating with, where I have travelled. I am presented with a road map of Yugoslavia which I have never seen before. It has a number of highlight markings on it, tracing a number of towns and villages. They demand to know what the marks are but I don't have a clue.

It is early evening and we are really getting into it now. One of the policemen screams at me, in fact he bellows — the same big oaf, I think, who roughly splayed my legs and arms on arrival. They insist the map is mine, that it came out of the vehicle. I have never seen it. This is the truth. Was it in the vehicle, did it belong to one of my field staff? I doubt it; the markings on the map were too random to mean anything, there was no pattern relative to the spread of our refugee centres. Suddenly, Oaf slaps me over the back of the head with the map, repeatedly — it does not hurt, but the gesture is violent and humiliating. He screams into my face and I notice, despite my revulsion and fright, in an amused, detached way that his eyes are bulging out of his head, like a frog's eyes. Frog Oaf.

I continue to deny knowledge of the map and Oaf belts me with an open hand over the head. Repeatedly, back and forth. He is a big man and his blows are effective. I firmly call back denial. I really have never seen the map and my instincts tell me that it would be suicide to simply give in for the sake of peace and quiet. The senior policeman leaves the room. The questioning continues along the same lines, and this time my denials bring a flying kick from Oaf, who kicks to the right hand side of the rib cage, with such force that I am propelled from my chair, straight to the feet of the interpreter. The interpreter, I notice, is looking pretty uncomfortable about all this biffo. I pick myself up immediately — the blow was not as bad as I feared — and place myself back on the chair. I am extremely unhappy; there is a mixture of rage and fright bubbling away inside me. Another blow to the head, another flying kick, but I stay upright in my chair. I think, you fucking cowardly bastard, kicking and hitting from behind!

I continue to deny any knowledge of the map — what am I to do, to say? I cannot very well make up some story about a map and its markings about which I know nothing. Not even a story that will please them. Have they planted the map? They must have. They are now insisting that the map has NATO target markings on it. Ridiculous. Any fool can see that this rubbish could not stick. The blows and the questioning go on intermittently for three more hours. Occasionally they slip back to a less contentious subject, usually revolving around my CV, the only other thing they seem to be worried about. The questioning during this period is comparatively civilised, but then Oaf comes back on and resumes his more brutal approach.

After three or more hours, I have lost count of the number of blows, including now plenty of stinging back-handers right over the face. I am thankful that so far none of the hand blows has been with closed fists or deliberately aimed at vital points such as nose, mouth or eyes, and I have not bled externally, although inside my mouth I am bleeding at the corners of the lips. My right ear is extremely sore, and I think one blow too many over the ear has injured something inside. My ribs are very painful but seem to be intact. My right leg has taken a lot of kicks and feels deeply bruised along the outside of the calf. Bug-eyed Oaf, a total animal I think. Overall, they seem to be careful not to injure me seriously, and most of the belting and kicking occurs when the senior policeman leaves the room. On two occasions on re-entering the room he has caught Oaf in the act of belting and pulled him up with a loud rebuke, I notice. Charade? Who knows.

There is a break of about another hour, and I judge that I have been in this chair and questioned for about eight to ten hours. No drinks, no toilet, no nothing. I am proud that I have not pissed myself, despite my growing fear. The police come back into the room. The questioning is about to recommence. I notice that my legs are shaking violently and I begin to feel a little ashamed. I hope these arseholes cannot detect this — I think they haven't, due to my quite baggy jeans. I pull my head up and try and square my shoulders. It seems to be about midnight. I wonder where everybody is? Samira, I think of her again, poor pregnant Samira. What about CARE? Are they onto this yet? Have questions and pressure been placed on the Government? I still have hope that this is just a terrible misunderstanding, inflamed by nervous, angry and paranoid policemen who are entirely ignorant of who and what I am.

The air raid siren booms away, the signal for Oaf to belt me again over the back of the head, screaming, 'NATO!' My legs shake like crazy now. I am finding it particularly hard after twelve hours of this to be brave, but I am trying. This time the police leave the room quickly, after having handcuffed me to a wall heater. Peace at last! But I reflect grimly on my situation and think as quickly as I can. Where do we go from here? Where is Peter? There is no mention of him in the interrogation, which is odd.

During the afternoon of 31 March Samira waited patiently in the suite she was sharing with her hosts for any news from Don Foley, or a telephone call from me or Peter. She did not eat, she did not dare leave the telephone, and she did not call anybody, trying to allow things to calm. She called Don Foley at 5 pm to see whether there was any news. '... No there is not,' he said. He was still trying to contact the Yugoslav Ministry for Foreign Affairs. Don asked Samira not to worry. At about 5.20 pm he called Sam and advised that the

Australian Belgrade embassy Serbian staff, whom Don was in contact with, had tracked down the telephone numbers for the Lipovac border post and were trying to contact the authorities there. But Don said he thought Peter and I must have crossed the border and must now be driving through Croatia. Samira said she knew her husband and his strict protocol well enough, and that he would have called her and called CARE Australia, through whatever telephone means and regardless of the time. Meanwhile Samira's host was busy trying to raise me and Peter on the mobiles. He regularly chased Don for updates and consulted with him on what may have been happening and where they could possibly check. Sam noticed that he was worried as he beavered away on the phone. Eventually he decided that, despite his confidence in Don 'to keep chasing the matter', he would try his own avenues, so he called the British consul in Zagreb. He asked them to get onto the Croatia border post at Lipovac immediately and inquire about me and Peter. He received an early answer, about 7.30 pm, when the Croats confirmed that Peter and I had not crossed the border. He reported this to Don Foley immediately.

The questioning goes on through the night, with the odd break of an hour, or thirty minutes. Sometimes the hour of questioning is civilised, occasionally with beatings, although well measured so as to keep me focused and conscious. The questioning now starts to concentrate on my Serbian staff as well as on my international staff colleagues. They have one of my staff lists from my files and closely question me about each individual. It is easy to explain in detail what each of these people does in the organisation, and for the most part the senior policeman accepts all of this with a deep, satisfied 'dobra, dobra' (good, good).

Close questioning follows on the movements of my field staff — where they go to and how often. These are the staff who have vehicles and therefore mobility, so initially it is they who attract the attention. I answer as carefully as I can, thinking that I have my faculties about me. I am careful not to say anything which will be misleading, and try very hard to ensure that the descriptions of our staff are entirely professional. This is easy to do, and certainly the coppers do not seem to try to distract me from my path.

A dreadful feeling of helplessness comes over me with respect my Serbian staff colleagues.

It occurs to me that this ruthless regime will do and say anything to achieve their objectives, and if this means falsely incriminating my staff, so be it. They will not give a toss about innocence. I know this, and have already developed a deep conviction that they will use our Serbian staff. I figure they will arrest many, interrogate some, scare the hell out of all of them and turn some of the staff into 'state witnesses'. I know this as surely as I know night follows day. I have heard enough about the regime and the police in this country over twenty months to be absolutely certain about this. It remains to be seen how far they will decide to go in their interrogation of me and my colleagues, indeed in any investigation of CARE Yugoslavia. Will there be Serbian Government intervention to stop this farce or will they loosely condone it — does anyone in government actually even know about our arrests? I also realise that 'out of the stream' police factions may have taken the initiative to arrest and to continue an investigation without approval or sanction from higher authority. If the Department of Humanitarian Affairs and the Department of Foreign Affairs, who know me and CARE well, are aware of this farcical arrest, I am sure they will intervene.

These thoughts go racing through my mind as I try to think fast and anticipate what will happen next, to see whether there is any useful tactic my tired brain can employ. But I'm beginning to arrive at the bitter conclusion that there is nothing I can do. This is more likely to be a case of 'roll with the punches' and minimise the damage. Survive. Survive to see my wife and family again. Minimise the damage to my staff, reduce the number of arrests. They have not yet begun to question me about my Albanian Kosovar staff. God, that will be a picnic.

At 8.15 pm Don called Sam and her British friends, to tell them — with a worried voice, Samira recalled — that there was no news. Having finally got through to somebody in the Yugoslav department of Foreign Affairs, he had in fact, been roundly abused. 'You are not even in the country and you are asking for assistance,' the official snapped back. The call was terse, ill-mannered and non–co-operative. Don said he had decided not to alert DFAT Canberra yet, as he thought it still possible that Peter and I 'may be on the road'. He advised Samira not to worry, that everything would turn out. 'You know Steve, he is experienced at these things,' Don said, adding that with our Australian passports nothing could go wrong for us. At worst, he felt, we may have been temporarily detained and perhaps my 'highly coveted' Land Rover had been confiscated, in the time-honoured tradition of the Serbian authorities. Don again stressed that he thought I was on the road or in a Croatian hotel, and he repeated that he would not yet contact DFAT.

Samira was not satisfied with this, and thought Don was 'too casual'. She immediately contacted CARE Canberra to raise the alarm, although she secretly hoped she was overreacting. Now driven by her worst fears, Samira also rang and got through, miraculously, to Mikhail in CARE Yugoslavia. Mikhail was worried, but could not do much at that time of the night: the air raid sirens were booming again, there was a curfew on, it was raining, and he, according to Samira, sounded a little frightened. In fact Sam learnt from Mikhail that Peter, as agreed with me in discussions that morning at the border crossing, had called Mikhail seeking his support to notify the Ministry of Humanitarian Affairs of our changed border crossing plan. Mikhail had tried all day to raise Buba Morina and her staff, but to no avail. Sometimes the phones had not worked, but often he had been told that Morina and her key staff were downstairs in the office bomb shelter and uncontactable.

Samira was galvanised into action, but was very frustrated and very concerned. She knew that I would have called her and Canberra, and felt that I must have been detained. Dead ends all the way round. She was deeply and instinctively worried, and could not eat with her hosts, who in turn worried about her. She worked well into the night, then sent her version of a SITREP to Robert Yallop and Charles Tapp.

In this SITREP she summarised the events of the day. She attached a copy of the Buba Morina 'safe conduct' letter. She asked Canberra to contact Ambassador Christopher Lamb (Australian ambassador to Yugoslavia, who had been back in Australia on leave for some weeks), who Samira knew had wide and unconventional contacts in Belgrade. She asked CARE to convince Lamb to get in immediate touch with his Belgrade contacts and pursue news of our whereabouts. It was now early afternoon in Australia — Wednesday, 31 March 1999. Sam was deeply worried and feeling 'horrified'. At 1 am,1 April (Budapest time), Samira called Brian Doolan at CARE Australia to officially report her worst fears about Peter's and my whereabouts and safety. She broke down on the phone and Brian tried to calm her. Brian called Ambassador Chris Lamb. Sam slept fitfully after calling Brian, convinced that something serious had happened to Peter and me.

It is morning on the second day, Thursday 1 April. We have been going at it all night. Mercifully the beatings have slowed. I consider myself lucky that at no time have the beatings been severe, otherwise I reckon I would not have survived the night. I have not been broken on the issue of the bloody map. There is little else I could say; the truth is stark and simple. I have never seen the map, and I have not been cruising around the country assessing or selecting NATO targets or anything remotely like that. Not even the most vindictive witness could fabricate such a story. All my travels over the months have been directly to humanitarian work sites, and for the most part with staff drivers. The interpreter is absolutely knackered — clearly he is the only English speaker in the whole building. What a useless bloody police force, I think!

After a short break the questioning resumes. They have grown tired of the NATO map/bomb targets line of questioning; they have also let up for the time being on questioning me about my staff. The senior policeman appears to me to be accepting my version of the truth regarding the CARE organisation and who my staff are. I feel a little more comfortable but remain extremely wary. The questioning now goes to my northern Iraq, Yemen and central African experiences, and they closely follow my CARE experiences in these places. The police are well informed about the strife and civil wars in northern Iraq and Yemen, and boast about their knowledge, and question me against that background, but at the same time display total ignorance about Rwanda and Zaire.

These police seem to be astonished that a bloke like me has spent six years working at the middle managerial and country director levels in these complex emergency arenas, in situations where there was always fighting. They are, it seems to me, both suspicious of my actions and motives in these strife-torn and desperate places and just a little awestruck that I spend so much of my life away from the comforts of home. The police boss says this. During a quieter moment, a relatively peaceful hour when the sun breaks in through the ornate windows, he reflects in this fashion. He appears genuinely interested, and for a while at least seems to accept my humanitarian track record. Where the hell is Peter? I ask again and they tell me this is none of my business, and order me not to ask about him again. Alongside this, I also have the sinking feeling that police raids have probably been conducted through the night on my staff's houses, the poor buggers dragged off down to some dreary Cold War police dungeon. I shiver at the thought and feel deeply sorry that this may have happened. I am to find out months later that this was indeed what happened.

On the afternoon of 1 April in Budapest, Samira was able to meet the Serbian staff member of the Australian Belgrade embassy, the woman who twenty-four hours earlier had accompanied, in Eduardo's car, Peter and me in our aborted attempt to leave Belgrade via the road to Budapest. She and Eduardo had managed to get down the road and cross over into Hungary during the night. She confirmed to Sam the events of the previous morning and the fact that yes, we had turned toward the Lipovac border. Samira had decided to go to the Australian embassy to see what could be done and what had happened. She met Jason, an Australian Belgrade embassy staffer, a man she knew. He was manning the Belgrade desk in exile. The Australian Belgrade embassy office had re-established itself here, working out of the Budapest embassy. Samira asked Jason to brief Ambassador Heggie, Australia's ambassador to Hungary, to request that Heggie approach the Yugoslav ambassador to Hungary with a formal diplomatic request for news of our whereabouts and guarantees of our safety. Samira felt she wanted to request this herself, but did not know Heggie well, so she left it to Don and

Jason. She perhaps innocently believed that diplomatic action at ambassador level ought to be automatic, and was operating on the basis that every little bit would help and that time was of the essence. Jason responded kindly and positively, and said, 'Whatever you wish, Samira, we will see what can be done.' Samira was reassured by Jason's manner.

Many days later Samira was disappointed though, and felt concerned to hear from Ambassador Heggie that he had known nothing of the disappearance of Pratt and Wallace on the actual day it happened and only heard about it later, apparently at Samira's request. Samira felt at that moment that the gravity of the situation had not been fully impressed upon some of the authorities. She had hoped that broad pressure could be brought to bear on the Yugoslavs, at a time when somebody might have been seriously threatening the safety of one or more innocent Australians. Samira heard later that there had been a death in the diplomatic staff; obviously this would have added to the woes of and pressures on Don Foley.

The interrogation fizzles out about mid-morning. I calculate they have had me under the hammer, through the night and with short breaks, for about twenty hours straight. I am tired, tired and tired. My head throbs from the beatings. All I have had is water, with nothing to eat. I am fairly scared, and my knees still knock from time to time, a reaction to the beatings, I guess. But my voice is steady, I have not cried out or broken down, which continues to give me satisfaction. Occasionally I am taken handcuffed down the hallway to a stinking toilet. They always check to make sure the hallway is clear of anybody. I am totally hidden from anyone in the police station except the six or so policemen attending my interrogation. Why are all institutional and public toilets in Serbia so incredibly filthy and foul? — a silly irrelevant thought crosses my weary mind. Through the rest of the morning and into the afternoon I am left alone, handcuffed to the wall heater.

Eventually the senior policemen and the interpreter return with a four-page statement written in Srbski. The interpreter slowly takes me through it, and I am totally surprised to find that the statement simply follows my life story, per my CV and my description of my CARE humanitarian work and duties. My version. There is no mention in the statement about the road map or alleged bomb target analysis, or about intelligence agents. Gratifyingly, there is no incriminating information, no allegations in the statement about the Yugoslav staff and no mention of Peter at all. I am stunned, having expected a trumped-up statement; after twenty hours of tough questioning and beatings it seemed logical that that was what they were going to produce. What is going on? They tell me to sign the statement, and I just hope that it is fine; their verbal translation had better be right. It seemed, the way the interpreter was struggling through the statement word for word, that this was the case.

The senior policeman then announces: 'Everything will probably be OK, there may have been a misunderstanding. In future with your work stay in close contact with the police, regularly brief them on your actions and there will be no problem.' He goes on, 'Do not rely on the Department of Humanitarian Affairs to cover for you, ah, Buba Morina.' He laughs, the interpreter laughs, I laugh, nervously. What a joke! As the warm sunlight streams through the window I feel an atmosphere of 'hail fellow, well met' — an illusion, but tired as I am, any respite from this madness will do. I still cannot see the chief, have never seen him. He continues to sit behind me, but now he is talking quietly and is relaxed. What is going on?

The chief tells me that I will probably be detained for about three days, then let go. Maybe there will even be a short court case before I am thrown out of the country. This makes sense to me, this is how I have envisaged things going. Unfair and brutal, but that is the best I can expect. I begin to experience a great feeling of elation. Shit, everything will turn out fine. Do not worry, Samira, I am on the way!

The interpreter is very relaxed now, and we talk at some length about our families. He tells me of his fear for the safety of his family in this town, although he still does not tell me which town we are in. The air strikes have the town paralysed with fear. As he works he worries for his wife and three kids — can they get to the bomb shelters in time? He is a very decent fellow and has been through the entire ordeal with me. He tells me he is sorry for the beatings and entirely disagrees with them. He seems to be genuine, but the thought crosses my mind that he might be part of a 'good cop, bad cop' routine. We talk about the NATO and Western attitudes and he tells me he has been surprised through the interrogation to learn that I have been against NATO bombing and that I have been internationally vocal about this. They actually found copies of my media releases illustrating this theme (in the files box) and had handed them to me for explanation. The evidence of my thirty-two international media and press conferences since October 1998 — in which I expressed strongly the view that it would be a mistake and counterproductive for the West to bomb the country, country-wide — had clearly stunned them. The interpreter is a much smarter and more sophisticated fellow than his colleagues who, except for the chief, look pretty thick to me.

Finally, the interpreter hands me back my wallet, minus the money but with the photos of my wife and Haydon. I am so grateful for this small mercy that my voice for the first time breaks and tears well up in my eyes. The young interpreter hands me a small packet of tissues and says, 'Do not worry, I am sure you will see your family soon.'

CHAPTER THIRTEEN
Under Threat of Death

It is late afternoon on the second day, 1 April (how appropriate, perhaps that written statement this morning was a bloody joke?). I have been in solitude for some hours, left alone by my tormentors. Handcuffed to a different wall heater, now I can see out into the town square. They do not seem to be concerned that perhaps people could see my face in the window, although I am some distance from the hubbub of the market square. It is a very pleasant-looking little town, with a range of respectable, well-kept and quite grand-looking buildings surrounding the square. People come and go; it could be any peace-loving medium-sized city anywhere in Europe. But how incongruous that away from this idyllic little park setting lies this monster of a jail with its seedy little toilets and prisoner bashings. I have begun to hear a lot of thumping upstairs and imagine that some other poor bastard is getting the rounds, enduring treatment much heavier than mine.

I bet all the (potential) 'enemies of the state' are being pulled in by plain-clothes secret policemen all over the country into these pleasant, ornate little provincial police stations. Journalists and opposition politicians will be questioned — pre-emptive strikes by the authorities to keep them in line, to warn them, in some cases to lock the 'troublesome traitors' away. I have no doubt that will happen, as I have heard plenty about the behaviour of the regime this last twenty months, particularly its reaction to the burgeoning democratic movement in this country. Again I am worried about my Serbian staff, who must be categorised the same way — working for these pesky foreigners puts them in the troublesome basket. And they get paid five times as much as the rest of the workers in the country. Jealousy reigns alongside paranoia, I reflect.

I am feeling incredibly relieved for the peace of the last few hours, and think that just maybe they have realised their mistake and will soon let me go. I am not allowed to see anybody, however, and my repeated requests to be allowed to contact the International Red Cross Committee or the Swiss embassy are repeatedly denied. A nice old cleaning lady brings me a hamburger and a Turkish coffee. I hate any coffee, let alone this poor version of river silt, but right now it is absolute heaven. The old dear pottering around my desk looks so out of place. Can she hear and know about the thumping going on upstairs? I pray to God that this will all end soon, for all of us. Fervent praying is not one of my habits, but I am rebuilding the practice right now; I have, I reflect, always been a believer, just a little remiss in the matter of worship in recent times. Is it hypocritical to be calling on God after taking him so easily for granted, I wonder? The afternoon sun beats into my face and I am grateful for small mercies — sun rays and river silt — as I ponder these spiritual and philosophical questions.

Now it is early evening and the nightmare begins in earnest. Everything so far has been a stroll compared with what is to happen next. Two strange policemen — I assume they are policemen — rush into the room shouting, and haul me to my feet. They handcuff me from behind and place a large grocery paper bag over my head. They are roughly impatient, hurrying me down the corridor and not too gently down the same concrete stairs I must have come up earlier. It can't be much after 7 or 8 pm. It is raining and I am bundled again into one of those little Yugo sedans, judging by its size and engine sound. Two police flank me and my head is pushed down viciously, the handcuffs pulled as far up my back as is agonisingly possible. Now I am breathing very fast, almost hyperventilating. 'Please God let me be safe!' I say to myself, almost panicking. It is all I can do to get a grip on myself, but I do manage, breathing deeply and slowly and reassuring myself that all will be OK.

The Yugo speeds quickly through the village streets, twisting and turning, and about ten minutes later comes to a stop. Except for the engine idling and the rain pattering down, there is silence; the police don't talk. One of them gets out of the car and seems to open a garage door and the car then moves straight in, a roll-a-door closing behind. Dead silence. I am bundled out of the car (not so gingerly this time — my head is banged two times on the door frame), I am squeezed between the car and the wall, and then I hear a weapon cocked. A chill races up my spine and I brace myself, the blood screaming in my ears. More weapon sounds, sounds like a magazine being detached — my initial fear subsides as it seems the goons are only clearing their weapons, perhaps 'making them safe' before entering the building. Bloody hell!

I am hauled up stairs, the bag is removed from my head and I find myself standing outside another room. I can hear muffled voices inside. The guards with me hold me patiently and silently while the driver enters the room and talks to whoever is inside. I am then brought, blinking owlishly, into the place. I notice nice lounges, coffee tables, billowing tropical pot plants and well-appointed wall units. The drapes are drawn. Three men sit around the coffee table on comfortable chairs and a blonde with a beehive-style hairdo and too much lipstick sits perched on a bar stool. I wonder whether I really am going crazy! The police who brought me quickly leave the room and retire to another section of the house.

I am faced by a thick-set fellow, medium height, in his forties, who is staring at me, unsmiling, over half-glasses. He has curly grey hair, quite long and tangled, and two days of grey beard stubble on his face. Later, when he does smile, he displays a kindly, professorial face. He is dressed in a dark tracksuit and track shoes. He is clearly in charge and I nominate him as 'Chief'. To his left — that is, to my right — sitting on a wide leather lounge, is a very large man, with an uncanny resemblance to the bulky movie star Steven Seagal, but without the ponytail. He has a very large, shiny head, appears to be in his late thirties, is tanned and clean-shaven. He is tastefully dressed in neat dark slacks and a dark cardigan. I call him 'Coconut Head'. To the right of the 'Chief', to my half-left, sits a much younger and smaller-framed man with a sneer on his cruel-looking face. He is dressed in jeans, blue denim jacket and track shoes. His face is pockmarked, a hangover of bad acne, so I call him 'Scarface'. I do not address these men in these terms, but this is how I mentally refer to them. I dub the woman, who turns out to be the interpreter, 'Beehive'. She has a terrible, over-painted face and outrageously wears the shortest of miniskirts and the longest stilettos I have ever seen. Perched on a bar stool the way she is, she looks nothing less than absurd. I didn't see any humour at the time, but I am able to recall this out-of-synch scene as at least having a comic dimension. There is little laughing ahead, I know. In fact I am very apprehensive, but happy enough for the moment to have got through the drive from the jail to this house. Alive for the moment, I now find myself taking life hours at a time and activity by activity. Later, I reflect on my fears at the time and wonder whether I had been melodramatic. I conclude they were well founded.

I am seated and Chief begins, through the interpreter, to question me, starting from scratch. It is immediately clear that the statement I signed with the police is now redundant. These people are entirely different and far more professional in their approach. They simply use the police statement as guidance, viewing it contemptuously. Chief curls his lip as he peers over his half-glasses, gazing down at the statement as if it were used toilet paper. Quietly and deliberately he asks his questions, at the same time peering very closely at me. He is only a metre away. The atmospherics are dynamically different in this interrogation.

Beehive remains perched on her stool at my left shoulder. Her black stocking-clad legs, little hidden by her miniskirt, are almost in my face, and I find this all a little bizarre. Does the Stalinist handbook for good comrade commissar interrogators direct that such distractions should be brought on so early in proceedings? Speaking of bizarre, I find these clashing odd and sometimes flippant thoughts rather off-putting, and wonder about my state of mind. Has it got to the point where I really don't care any more?

Beehive does not have a pleasant bedside manner. She shrieks as she talks, and with her beady, bright eyes, her sharp nose and angular face, almost takes on the appearance of a busy, bobbing bird, if of the carrion variety. Half an hour into proceedings she repeats Chief's very emphatically stated, 'Do you understand? You are in very deep trouble, trouble of the most extreme kind, do you understand me, do you understand me? You must co-operate, and very closely. There can be no mistakes. Your life depends on this, do you understand?' She parrots his emphasis but adds her own volume in a shrill voice over and over. While Chief speaks quietly, almost softly, examining me closely over his specs and firming the line of his mouth, Beehive continues to shriek into my face. Her English is very good, but she wears a nasty, twisted expression, and her eyes are intense. Her voice is harsh and throaty, presumably from too many cigarettes.

The other two in the room say absolutely nothing, just peer at me intently. I can feel their eyes boring into me. They take their time. There is no hurry — I know by the sudden turn of events, by the discarding of the first police statement and by what I detect to be their contempt for the police interrogation, that I am in for a long haul. So long as I remain useful, that is. That is how I assess it. I try to second guess what is going to happen, what steps I can or must take to get me and my colleagues through this incredible, outrageous mess. Out of this nightmare.

This interrogation also carefully picks through the details of my CV. There is no interest displayed by the Chief in my real job, nor in the roles and responsibilities of CARE Australia and CARE Yugoslavia. It is starkly clear that he intends to simply ignore our real work and the reason for my presence in this country. He quickly demonstrates a complete ignorance of the business of the international aid community — either that or he is profoundly uninterested. It becomes gloomily and very quickly apparent to me that the truth of my situation is entirely irrelevant to these people. I am told after the first hour of relatively quiet but deeply depressing interrogation that they are going to commence taking a statement from me, and that I am to co-operate closely in the preparation of that statement.

Chief says calmly and clearly that he believes I am the head of an espionage agency in Yugoslavia. He then describes how I have established the network utilising my staff, many of whom are in my employ as agents. He describes CARE Australia and CARE International as the international 'spy ring' to whom I am reporting, and he ludicrously states that Charles Tapp (CARE Australia national director/CEO) had sent me to Yugoslavia in May 1997 with clear instructions to establish such an espionage network and to prepare the collection of information for submission to NATO.

Chief calmly peers over his glasses as he spits out this diatribe, the poison flowing onto the table and leaving me with a sick feeling in the pit of my stomach. My hair stands on end and there is a ringing in my ears as the realisation strikes home that these bastards are quietly, and with determined deliberation, setting up a scenario in which I, my colleagues and my organisation will be the fall guys.

It is very chilling to hear Chief summarising his 'findings' after a mere hour of interrogation, in which time he had merely gone through my CV, a most unremarkable document in any case. He is most relaxed, seems to have all the time in the world and demonstrates all the confidence of a man who will get what he wants, or be rid of the problem, one way or another. Certainly he displays none of the frustrations, harrowed feelings and weariness of your average democratic society policeman trying to prove his case. Coconut Head and Scarface look on impassively and silently, although I see the glimmer of a satisfied smile on Scarface's face. Beehive punches out the translation with feeling; this bitch would love to reach down from her carrion perch and punch me in the face, I think.

It is now late in the night. My weariness accumulates; I reckon I have had only three to four hours' sleep in forty-odd hours, and none in the thirty-five or so hours since capture. Of this time I estimate I have been under interrogation for about twenty-five hours, on and off, and I am absolutely buggered. But my fear does not allow me to droop. Though I am not sagging in my chair, my brain feels very clouded; confusion is beginning to creep in and disorientation is increasing rapidly. It is pouring rain in the dead of night. A pall hangs over the place and depression surfaces. I hang my head, shake it, and say to Chief that he has got to be joking, that this is outrageous and a great lie. Chief, his grey stubble glistening against the backdrop of the coffee table lamp behind him, shakes his woolly head and with the first hint of a smile says that this is a very serious situation and, 'we are not playing games, Major Pret'. He actually for the first time speaks a little English, but this is not to be his habit — all his communications to me will be through Beehive.

I am horrified to see my office notebooks placed on the coffee table before me. These are your everyday, garden variety office books, the type any executive or manager carries. Following the traditions of military administration that I have learned over the years, my books are detailed and meticulous in their layout and information; they are not the tools of clandestine behaviour that these bastards are to allege. Chief goes through them. Clearly they have been studied for some time, as some of the pages of these conference notebooks and office diaries are flagged with pieces of paper. As well, photocopied documents sit on the table — they have been busy ransacking my briefcases, my office documents. They have clearly formed a view that whatever is in these documents and notebooks forms a case for some sort of skulduggery. My nausea deepens further.

Now Chief is again concentrating on one of my staff members, Branko Jelen. Chief has questioned me closely and resolutely about the most senior twenty staff on my staff list, which he has in front of him. He again returns to Branko, seems very interested in him. He points to a number of telephone conversations recorded in my book, discussions Branko and I have had. Branko, as my main field team leader in the south of the country, features regularly in my notebook.

In the first two weeks of the war Branko dominated the list of telephone conversations, due mainly to our joint concern about the danger to the Serbian refugee centres in the south, the area most vulnerable to NATO bombing. There had been those incidents of refugee centre bombings by NATO, about which Branko had rung me in outrage. We had talked frequently about them, and his name therefore featured regularly in my record books. He is now a marked man. I feel deeply worried for him because I also know that Branko is a target for another reason: he is of a mixed Serbian/Catholic Slovene background. I vigorously reject the line of questioning, trying to patiently and pragmatically explain the role and responsibilities of Branko and my other staff, but my knees knock at the thought of these loyal staff members being implicated in this bloody mess.

The questioning continues over the next hour, essentially centred around the events of my job, as illustrated in my conference notes and in the record of my telephone conversations with CARE staff, with Canberra and with other UN personnel around the place. It is clear to me, even through the curtain of my exhaustion, that I am dealing with a mixed bag of paranoia, ignorance and just plain cynical exploitation. These bastards could not for one moment believe the crap they are going on with. I can see it in their eyes — they are playing. They continually sweep aside all my references to legitimate matters. They still insist that I am British and a currently serving British Army intelligence officer, despite the fact that the original police interrogators had accepted my true professional and national status.

The kindest thing that I could possibly say about the people in this room, I ruefully reflect, is that they are paranoid, under some sort of pressure, and blindly and mistakenly ignorant. But I know that they are too intelligent for that and must know the realities of life, of UN and international NGO business, and so on. I was willing to give the police at the police station the benefit of the doubt and see them as frightened, ignorant and mistaken, but not these people. They are a different breed. It dawns on me that they must be military intelligence. They are cooler and more self-assured and they speak in a military language and about military things which I quickly recognise. These thoughts pound quickly through my head as I seek some rhyme or reason to what is happening, a way out perhaps, some grip on where they are leading me, how far they will go to achieve their objectives. I continue to argue and refuse to accept their line of inquiry. I say that I will not be making any statements to support their 'thesis', ask again to be allowed to see the International Red Cross. Chief for the first time laughs — what a joke, see the Red Cross!

Suddenly there is an exchange between Chief and the other two men. They jump up and reach over, haul me to my feet, then drag me out of the living room. They take me up half a flight of stairs to a split-level room which is bare of furniture and all niceties. Coconut

Head and Scarface hurl me against the wall and Scarface follows up to belt me in the stomach. The wind rushes from me and I double in excruciating pain, unable to recover. They hurl me heavily against the wall again, buggering my right shoulder, which has taken the impact, Rugby style. I try to keep my head clear of impacts. Scarface throws a flying kick which I take fully on the chest. He has the eyes of an enraged maniac, one who is enjoying himself. Coconut Head doesn't participate in the beltings, but stands back; he is not needed anyway, as I am so tired I cannot fight back or resist. Fear also saps me of the energy to physically resist, although I find sufficient mental strength and determination to 'firm up' and ride with the punches. (I am to reflect later in prison that my many years at the bottom of Rugby mauls and rucks, in Rugby League as an underweight school player, and in the rough and tumble of Army life, have partly prepared me for the hidings that I experience during this ordeal.) While Scarface knocks me around I am a little encouraged by the fact that, like the police at the police station, he does not direct his blows to vital areas; he does not appear to try to break my nose, eyes, teeth, ribs, genitalia etc. He bloody well hurts, though. I have no idea how long this goes on for — a minute? twenty? — it is all a blur.

Eventually I am dragged once more down to that tastefully appointed living room and held standing before Chief. The vulture-like Beehive stares at me as she spits out the translation on behalf of her boss. No shrinking violet this Beehive, she seems to be enjoying herself. Chief says, 'Major Pret, we can do this the easy way or the hard way, but either way we will get your co-operation. We will take you back upstairs and we will force you to participate in the preparation of our interrogation statement. Or we can all sit around here in a nice way, like the officers and gentlemen we all are.' This is Chief's first hint of his background — a military officer, military intelligence. 'We are both majors, you and I, we both know how to be sensible. You are an infantry major with intelligence links, we know this, and of course this means that you are ready to die for your country, we know this, and maybe, Major Pret, it will come to this,' he says chillingly.

My hair stands on end, my heart beats incredibly fast. I am sore, I am tired, I am lonely and I am just plain scared. My head throbs.

Does CARE or the Australian Government know where I am? I am roughly forced to sit, despite the fact that I have not replied to Chief's invitation. 'Pret, you are going to write your statement, sentence by sentence, as I dictate. I am running out of patience and we will not waste any more time. We want the truth,' he says. I reply that I have been telling the truth, and he says, 'Rubbish.' He says, through the vulture perched at my left shoulder, that he has his objectives and that I have my objectives: 'To live, to see your wife and family again. Forget about your organisation, forget about your country, your objective is to survive.' He says that we will join our objectives together and that things will go easier for me. Chief stresses his critical point: 'In telling the truth,' he says, 'you must play by the rules. The rules of the game are that you will tell us all about your espionage activity and that of your espionage colleagues and your organisation's espionage activities. The rules of the game do not permit you to mention anything about your job, your organisation's humanitarian business — do not waste my time mentioning these things. Dobra? You understand?' I reply no, I do not, that I have been telling the truth and have told everything in meticulous detail, which I have.

Chief slams the coffee table and roars like a bull, and on this cue, Scarface slams me across the face. Reeling and ears ringing I look up. 'Now look here, Pret,' says Chief, bending forward for emphasis, mouth set firmly, teeth gritted, eyes boring into mine. He begins a demonstration with his hand, as he is to do a number of times in the ensuing days. One hand horizontal, he places the other on top and vertical. 'This represents your life, Major. You are finely balanced and could fall to death in an instant. Do you understand?' barks Beehive, translating. He says words that are to echo in my mind forever after. 'I have the authority and the discretion to liquidate you tonight!' he hisses with ironic emphasis. His breathing is heavy, his eyes ablaze. You could hear a pin drop. I feel the situation at this very instant is razor-edge balanced. The blood is roaring in my ears, I am struggling to keep my breathing easy. He nods over his shoulder, indicating Coconut Head, and says, 'He will take you downstairs and kill you quietly in a few minutes; he will then use that plastic bag, and drop your body into the boot of that car down there.' A black garbage bag sits on the floor next to Coconut Head. 'We will not wake the neighbours. Then we will immediately take you down to the banks of the Danube, not far from here, and we will bury you in the soft river mud. It is easy. In the rain tonight, nobody will know. In any case it is none of their business.' He projects all of this straight between my eyes. These words, this scene, are burnt into my brain, and will haunt me in the months to come. To this day, the devils still rattle around in my head. He concludes: 'Let me remind you, Major Pret, you are on the missing list, nobody knows where you are, very few people even know that you still exist. You are expected to disappear!'

The rain continues to fall. This is a severely depressing and fearful moment. The truth is, I cannot give these animals what they want. I know it. I feel with a hugely heavy heart that I am staring death in the face, and I know they are not joking. I am to debate this for months — was this an elaborate, harmless charade to get their fabricated story, or was this reality? I am to conclude months later that these bastards would have been happy to kill me in a heartbeat, if I did not lie for them. What I did know from my experience in Serbia was that this military intelligence gang was one of many political, police, mafia and military factions vying for power and influence in the complicated spectrum of the Yugoslav landscape. I also conclude later that this military intelligence faction was probably out of control and not operating with Government authority, or at least not with the authority of either the Yugoslav Department of Foreign Affairs or the Department of Justice. Discussions with Australian diplomatic staff and even unusually frank but discreet discussions with Yugoslav legal and military people in jail, much much later, will lead me to this understanding.

The deciding moment, I feel, has arrived. What do I do? Preservation of course takes over. I am deeply focused on Samira and my family. My death will be the death of Samira, I know it. As strong as she is, she is dedicated to me and to our life — she has often said to me that she has nothing else. (Moved by the thought, during this odd moment of reflection, I wonder do I deserve such devotion?) But she could possibly deal with a long prison sentence imposed on me. I think of my son Haydon, and of my poor old Mum, who is seventy-five, and wonder whether she could ever cope with the shock of all this.

I am seated again before Chief. The dramatics of the previous hour have been allowed to die down and now there is deathly quiet. I ask them what they wish to do, and we commence the most ridiculous and awkward farce I have ever participated in. The first sentences are dictated to me. I hear a strange voice, which cannot be mine, agree that I am a member of the Australian Defence Force's 'Joint Intelligence Organisation', the JIO. They have asked me the name of the nearest organisation which equates with their fabricated story. JIO no longer exists, but that is the name I give them. I decide to provide false names wherever I think I can, without going to the point of being too obvious, of enraging them. I give them a false name of a lieutenant colonel, supposedly the branch head of JIO who is 'running me', to use their own spy jargon. I could not give them a real name in any case because these days, since having left the army, I do not have a clue who the officers in any departments are, let alone those in JIO, or DIO, or whatever it is called these days.

I sit there, head bowed, enveloped within this strange and contradictory exercise, obliged to create each sentence which is given to me in outline. I could not insert any credible information, because I do not know these things. What I am made to say is literally all lies, but there is some perverse satisfaction in coming up with clever things to say to save my shaking hide. It is curious that later they do not appear to confirm this 'information', neither the substance of the text nor any of the basic facts. I am to wonder whether the Yugoslavs ever directed their ambassador and their intelligence people in Australia to check and corroborate this fabrication which I had created. My theory later is that the military intelligence faction did not really give a toss, and simply concocted any old story as quickly as possible in order to force a conviction, or to justify an extra-judicial execution. To get their glorious moment in the sun. To do their bit for the war.

Sentence by sentence Chief takes me through the sensational scenario: 'Right, Major Pret, you will now in this sentence write who your agents were assisting you to collect the information about NATO targets. We would like you to state that you passed this secret information to your intelligence chief, "Shels Tep" (CARE Australia's Charles Tapp). You will in the following sentence describe how "Tep" came to Yugoslavia in May 1997 and gave you your espionage orders. Write this now.'

I protest, if only to say how ludicrous and unbelievable it sounds. Scarface comes around quickly and hits me over the side of the head, adding to the ringing in my head. 'Pret, I remind you that these are the rules of the game and you must stay with these rules,' says Chief, ramming it home, though I can hardly hear him through the ringing in my left ear. He demonstrates again the vertical hand over the horizontal, reminding me of my finely balanced life, as he would describe it.

We go on like this for two, maybe three, hours. I don't know how many exactly, I lose count. It must be 2 or 3 am, and it's still raining. The air raid sirens have gone off again but these blokes are not fazed. They don't bother to evacuate the house for shelter. In fact the sound of distant bombing crunching away somewhere, perhaps north near Novi Sad, seems to enrage Chief, and, for a moment, he even seems to believe his own propaganda. He rages at me: 'NATO! You have helped these planes!' But the other two and the interpreter sit placidly. Chief, I feel, is acting — all the show, bluster and wind are geared to impress me. He does. I am severely defeated. They have taken my soul and turned it inside out. I have lied, I have been forced to 'shop' my colleagues and my organisation.

These bastards have selected from my staff list the most likely candidates for the 'espionage network' — those staff who have held down the most important positions, in terms of either their function or their geographic location, and who therefore best fit the picture they intend to create. Peter Wallace and Jim, by dint of their nationality and the key positions they held in the CARE Kosovo program, are selected. Chief laboriously works away, questioning me about the relationships among these staff and their exact duties, particularly their movements and professional associations over the past months. He works away cleverly, I must say, fitting each of the key staff into key 'espionage positions'. The hypocrisy is breathtaking. The potential destruction of lives for the sake of Chief's cause is also breathtaking. I would never have believed that in the 1990s such things still existed. I can picture the old Soviet 'Star Chamber' of the 1930s, the 'fixing up' of Stalin's 'enemies of the state', outrageously charged and led away to the gulag or their deaths. The model lives on in Yugoslavia, I now know. My distress deepens as I ask myself what is going to happen to these people of mine. To what degree will Peter be implicated?

Chief expertly works Branko Jelen into the alleged espionage network. Branko is selected because of his field role in the south, his long association with me and his key responsibilities over so long a time in Kosovo. As one of my and Melissa's four field team leaders in the country, Branko was the one responsible for monitoring humanitarian deliveries to the 147 Serbian refugee centres which had been located in Kosovo for two or more years. I am to say to Chief that 'Branko was my right-hand man for the distribution of refugee assistance in the entire south of the country ...' The selective quote, 'Branko was my right-hand man ...' is to come back to haunt me later, as a quotation they will read back in court to justify Branko's arrest. It is also a quote the secret police are to throw into Branko's face in a jail cell in Nis in the south of the country, two or three nights later. Understandably, Branko is to carry anger against me for this, but he is not yet to know the true context in which these things were said.

Branko has also been our key field staff supervisor for the running of programs supporting six medical centres in the Kosovo refugee centres. These programs had essentially serviced Albanian Kosovar displaced people, but also displaced Serbs and gypsies, casualties of the 1998 guerilla war in Kosovo. Because of the nature of his business, Branko Jelen's name was frequently recorded in my telephone conversation records. It was a simple matter for the military intelligence people to take these recorded conversations (all related to our refugee and displaced people work, the delivery of food, winter heating fuel and medical supplies, the bombing of the refugee centres by NATO, for example) and twist them to fabricate conversations about espionage activities. Allegedly, and in their twisted logic, Branko and I were discussing the results of NATO bombing on 'strategic military targets', when we had actually been discussing the tragic bombing of the refugee centres. We had discussed this most energetically and frequently in the previous two weeks. Furthermore, discussions and meetings that Branko and I had had in late 1998, where we had talked about the deteriorating security situation in Kosovo — which were about identifying those areas that field staff and contractor supply convoys should avoid — now become the basis of new fabrications.

I continually try to steer the interrogation back to a description of Branko's real duties. During one deeply bitter moment, as I am being dictated a particular piece about Branko, I rebound, refuse and say to Chief, 'I cannot say that about Branko, because that is untrue and will be incriminating.' He responds, 'Major Pret, do not worry about Jelen, you must worry about yourself and you must worry about your family.' This becomes a regular exchange in what becomes a futile and hopeless battle to salvage Branko and other key staff. I brace myself for Branko's arrest. This greatly saddens me, because I reckon they will give Branko a terrible time. Curiously, very little is said to me about Peter Wallace, and I am perplexed by this. I am able to steer a lot of the questioning in Jim's direction, knowing that he is out of the country. I wonder at the time whether Jim will mind this.

I am able to repeat this exercise later with the two key Albanian Kosovar staff, whom I know (from information we received some five days earlier) have crossed the borders out of Kosovo. I am thus to take a little heart in reducing the damage by some small degree. The beatings have continued sporadically, and once more I am taken up into the 'beating room' for, mercilessly, a short working over. It seems to be a reminder beating after another argumentative session, to stiffen me up and put the fear of God back into me, which it does. I am frightened, battered, completely dispirited, fatigued, feeling powerless and at the mercy of these mongrels. At some late hour in the morning they finish the session and return me to the local jail. Back at the jail I am handcuffed uncomfortably to the wall heater again. I try to sleep on two seat cushions tossed at my feet, with my arms at an odd angle and raised. I am exhausted and sleep fitfully, but wake what seems a few hours later to streaming sunlight, and with badly twisted and aching shoulder blades. My head throbs, I am in pain all over. I realise with a shudder, it has all been more than just a bad dream.

Through the morning I am seated and handcuffed and left to my own devices. I doze on and off. The pain slowly subsides, which is a good thing, because there is no medical attention. Scant food and the odd Turkish coffee is brought my way. The mood of the police hardens; indeed the English interpreter from the first of the police interrogations now scowls at me, all friendly banter gone. 'So you are a NATO spy after all,' he says with contempt. Occasionally the police look in through the door to check whether I am still there, or still alive.

In the afternoon, as I am again seated facing the wall, about five policemen come into the room, gain access to a large safe and start loading pistols and AK47s. They all do this while at the same time watching me with contempt. One of them motions to me with his weapon that I should be, or will be, shot. Much pushing home of firing actions, sliding of bolts and clacking of ammunition cases. I wonder whether this is just a show to put the wind up me, to soften me up for the next round of questioning. Probably. But that chill goes racing up my spine again. How long, I wonder, can this nervous system of mine put up with this, the regular references to death and the worry about others?

Through the afternoon I constantly think about Samira, and I pray quietly and often. I now strain my ears and imagine I can detect Peter's coughing. I am pretty sure I can hear him one or two rooms away, and this is somewhat encouraging. Hoping he is OK, I am at the same time discouraged, for I had hoped he would have been let go. To get away, to get help. At one stage it seems that I can hear Peter being interrogated. Just faintly I think I can make out his voice. I cannot decipher what he is saying, but the voice sounds English and I am sure I can pick that tone which is so different from the harsh Serbian tongue. If it is Peter, he does not sound stressed and his voice is even and calm. I do not hear the same dramatic police shouts and yells that accompanied my interrogations. I am to find out some three months later, in my first discussion with Peter, that his ordeal, while no picnic, has been different; significantly less stressful and far more peaceful than my experience. Peter is to eventually tell me that he was not beaten and that he was questioned mainly about me. Using Peter to gain additional information for my interrogations, they seem to indicate to him that they consider him to be the 'unwitting' junior partner accompanying that dreadful bastard 'Pret'.

We are to have a good laugh about all this when we are reunited. But of course when the indictment is struck, months later, Peter is banged up as a little more 'witting' than the police and the military intelligence have indicated in these early days. Despite the absence of beatings and the shortness of interrogations, and the more pleasant interchanges between prisoner and interrogators as described to me by Peter retrospectively, his life may well have been in just as much danger as mine, if only because getting rid of me may have had an automatic 'knock-on' effect for him. Get rid of them both, their vehicles and all possessions may well have been one of the military intelligence team's scenarios. I think the jury will be out forever on the question of Peter's fate. Unpredictable possibilities, perhaps. Thank God the worst was not to be.

CHAPTER FOURTEEN
Military Non-Intelligence

In the early evening of day three, I believe it was 2 April, they come for me again. I experience the same car routine, and just as roughly. Once more they place me in front of Chief. Chief looks at me coldly, then motions to the other two men, who spring up and take me away again to the beating room. I feared this would happen. They do me over, but a little less savagely, certainly careful again not to cause major damage. God it hurts though, and I grunt with every hit, except across the face, when I just stare straight ahead. I do not cry out, but it is a hell of a battle not to. I am now shaking uncontrollably; it is getting much worse than before. My legs shake so much I can hardly walk straight. They see this and laugh. I am humiliated, and left feeling deeply bitter and entirely hopeless. I am taken back to the seat and we commence a new phase of interrogation.

The interpreter has been changed. Beehive is gone and in her place is a more competent interpreter, and a more pleasant woman at that. She is attractive, younger, auburn-haired and tastefully dressed in dark blue slacks and a dark cardigan. She looks intelligent, even vaguely kind, and I wonder how the hell she ended up in this den of thieves. 'Auburn' even speaks pleasantly and calmly, although she still conveys the death threat with clarity. She does it more euphemistically, avoiding the harsh words, saying, for instance, '... you know, they are serious and would have to do something extreme to you ...'. I am sure this is another case of 'good cop, bad cop'. She even apologises for the evening preliminary beating, and seems genuinely sorry, smiling gently and tilting her head. Jesus, what a bloody nightmare! I think I am losing my mind. But I strive to maintain my dignity, fight to keep my calmness and to keep my head. Even if I have to lie and contribute so damagingly to this charade.

The questioning and the bullshit statement writing goes on in much the same way as the night before, although with a greater emphasis now on my weekly and sometimes daily situation reports, particularly those I had sent to CARE Australia in the last few weeks. Of the forty-odd SITREPs they have in their possession covering the last twelve months they single out six for special attention. These are on average one and a half to two pages long, consisting generally of ten paragraphs, and are the same as the CARE Australia country mission SITREPs that I had routinely written over the six years of my CARE experience. The objective of these reports was to summarise all major happenings in the country mission for the period covered, usually a week, sometimes a fortnight. When the situation broke down into a severe and complex crisis, I would produce SITREPs daily and often twice daily. 'As the situation dictates', as we were fond of saying in the military, and now a basic practice of management in humanitarian emergency work. The SITREP would routinely cover such matters as the general state of the humanitarian mission, the progress of current aid programs specifically, updates on newly identified humanitarian needs, future aid program intentions, administrative and logistic imperatives affecting the mission and general observations about the country situation impacting on the country mission, including the safety and the prevailing security situation.

These SITREPs were sent in addition to other regular mission reports such as program progress reports, humanitarian 'needs assessments' reports, financial and budget reports and other administrative and technical reports. I would often write these documents myself, but often, too, I would delegate the preparation of the technical reports to my colleagues. In such cases I would approve and sign off on them. Often the SITREP would summarise the key points of all of these other reports, thus allowing head office staff in Canberra to, at a glance, update themselves on the situation of the particular country mission. The same SITREPs would also, but not always, be sent to CARE sister organisations around the world, depending on their current involvement or imminent involvement in our country mission support and funding support. This is the way the CARE federation best functions, through a sharing of knowledge and pre-emptive advice.

The last four weeks of SITREPs and two covering the October 1998 guerilla war period had a heavy component of safety and security information in them, although taken in their entire context, they read as balanced mission reports. This fact was not to be brought forward by the Yugoslavs or even the media in Australia, where sensationalised assessments were to be made of these reports. The SITREPs were the urgent medium for alerting my head office, and the CARE organisations round the world directly involved in supporting our Kosovo mission, of the acute danger the mission was in. They were the means by which we could let others know about the safety of staff, the dangerous potential for the disruption of programs (which included the potential loss of up to US$2 million in donated funds), and, most importantly, the dangerously deteriorating situation with respect to the growing human crisis. Naivety and ignorance, in the ranks of the Yugoslav military, in the Yugoslav judiciary (and regrettably also later in an immature Australian media), will mean that a handful of these SITREPs are misread and twisted into documents of alleged 'espionage'.

During the critical phase leading up to war and then during the war itself my knowledge grew, being built on by regular discussions with my colleagues and other field staff, and by update information acquired at UN and other agency meetings. Furthermore, I had relied greatly on the UNHCR and OSCE KVM daily safety and security bulletins for vital information on incidents which had occurred in CARE's area of programming. These UNHCR and OSCE bulletins had been distributed by e-mail and hand mail daily, often twice daily, right across Yugoslavia, available to all fifty-five international NGOs and UN agencies. And also sent to the Yugoslav Government!

So it is with an incredulous shake of my head that I am to greet Chief's ignorance of these information bulletins. The knowledge they contained contributed to the daily picture I could present through the SITREPs, allowing CARE Australia to make very timely emergency policy decisions. Sister CARE organisations around the world supporting the country mission were able to contribute immediately to the 'strategic humanitarian planning' undertaken relative to the Kosovo overspill emergency that affected the Balkans generally. The SITREPs had thus become an integral part of the emergency planning during the months and weeks leading to war, and beyond. Information about military activities impacting on CARE's safety and influencing the unfolding humanitarian disaster had formed a minor but vital part of these reports. It is these few paragraphs about the fighting, a few hundred words taken from forty-odd SITREPs, which become central to the military intelligence interrogation.

During the interrogation I do not deny the contents of these six SITREPs. I deny that the information represents 'secret military information', which Chief insists it is. I argue that the information included in the SITREPs was not gathered secretly. This is not secret military information, it is information about fighting, widely known in the humanitarian community at the time. It was discussed daily in detail in crisis meetings amongst international agencies and it was reported daily in UN and other agency safety information bulletins. Included in the safety information bulletins were the details of military forces, where they were fighting and which way they were heading. I argue until I am blue in the face. Chief tires of this strident arguing and reminds me of the 'rules of the game'. He wins the argument and I am forced to write into the statement that these SITREPs, sent openly and filed openly, were 'espionage reports', which were sent to my 'espionage headquarters' in Canberra (ie CARE Australia). The bitter charade continues.

A degrading episode — but nevertheless a respite — soon occurs. Chief is obviously happy that he is making progress. He breaks out the plum brandy, and I am staggered to be offered a drop. Even Scarface is smiling. Scarface then brings out a platter of sandwiches, cheeses and cold meats. It must be well past midnight; we have been at this for hours. It suddenly occurs to me that I have not been beaten for hours, a small luxury. I am utterly drained once more and fuzzy in the head, but I wolf down the food which is offered. I cannot believe my eyes as, with polite ceremony, they offer the food to me before they themselves partake. Suddenly I am actually reminded of that part of Serbian culture and community I have to come to like — the eating, drinking and merriment. Serbs are very good hosts. These villains who were bashing me some hours ago are now my very kind and warm hosts! The transformation is staggering, and there is genuine warmth in their eyes when they offer me a beer. 'Ah, you Australians (what happened to the British agent?) love your beer. Yes you must have a beer with me,' says Chief. But why should I be so surprised at this transformation, this unpredictability? This is what I have come to expect in this country, this society, this culture. The mood swings here are savage, and there is a penchant for going to war, a penchant for killing at the drop of a hat.

After the food, there is an air of relaxation about the place. Why not? I ask myself. After all, I am, sentence by sentence, co-operating with their concoction. My hopes are raised a little, although the situation is so unpredictable I could be just as well taken out and got rid of, if it suited them. I am taken back to the jail, at God knows what time. I am so bone weary I do not care about anything much any more. The food and the beer were bloody good though, helping a little to fortify me. I am chained to the wall, as usual, but now on three chair cushions (I seem to have graduated). I collapse into a deep sleep.

I am woken again by the rough and noisy entrance of two plain-clothes men. Not too gently they un-handcuff me and then order me to put on a jumper which they have brought from somewhere. My jacket, which I treasure, is inexplicably removed. I am told to hurry, hurry. I am dragged outside again, into pitch black dark. I am very tired and half-conscious, the result of a combination of very little sleep, hours of stress and now one beer, which clearly went to my head. Bundled into a car, a larger car this time, and very roughly handled by this absolute bastard, who takes delight in ramming my arms, handcuffed behind me, right up my back again. The cuffs are very tight and cut into my right wrist. I have to fight the returning panic again, to keep telling myself 'It's OK Pratty, everything will be alright!' But I am heavy breathing again and frankly shit scared. This is the small hours of the morning — where would they be taking me now? Was that lovely supper and beer the 'last supper', some quaint Serbian pre-execution ceremony, perhaps for army officer prisoners of war? I fight with my mind to rid myself of these silly thoughts, but it is a battle. 'God save me,' I mutter. I must have muttered aloud through gritted teeth, head bent in bag, because I get a sharp elbow in the ribs, accompanied by a guttural grunt.

We pull up about five minutes later. It is raining again and I sense the car veer off the road. Police or military agents, whatever they are, get in and out of the car. Much discussion and muttering. Another car pulls up behind us. Lights are killed. I can see enough under the bag to sense these things. What now? Am I to be pulled out of the car and marched off into the scrub? Is this the river bank of soft mud? I await the harsh sound of gun metal, the sliding of bolts and the clash of hammers. I can hear the wind blowing heavily through a thicket of trees and have the impression we are on a stretch of lonely country road, in the darkness of the wee hours. It is bloody frightening. I am breathing deeply to try to control myself and manage to slow down my racing heart. I sense a number of men milling around. I suddenly hear a vehicle's alarm going off and recognise it as that of my Land Rover. Interesting. I patiently wait for whatever fate is about to befall me. I silently make my peace. I pray for Samira, Haydon, Mum and others I hold dear to my heart, but especially my immediate family and the unborn child. My head is forced between my legs and in my tight little world between two car seats I ask God to take care of my loved ones.

Suddenly there is rapid movement, men piling into a number of cars, doors slamming, and we are off. I calm a little. I now get the sense that we have turned onto the freeway, and I further sense that we have turned east. After about ten minutes of driving I am sure we are on the freeway and I reckon we are heading towards Belgrade. My mood improves; this is a good sign. I complain about the handcuffs, which are viciously biting into my right wrist. I hear a voice and recognise it as the English interpreter from day one. He snaps at the goon next to me to fix the problem. Then he snaps at me and says, 'Why didn't you say something before?' Because I was in my own little world of shit-scared fantasy, you idiot, I want to say, but don't.

The car sounds and performs like a medium-sized BMW, purring along at high speed. I judge by the increased light penetrating my paper hood and the time taken that we are in Belgrade. I hear the sounds of the sirens go off, accompanied by 'shit!' exclaimed by the guards. We accelerate quickly. My feeling is that we are crossing the bridge over the Sava River, which they want to get off in a hurry, as the bridges are already targeted by air attacks. The mournful sound of six or so air raid sirens echoing across the city confirms for me that we are in Belgrade. There is some hectic driving around wet streets and we arrive at our destination.

Out of the car, pulled roughly, cursing me. Again roughly handled. Shit, I am shoved up against a wall, still blindfolded — dead silence, and then more cocking of weapons. Low murmuring. Head pushing against the wall, hard, and held hard — I can hear the bloke breathing close to me. I tremble, is this it?

I am hauled inside a building and shoved onto a comfortable bed of some sort. Again there is the sound of weapons being cocked — or unloaded, I am not sure — and as always it puts the wind right up me. But I am too tired now to wonder what is next. Do not give a stuff. Another mock execution preliminary? Hooded, I am forced to lie on the bed. Then I am handcuffed (one hand) to a bar behind my head. The idiot who put me on the bed, forces the hood back onto my head and I lie there in complete darkness. I feel comfortable, for the first time, and soon fall into a deep sleep.

I awake on what must be 3 April, woken by lights being turned on in what must be my cell. With my one free hand I tentatively remove the hood a little. I see that I am in what appears to be a motel room — carpeted walls, bunk bed, table and even an ensuite bathroom! It seems to me to be a motel room converted to a prison cell. The two windows are small and high above my head and I have the impression this cell is half below ground level. There is very little light coming in through the windows. Suddenly I hear the clash of keys on doors and two doors are opened, an outer first, then an inner, grilled one. An old man with a torch enters the room and places a tray of food on the table. He undoes the handcuffs and motions to me to eat. He brings me some sort of coffee, and while I still hate coffee, again I wolf it down. The food is not actually too bad, although I suppose compared with the shit I have consumed and the general absence of food, anything will do. Mashed potato, slab of meat and gravy, hard bread, but all filling, which is important. I need to get my strength up for the sake of survival.

Out of the blue, Chief and Coconut Head come in to the cell. They sit down and without an interpreter (and in very broken English) ask whether I am OK, have I eaten, 'da, da, dobra, dobra …' Chief is friendly, indicates that the interrogation will soon recommence. They leave. I reflect on my position. It seems they have decided that I am useful; perhaps they can create some further scenario with me for their political purposes. They have brought me back to the city to develop their plan. For the time being I suppose I am useful. I take a lot of heart and now believe I have a reasonable chance of survival. I think again of Samira and the family, and through whatever kind of telepathy I can muster, I will them not to worry, to take it easy. I can hear somebody coughing in the distance, and think it is Peter. Too far away for me to call out to him. I hope he is OK, and wonder what state he is in, how he is coping. I cannot do a thing for him, cannot discuss him with Chief; I am powerless to help him or, for that matter, myself. The cells are muffled, a side effect of the carpeting.

I am very, very sore, all over. I have a sickening pain in my head which nauseates me, just throbbing away, the product of too many blows across the head. My mouth feels tender — there are some lacerations inside. My ribs are really hurting, although I notice that breathing does not hurt, which is a good sign. The chest is OK where Scarface had landed his flying kick, sore but not too bad. My right ear though is giving me hell, as are my right wrist and right shoulder blade. This stocktake of the body reveals that nothing seems to be broken. I am not pissing blood, nor do I feel any untoward lumps in my stomach, which might indicate some sort of internal damage.

For the first time I am un-cuffed and free to move properly. A small demonstration of hope. Hope, hope, hope is what it is all about now. I am still in deep trouble, still very much on the razor's edge. I must be, because this is a very tiny jail, which I suspect is secreted away somewhere, a hidden institution deep in the bowels of secretive Belgrade. I sense I am very much on the missing list still, my fate most unpredictable.

It is 3 April and the interrogations continue. They have added three more intelligence agents to the team and two young female interpreters. The interpreters are as innocent-looking as any of my own young female Belgrade staff; they look to me like university students brought in for the occasion, but I doubt that, given the secret nature of the work. Thankfully, they speak good English. Two agents now do most of the interrogating, with Coconut Head attending occasionally. I am taken once a day to see Chief. The pattern of forced statement-making continues, and sometimes I am hit savagely over the head, without warning and on impulse, but as before, with an open-handed hit. Small mercies. The hitting, while frequent and continuous this next few days, is much less intense than that of the first forty-eight hours. But the death threats are just as frequent and the psychological torture now even more intense. The interrogators enjoy leaving me with the impression that I am a doomed man.

On one occasion one of the young interpreters appeals to me to tell the truth, to revisit what I have said, to provide more in-depth information, to confess to 'marking the targets and guiding in the air force bombers; for God's sake and for the sake of your life you must co-operate!' She finishes in tears and shaking her head, and is led from my cell by her female companion, leaving me blinking in wonder. This pattern of behaviour on the part of my interrogators goes on for two days and nights, interrogation after interrogation, often going over the same old ground, occasionally writing the next phase of the so-called 'interrogation statement'. The statement continues to be prepared sentence by sentence, usually produced by Coconut Head and/or Chief. Then the younger agents and their interpreters return for a session of plain questioning, often referring to the coerced statement most recently written. They have me entirely confused.

The young agents demand to know the truth and often accuse me of lying. They will scream and threaten me with billy-clubs and 'demand the truth'. So I find myself dancing between their labours to 'prove the story' according to 'the rules of the game', and their sometimes genuine questions about my real life and work in Yugoslavia. I confuse them and, often at 2 or 3 am in the morning, I confuse myself. And get beaten up for it. The two young agents are tough, although at times there are moments of humour. If they are happy with the session just completed, and if during an occasional moment of actually telling the truth I am able to describe the work that CARE and I have really done, they allow themselves to become fascinated, impressed that so many Serbian refugees should have been well cared for, for so long. They relax, they listen, they confuse me. But not their seniors, not Coconut Head and Chief. They have no sentimental capacity at all and resolutely march towards the goal of completing their fabricated story. I am wary of these starkly different sets of attitudes from the two teams conducting my interrogation. I don't wish to make light of the viciousness of the younger agents, though — they are more prone to bash me and they are cruel in their psychological torturing techniques. It is simply surprising that they also appear so interested in the truth of my work and existence in Yugoslavia. They happily question me about all that. The reality is, however, that they too adhere to Chief's template for the 'rules of the game', and ruthlessly work away to the game plan. They put me under intense questioning and clearly are looking for ways to pin on me the role of 'NATO bombing scout'.

Though the interrogations go on around the clock, they allow me four-hour blocks of sleep at night. They concentrate on my seven most senior Belgrade office staff, and for hours and hours I am on the defensive about these people. I am accused of setting these people up as 'espionage agents'. They seize on my office pay records and focus on the overtime payments. I am accused of paying additional wages, ostensibly espionage allowances disguised as overtime. How bloody ridiculous, I respond. I am now way beyond the point of good manners, and point out that espionage agents would surely get paid more than 100 dollars a month for the type of dangerous duties which we are being accused of carrying out. They do not get the point at first, and this overtime payment factor, which they seem to consider a goldmine of an opportunity for their fabrications, just refuses to go away. I have a strong sense now that they have pulled in some of my staff for questioning. I can sense that the financial and administrative staff have been questioned about the overtime payment system. It hits me time and time again just how ignorant these so-called military intelligence people are. They have no concept of how international organisations work, no idea of their administration, code of ethics, administrative parameters or, most importantly, their operational safety needs. How do these bastards get themselves paid and administered, I wonder? Via Genghis Khan, no doubt! I see there is little hope in appealing to anybody's commonsense and decency in getting myself or my staff out of this mess. I remind myself yet again that I am dealing with ignorant, paranoid and dishonest fools.

The air raids now are intense, by day and by night, increasingly by night, indicating to me that NATO is stepping up its air raids (as against cruise missile strikes). Anti-aircraft fire now increases, but only during the night, when they must feel that the anti-aircraft batteries are less vulnerable. There is a cacophony of anti-aircraft batteries booming away. Ear-splitting noises of cannon and machine gun fire — clearly some of these anti-aircraft units are very close to this prison. Hard to resist the thought that a lot of the anti-aircraft fire is just bravado, to impress the civilians, to make heaps of morale-boosting noise. I wonder whether I am to be trotted out as a target hostage, lashed to a television tower or something like that. The deafening, deep, slow cyclic throb-throb-throb of the heavy millimetre cannons booms out. This is interspersed with the hair-raising sound of the fast-firing multibarrelled heavy machine guns, like metal sheets being ripped apart. What a symphony. Even the interpreters give up trying to question me. The noise is deafening, the echoes reverbrating through the canyons of the city. I recognise the sound of the weaponry, all so familiar from the fighting in northern Iraq — it's the same Soviet equipment. In the background I hear again the deep 'crump – crump – crump' of falling bombs.

CHAPTER FIFTEEN
The Confession

It must be the early morning of Sunday, 4 April. The bombing and responding anti-aircraft fire has woken me twice during the night, but I have had some substantial sleep, for a change. Regardless of exhaustion, getting to sleep is not easy. I have devils racing in my head that make sleep difficult. Last night the television upstairs was booming and I recognised the voice of the Yugoslav Foreign Minister, Juvanovic. While I was unable to decipher much of what he was saying, my limited Srbski picked up sufficient to recognise what was a ranting, raving and I suppose stirring address to the nation. When I can hear the TV upstairs, these addresses seem to dominate the television. Juvanovic screams as he presents solid propaganda. I am surprised at the strength and constancy of his screaming, having never heard anything like it in my life. No doubt a stream of invective against the state's enemies, which no good citizen would dare question, especially not if he were in company.

During my wakeful moments at night I have fantasised about escaping; such thoughts and dreams have come to dominate my thinking time, between interrogations. I swear to myself that given the chance, I must escape; I am not waiting here to die like a dog. I have imagined disconnecting the long chrome metal tap faucet in the toilet, the only item I can see in this whole cell that I could possibly work free. I have imagined hiding behind the toilet door with blankets rolled inside my bed to represent me sleeping. I have then imagined the poor old fellow who delivers the tucker coming in early in the evening, delivering my dinner tray and shaking me awake. I will step from behind the door and clout him with all my strength, hoping to kill him. I bank on his confidence that I am knackered and dispirited, and at age fifty no sort of physical threat anyway. So far he has always come to my cell alone.

This fantasy of willingness to kill does not shock me at all — I have always known that I would consider such action at a time like this. This willingness only reflects my desperation and desire to survive. If I stand a chance of being killed by execution, then I am prepared to kill, and I have made peace with myself on this score. I imagine dragging the body into my bed and covering it with the blankets to represent me. I take his keys and slip outside, hoping that the exit is easy. I have worked out that there are no more grilled doors beyond my cell. In the stumbling walks that I have taken up to Chief's office I have never passed through locked doors. I have heard the parking of vehicles quite close to my cell, uninterrupted in their approach and exit to this interrogation complex. I judge, or imagine, that this military interrogation centre is in the middle of Belgrade city. I conceive that there will not be any guards posted, as I have not heard any regular movement of people around the outside of this cell or the surrounding building.

My fantasising at this time knows no bounds. I imagine running in the night (holding up my jeans without the belt and awkwardly keeping my laceless shoes on) out across the street, and reckon I have a few hours free of discovery in which to get clear. It seems to me, from the sound of river transport noises close by and the sound of trains below me, that this little prison could possibly be above the confluence of the Sava and Danube Rivers. I wildly and recklessly imagine running down the hill and flinging myself into the Danube, swimming out to a coal barge and burying myself in one of its holds. Riding with the barge down the Danube I imagine crossing the border 30 kilometres downstream into Romania. Voila!

Too simple and fanciful, I admit to myself, but as the weeks pass the plans are to take on substance and a little more realism. The reality is, however, that escape seems nigh on possible. But still I dream and hope, and hope. To try to relieve my anxiety — and, more importantly, to pump myself up, to inject positiveness — I pace my dark little cell. The lights in my cell are rarely on, by day or night, except when they wish to shine the bright beam of one particular light into my eyes. Otherwise I am left to my own devices in the semi-dark, which is the most light I ever see through the entire day. I have mapped out a 7 metre walk, with a slight curve to detour the bed and maximise the available space. I learn to pace quickly, turning quickly on the ball of my foot at each wall. Hands in pockets and moving my shoulders vigorously in a shrugging movement to ward off the cold, I talk myself into a positive frame of mind, reassuring myself, talking to my family. It is a constant battle, however, to retain any positive feelings at all.

Over the next 48 hours little changed. Absolutely no news from anywhere about Peter and me. Strong encouragement and support continued for Samira from the Australian embassy, including the Belgrade office team, and from CARE Australia. Samira was advised by Brian Doolan that Ambassador Chris Lamb was to return from his leave in Australia to see what he could do. Samira heard that CARE CEO Charles Tapp would accompany him. They were expected to arrive about 3 April. She also heard, and was encouraged by this, that Malcolm Fraser was making plans to come as soon as possible to enter formal negotiations to determine our whereabouts and our fate. Samira's spirits began to lift. There seemed to be action and everybody was aware of the problem now. Something had to break soon.

But the thundering silence from the Yugoslav authorities continued, with all knowledge of our whereabouts or previous movements emphatically denied. Samira was to feel the same deep frustrations and anxieties as both CARE Australia and Australian diplomatic staffs felt over these next four to five days, when there was not the smallest hint of our movements or fate from anywhere.

She again called Mikhail. He had nothing to add, and was understandably very pressured. He, to use Samira's description, 'cried' about the NATO bombing. He was both fearful and angry about the bombing across the country. Samira sympathised; like me, she did not agree with the West's country-wide bombing campaign, but she was more fervent than me, for Samira was passionately anti US military aggression. She deeply sympathised with the Iraqi people, for example — victims, she insisted, of bone-headed, reckless US military action. Amidst her own grief and worries Samira shared Mikhail's woes for a minute, comparing the plight of the Yugoslav civilians with that of the Iraqi civilians, all victims of pariah regimes.

On Saturday, 3 April Jason had reached the Lipovac border. The Croatian authorities were adamant, telling Jason that no Australians in UN vehicles or any other forms of transport had crossed the border since the outbreak of war. Jason was treated with a heavy hand when he approached the Serbian side of the border; he was refused entry and found it difficult to speak to anybody. He spoke quite competent Serbian but found himself severely stuffed around. The border guards and plain-clothes officials who spoke to him made fun of him and abused him. They denied all knowledge of the existence of myself and Wallace, denied that we had ever approached the border. During a weak moment one policemen let it slip that he may have seen us, but he was sternly and quickly overruled. Jason, persisting, was confronted with the waving around of weapons and the cocking of weapon bolts and hammers. He was forced to leave.

It is late in the small hours of Sunday, 4 April. I am woken by new noises — I can hear movement upstairs. I begin to tremble, wonder what is going to happen next. I instinctively know that this burst of sound — now I can hear the voices of two or three people — relates to me. I wait in anticipation, shaking from head to toe and struggling hard to control myself. Eventually it subsides but I am deeply troubled: is time running out? I am at my worst in the early hours of the morning, the traditional (and real!) time of dark and dirty deeds. The talking and banging around goes on for about twenty minutes. I hear movement down the stairs, and muffled voices. The noise heads in my direction. My heart is racing, I steel myself.

THE CONFESSION

The noise of keys clangs in two doors. Suddenly the door is flung open and there is much shouting. Torches flashing all over the place. I am blinded. The young agents, Red Jacket (he is never without one) and Marlon Brando (a likeness to the great star) come rushing in. Red Jacket, with his peculiar shrill voice sounding off, wallops me once over the shins before I can even sit up. Jesus that hurt! They pull me out of the bed and tell me to stand against the wall. They are accompanied by a short bull-necked man, also in his late twenties, whom I have never seen before. All three of them carry short black and brutal-looking billy-clubs. I am prodded by them. They all rant at me loudly. I haven't a clue what they are saying, except, 'NATO spy ... liar, liar'. Bull-neck raises his club as if to strike, a vicious look on his face, but is stopped by Marlon Brando, who speaks a little more calmly but firmly. I am told to sit on the small bench opposite my bed.

In walk the two young female interpreters, who had waited outside until the preliminaries were over. I am told that I have been lying, that my whole statement is rubbish (of course it is, I remind myself) and that I have very little time this morning to co-operate, to 'get to the bottom of the truth', or I will be taken away and 'liquidated', as 'earlier promised', before the sun comes up. They question me brutally, while the interpreters take it in turns to translate, and are very tense — they are obviously not happy to be here and their unhappiness disconcerts me. The interrogators punch away again on the question of NATO bombing in northern Serbia, around Belgrade and the surrounding districts. They continue to try and pin my Belgrade staff, insisting on their roles as espionage agents. I am shaking, I am responding quickly, this is not a good moment. I sense again, rightly or wrongly, that I am running out of time and may be on the edge of death — then almost immediately, and for the umpteenth time, I wonder if I am exaggerating my concern. I will never know. But even if I decided to tell them whatever I thought they wanted to hear me say — for example, 'yes, we were all spies and these blokes did this and this and I did this, and so and so ...' — the story would not stick anyway, could never be tested. So I make up my mind to try to continue with my defence of the truth whenever the opportunity presents.

I have now entered an entirely surreal world. On the one hand, both intelligence teams continue to force me sentence by sentence to write the fabricated statement, mainly centred around alleged activities gathering 'secret military information' in Kosovo. On the other hand, one of the two teams continues to question me about my actual humanitarian activities and duties, albeit to try to tie these to new allegations of espionage related to NATO bombing in the north of the country, but still in a less cynical way. I decide that there are two distinct games being played here, but I am so bone weary, frightened and just plain punch drunk, I cannot pick what is going on.

One conclusion I arrive at is that maybe Chief and his team have no idea where they are taking this whole exercise, beyond their desire to fit me and others up with some 'crimes'. They know this is all bullshit, and are cynically creating a big fix. They may well be genuinely angry, but they are also just probing to see what they can exploit, to see what intelligence opportunities might pop up. And I happen to be the best and only bunny they have. It is as simple as that, I reflect. I am convinced that this is the fundamental basis of my capture and interrogation. The only remaining question is how many of my staff will be sucked into the vortex along with me?

The frantic pace of questioning with the younger team continues for the best part of an hour. The place is very tense, the atmosphere very dangerous. The interpreters struggle to keep up with racing emotions and with the tempo of the questioning, as much as they struggle to return my fast responses. I respond instinctively, quickly, encouraged by the billy-clubs being slapped in the hands of their owners. Occasionally one lunges at me, a thrust into the ribs, prodding more than injurious. They are angry, and accuse me of lying, but all I can honestly and indeed practically do is go over my previous answers. Finally the tempo slows. They put out the torches and light candles. They will not turn on the cell lights because of the air strike threat.

We sit there in this dank and dingy cell, black as the hole of Calcutta, all of us in three-quarter shadow, our body outlines tinged by the soft amber glow of the three candles. The candlelight only adds to the gloomy atmosphere. They notice that I have not strayed from the truth of my story. When they point out the obvious contradictions — the truth of my Kosovo experience, which I tell now, as against the fabricated statement dictated to me by Chief — I just laugh, the first laugh for days. 'You blokes have told me at pain of death I must play by the "rules of the game",' I say. 'One story is as per the "rules of the game", and what I am telling you now is the truth.' They shrug their shoulders. What is going on? They continue to question me for another hour, going over and over all that has been previously addressed. They revert at times to the 'rules of the game' and dogmatically stick to their fabricated plot, sneering when I contradict that position. At least, I ponder, these young blokes let me talk about the truth, even if they reject it, unlike Chief and Coconut Head. Again I am told to 'co-operate, co-operate', to 'tell the truth', according to the 'rules'. I have had this banged into my head ad infinitum now for four days. The pace of interrogation is slowing; I feel some of the sting going out of it. They are relaxed now although two of the agents sit very near in close scrutiny, while the other questions. If they do not believe me or do not accept my version they at least show an interest in what I have to say. The interpreters are more relaxed and are fascinated with some of the answers about my personal position, my careers, my marriage and life experiences, especially my experiences in humanitarian operations in Iraq, Yemen and central Africa.

I cannot fathom the moods, attitudes and motives of these people, and find the whole unpredictable experience of these interrogations weird, as well as deeply onerous. I shake inside still — my knees are noticeably shaking — but I keep my chin up and continue to look right back into their eyes. I feel a second wind coming on and find a little more composure. The storm seems to be subsiding for the time being.

The air raid sirens go off. Mournfully booming away, they make my hair stand up on end again. So does theirs, judging by the reactions. It must be just before dawn, although with very little natural light filtering into my dingy little half-underground cell, it is difficult to be sure. They quickly blow out the candles. Red Jacket only puts on his torch, the light masked by his hand. He tells me to stay on the bench and not move. 'No bed!' he says. They all quickly file out, as the first anti-aircraft batteries thunder into action. Deafeningly close, although I notice that some of the batteries firing tonight have changed position. It seems they have these batteries mounted on trucks, and move them nightly to confuse NATO reconnaissance. Judging by where I think the firing is coming from, it seems to me the Yugoslavs are parking these truck-mounted batteries in areas close behind the residential apartments which dominate the inner areas of Belgrade. Very cunning, I think, though not particularly brave.

The bombing is getting closer. For the first time I can actually hear aircraft overhead. They must be of the medium fighter/bomber variety, I reflect, putting my old military hat back on. Nothing else to do right now. I hear these planes streaking through the dawn sky, clearly diving and then pulling out into steep climbs, the boom of afterburners discernible amidst the cacophony of the anti-aircraft fire.

I have snuck back to my bed. I feel safer there. Stuff the intelligence goons. Suddenly I hear the whirr of propellers. That means one of two things: either laser-guided bombs with their fins deployed or cruise missiles. The wind is right up me now. Christ, do I need this? There is a deep, thundering roar not far from me, then a mighty impact that shakes the whole building. Propellers are still whirring, the sound is closer ... another tremendous impact, even closer. The shock wave lashes my cell. I am huddled on my bed, nowhere to go. More propellers, now the sound of multiple propellers, coming closer, louder than before, impacts and greater shock waves. God, they are getting closer. No sound of anti-aircraft fire now. Whoomp!! An enormous blast and a blinding flash of light, so close that the shock wave seems to pick my cell up and shake it to pieces. The small ceiling-level windows are blown off their hinges, blown across the room and I am thrown from the bed to the floor, against the wall with the fallen windows. No broken glass; being wire impregnated it has stayed intact. Ringing ears, cannot hear anything, spots in front of my eyes, difficult to see, the deep stench of burnt something. I judge the last explosion, the last in a series of four or more which marched towards my cell, must have been within 100 metres. I can count my lucky stars that this cell is essentially below ground level, otherwise I may have been done for. As I pick myself up I can hear the crackling of something on fire, perhaps a building burning close to this prison. Oh God, I think, let this prison catch fire and burn down, let me escape!

I sit quietly against the wall as dawn breaks. The air-raid seems to have passed, although the all-clear sirens have not sounded. I am shaken to the core, the butterflies in my stomach hammering away. My whole body rattles intensely from head to foot. That air strike near this jail was a close thing. I hope Peter is OK. I wonder how long I can continue coping with these scares. Now I await the return of the interrogators; they have promised to be back to finish the business, to push the line that they want, the so-called 'truth'. They departed a little calmer than they had arrived, when they had charged into my cell threatening death and prodding away with billy-clubs. What will they do? I start to shake violently again in anticipation of the next session.

Return they do, goggle-eyed at the fallen windows in the cell. But they are not concerned about my escaping, as squeezing out through the now open windows would not be possible; the windows are too small and the exterior is boarded up. The questioning is resumed, firmly, and billy-clubs are waved around, but they definitely seem calmer than before. I am relieved, although the stomach butterflies continue unabated for the next couple of hours. Strangely, they do not seek to continue, in the coerced statement, with any detailed fabrication concerning the allegations of NATO bombing in and around northern Yugoslavia. They vaguely allege 'must have been involved in NATO air strike planning' but have decided not to create the same sort of ridiculous story that they have for other allegations. It now seems that they will not seek to write into their plot the involvement of any more staff, at least no more than those already irretrievably implicated. Branko Jelen, Peter Wallace, Jim and the two Albanian Kosovar staff (Jim and the Albanians I know have fled the country) are now clearly implicated, although it is not to be for some weeks that I confirm that Branko has been arrested.

The questioning goes on relentlessly. More breaks, even a half-decent breakfast, but always returning for additional questioning, sometimes going over all that has been discussed, sometimes exploring new avenues. Red Jacket and his offsider, Marlon, are very firm, probing, their blazing and their fixed gazes burning into me. I am forever on edge. Three or four times during the day the atmosphere will suddenly turn nasty, with shouting, billy-clubs waved and a number of prodding blows. For the most part, though, the violence has abated.

I have concentrated, for a day and a half, on offering no new information, not even on the most remote and innocent issues. The damage, I feel, has already been done with respect to the coerced statement, and this will be irreversible, but I am damned if I am going to exacerbate the problems of my position. However, I have no control over their ridiculous interpretations of my office records, and they have much to choose from, for now I know they have raided my Belgrade office and confiscated files and records. Chief has also forced me to give him my entry codes for my laptop and palmtop computers. Each day now in interrogation new items freshly gathered from the office material are presented to me with the most laughable allegations made about them. Dozens of records are thrown in my face with an explanation demanded, such explanation always being met with much scoffing and mirth: 'We do not believe you, Pret, these must be espionage messages.' This goes on hour after hour. The cruellest of these is the record of a telephone discussion between myself and Branko Jelen, concerning an incident in July 1998 when he and his team had met with difficulties at a Serbian refugee centre in central Kosovo. The telephone record indicated that Branko's team had been unable to get through and complete their delivery tasks because of the presence in the area of Serbian militia fighters, apparently members of 'Arkan's Tigers'. There was a concern that these militia were likely to return to the area, which would make the continuation of our programs in the area impossible. Branko, as I had directed him to, had reported this information to me and I had then warned all other CARE field teams to avoid the area until further notice. Chief alleges that the record of telephone calls on this issue were detailed espionage assessments where CARE had allegedly followed the movements of the Arkan militia, though the notes clearly report the contrary, and are an attempt to warn CARE staff to get out of the way.

These allegations, like all the others, are complete rubbish. CARE has never been so stupid or unprofessional as to do anything about sightings of fighters or fighting except report the facts in order to warn others of the danger. Chief's theme is repeated four or five times. Chief nominates other incident reports where again various field staff, often Branko, have urgently called in to warn about fighting and movements of either KLA fighters or Serbian police which were potentially cutting across CARE humanitarian deliveries, or actually disrupting medical distributions and food deliveries. These reports had warned of the consequential dangers to CARE field staff. My notes on these calls or on conference discussions of these issues are cryptic and brief. Chief cleverly and meticulously weaves a fabricated story around these. I can only hang my head in defeat as he does this. There seems nothing I can do as the most outrageous interpretations are made of my office notes. As is the practice in the interrogations, I am then routinely forced to dictate, sentence after sentence, alleged accounts relevant to Chief's fantastic new allegations, created from the notebooks. Branko Jelen, I realise with a sickening crunch, is steadily being woven into the plot and has now surely been fully implicated in this farce.

The interrogations go on and on, again late into the night. Sometimes the interrogators are Red Jacket and crew pushing into my cell; other times I am dragged off to see Chief for the next fabrication instalment, the next Steve Pratt notebook or file exposé. Air raids bring the only respite. The irony of this is not lost on me. Whenever I waver from the fabrication task at hand I am reminded of the threat of burial in the mud flats and banks of the Danube, said reminders usually offered by Coconut Head. Occasionally, to break the routine and throw me right off guard, I am even given a plum brandy, sometimes a beer.

The next day, 5 April, holds terror, my undulating ride of the last four days plunging me today back to the depths of fear. 'Pratty, how the hell did you get here?' I say again to myself. I have been handled more roughly than usual, hooded, handcuffed and dragged up to Chief's office. I am surrounded by about six intelligence people. Scarface, whom I have not seen for some three days, is back on stage and has been backhanding me for about ten minutes. Knocking me around as only he can — effectively, but making sure not to break anything. He is a right mongrel! I have adopted the violent shaking of the knees routine again, too much a feature of my living lately. I'm thinking fast, or as fast as I can given my weariness. A short while earlier I had been shown a statement, explained as a summary of my 'confession'. Indeed, it seems to summarise the six or more pages of lies which have been created over the last four days. So it has come to this. They have arrived at their end game, they have what they want. How useful am I now? What will be my fate? I am instructed by Chief to rewrite his summary in my own words. We struggle through this farce. I am now instructed to get myself ready to present the statement to the senior intelligence officer, the commander. I am to memorise the one-page rewritten statement. To assist me, Chief takes me through it by way of a 'rehearsal' of the presentation. I am keenly watched by the gaggle of six agents, most of them smoking hard, the youngest of them manically chewing gum. All peer at me closely and unremittingly. Scarface has his pistol on the coffee table, pointed at me, and a blue uniformed MUP officer sits at the back of the room with a Kalashnikov cradled on his knees. A strong delegation is with me in this room today for the show. It is a very chilling feeling; they all watch me closely, very silently, with little satisfied smiles. There is an air of expectation, and it all feels horribly final to me. My heart, as so often these five days since my arrest, races quickly. I silently say my prayers, give my best wishes to my wife, family and friends. I consciously do this in case I do not have the time to do so later. This does not seem melodramatic to me at the time, just something which is necessary. Such is my little, narrow, dark world at this precise moment.

Chief, through gritted teeth and enunciating slowly, via the interpreter, tells me that my moment has arrived. He tells me I have a chance to live, that if I impress his commander, the commander may decide to recommend to his superiors that I remain alive, come off the missing list and be sent to trial. I ask about Peter Wallace, and again I am told not to talk about Wallace. Scarface punctuates this response with a stinging open-handed belt across the side of my head of such force that my head is rocked violently to one side. The others sit quietly and just stare, with those stupid little smiles. Chief lets me compose myself, they take their time. Chief chillingly tells me that for my family's sake too I must co-operate. He does not say it — nobody has ever said it directly these last five days — but the implication is there that somebody just might reach out overseas and harm my family. Fucking bastards!

The commander walks in. Chief makes a great play of briefing him on what is about to happen. The crew-cut styled commander is dressed in khaki slacks and wears one of those old Vietnam-era green GI bush jackets, an American-made piece of apparel. He frowns and looks very serious. He's a fit man in his forties, ramrod-backed and very formal. Lots of deep guttural 'Dobra. Dobra'. I am to wonder later whether the commander was indeed simply the cameraman, whether Chief indeed was in charge, and this was simply another charade. I do learn later that this interrogation and reading of the statement by me to the commander is filmed, by what must have been a hidden camera located in the next room. With weapons cocked and pointed at me, still seated and looking to the commander seated to my half-left, I go through my memorised statement, saying words to the effect that 'I came to Yugoslavia to carry out espionage activities on behalf of my country and for NATO against the people of Yugoslavia. I established an espionage network utilising the staff of CARE Yugoslavia. I was directed in my tasks by CARE Australia. I also reported to JIO in Canberra ...'

The diatribe goes on. I sit there dressed in baggy jeans, by now very baggy and almost falling down, such has been my rapid weight loss. Over an old ski jumper sits my pinstriped dark blue suit coat, which they have insisted I wear for the occasion. I lean back in my chair, speak in an exasperated voice, gesture occasionally. At the time I think that this so-called confession is being audiotaped for world consumption, so I attempt to indicate that I am deliberately lying and doing so under duress, by body language and by the use of blatantly incorrect statements. I nominate in the statement — indeed I have asked Chief if I can specifically 'enhance' my statement by including this — the term 'JIO', which in fact is nonexistent. The exercise is short. The commander nods seriously and walks out.

I am hoisted to my feet, hooded, handcuffed again, and taken back down the curious external spiral staircase to my cell. I sit in the cell brooding, plain scared and waiting for what must be some sort of verdict. Useful statement or not? I am sure they are thinking, can we make any further use of this guy, will he be even more exploitable, can we make some sort of a credible case which will be of propaganda use to the state on him? I am absolutely sure these are the 'Terms of Reference' the military intelligence people are operating to and that right now they are assessing my future worth. I have no doubt they are also assessing the embarrassment factor for the state in terms of the secret arrest. Should I, or we, be got rid of, or do they have something to play with? I am sure my 'confession' is being closely assessed. I sit crunched at the bottom of my dingy little half-dark cell awaiting my fate, with a throbbing head, an aching and still ringing right ear, and struggling to control my shaking legs.

CHAPTER SIXTEEN
A New Nightmare

I sit on the floor of the cell for quite some time, and occasionally rise to walk the cell, to try to 'gee' myself up. It is difficult. I am entirely exhausted now, as it has been a torrid and terrifying four days. Hours pass with not a sound anywhere. The cell is more than half dark although it can only be mid to late afternoon, judging by the small ray of sunlight piercing a small crack in the outer wall, which is some five or more metres from the windows. I do not know what to anticipate but feel that I have come to an important milestone in this horrible journey. I think deeply of my family and friends, and silently tell my wife over and over that I love her and the little unborn 'possum' she is carrying. I wish her strength to carry on, no matter what.

The rattle of keys, the complicated door-opening ceremony. Christ! Here they come! Doors bang open and standing there are the two young agents, Red Jacket and Marlon Brando, with one of the interpreters. The blood is rushing through my beating temples. I am braced, stomach muscles knotted. Marlon says in rough English, calmly, 'You will go to trial, you are a lucky man.' He says this in a friendly manner. The young female interpreter says, almost buoyantly, 'What he is saying is that you will now go to prison to wait for your trial. You are taken off the "missing list" and now you will be officially a prisoner of the state.' And she adds, rather sweetly and genuinely, 'I think you will see your wife and your son again.' She smiles warmly and walks out.

A sensation of incredible relief washes over me, though I am still extremely cautious and untrusting, and do not wish to entertain false hopes. Red Jacket and Marlon step back into the cell and tell me that I will be transferred tonight to 'another place'. As he steps out Marlon hesitates, looks me straight in the eye and with a small but relaxed smile says, 'Now at least I do not have to kill you.' He gives me a knowing look, head tilted, and quietly walks off, crashing the doors behind him. I am left blinking in astonishment as the echoes from the crashing door bounce around my cell, standing there like a stunned mullet, not sure what to think. So, not wishing to dwell, I break into a frenzied walk. I tell myself that I do not care if they jail me for years, as long as I know that I will get out alive and that Samira knows this as well. The confidence that I will at least get out of jail alive will sustain me. If a jail sentence is what this nightmare is going to come to, I will survive it. I will have the will to survive it, I tell myself, and I will see my family. I do not deserve five minutes in jail. At worst I might be obliged to face a good talking to for being 'offensive to the regime', but I know the game is that I will be framed, charged and sentenced to prison. Dark questions about capital punishment in time of war flutter into my head, but with a shudder I force these to the back of my mind.

Samira continued to call Mikhail, though aware that he was under great pressure. He indicated that he had been on the phone regularly with Robert Yallop and Brian Doolan in Canberra. He said that there was nothing he or the other staff could do for me and Peter. They of course could not drive to the border to check the trail, and Samira understood that. Nobody was game to leave their house, let alone drive down highways. Definitely they were too frightened to visit and talk to the police, at the border or anywhere. Mikhail sounded tired and stressed. This was understandable under routine war conditions, but she wondered whether he had also been questioned by the police, or was being watched by the police. Samira realised that she could not make any more telephone calls to the CARE Belgrade office.

During the early evening they come. They hood and handcuff me for the trip to what turns out to be Central Belgrade Prison. I am stripped of my pinstripe coat and travel in jeans and jumper. The trip theme — head bent in the back seat between two guards — is repeated through the streets of Belgrade, and I recognise the all too familiar sounds. Both Red Jacket and Marlon are with me, and they and the driver talk quietly, chatting away. The same BMW-like car carries us through the centre of the city, I am sure. Lots of short steep hills, sharp bends and cobblestoned streets. Pedestrians everywhere, our driver muttering and swearing as only Serbs can in Belgrade traffic. I am tense, but for the first time on one of these car trips I am a little relaxed. I talk to myself to gee myself up. 'Everything will be fine,' I say to myself, again and again.

Another dramatic halt and I am pulled out of the car. Red Jacket, now talking to me to calm me, pats me on the shoulder. Odd bit of affection, I think. I am escorted into the prison. Through the paper hood I can see a flood of light, light everywhere, warm, amber light. The first decent light for days. There is a general hubbub of noise, many people talking, echoing voices along long corridors, much clanking of keys, all types of industrial noises. I sense that I am in the company of a great many people and in a very large and very open complex. It is an oddly pleasant feeling and soon I am almost ecstatic. Relief begins to turn into a sense of wellbeing; crazy, I think to myself, considering that I am going into jail. But I remind myself, 'One thing at a time. Perhaps I am on the road to return, the road back from the edge of the abyss.'

After being escorted by them for what seems like hundreds of metres, Red Jacket and Marlon put me into a small single cell. They treat me kindly, tell me to get some sleep and they will see me in the morning. It is a horrible little rectangular cell, 5 metres long and 1.5 metres wide. There is a wide, meshed window about 2.5 metres up, above the heavy, metal, blue painted door. There is a small wooden bench, which is the bed, with a minute table built into it at the foot. One strong, almost strobe-quality, light bores into me through the window but I do not care. I have had three and a half days in pitch darkness or dank gloominess, and this almost feels like being at the beach. Nobody else looks in through the door slot — strange, given the number of guards I can hear walking up and down outside. The guards are all shouting orders to each other and calling out commands to the other prisoners, little of which I can understand. I welcome the respite, lie on the paper-thin palliasse with its one blanket and fall into a deep sleep, light or no light.

On Sunday, 4 April Ambassador Lamb rang Samira. He was cheerful, the same old Chris Lamb that Sam had always known, the eternal optimist and non-stop joker. I was to think later that this behaviour was a good ploy, and I was grateful to Chris for dealing with Samira in this way. He was now in Croatia, having flown in through Zagreb, and had set up base at Vukovar, not far from the Lipovac crossing. He told Samira that he had no news but explained his actions and what he was trying to do. He carried his mobile, would drive daily to the border post to try to negotiate with the officials for information, while at the same time calling anybody he could in government ministries and elsewhere. He explained that their national staff in Serbia could play only a limited role, but promised they would do all they could. The regime was being unduly tough on and paranoid about all foreign organisations, including embassies. Samira was frustrated and wondered why the embassy staff were not crossing the border to go and personally see the Government. This frustration was with her daily. She knew that it could not be a matter of visas. Were the border authorities simply refusing to allow them to cross back? But that did not make sense — the Yugoslavs should have welcomed the ambassador of a 'neutral' country to witness the effects of 'NATO aggression'.

Samira was to find out some six weeks later, during a vigorous telephone conversation with a DFAT staff member in Canberra, that DFAT had indeed prohibited Lamb and his staff from crossing into Yugoslavia before 8 April. Understandably, DFAT feared for the safety of the Australians. Samira (then in London) was to hear from the DFAT staffer that DFAT officially still had no idea about the route, timings, movements, details of last mobile telephone calls etc, or even the actual border crossing, which had featured in our disappearance. The staffer was surprised, indeed shocked, when Samira briefed her on the details of that first twenty-four hours, all of which should have been clearly known to DFAT at the outset.

On the Sunday evening Samira had dinner with Ambassador Heggie and one of the guests was Geoff Kitney, the *Sydney Morning Herald* London-based journalist. Geoff and I had had beers together on my last evening at the Intercontinental Hotel, the evening of 30 March. He had conducted a lengthy interview with me, the only time I have ever been formally interviewed over pleasant jugs of beer. The objective of that interview had been to describe CARE's humanitarian programs in Yugoslavia and CARE's assessments of the growing humanitarian problem in Kosovo and the neighbouring Balkan states. Geoff was anxiously awaited by the Ambassador, Samira and others to tell of his last meeting with me — perhaps some clue might arise as to where the hell we had got to. Interestingly, I had seen Geoff go off to interview the infamous Zelko Raznatovic, or 'Arkan', the faction warlord, who had been sitting at the table next to us. Geoff had, coincidentally or otherwise, been thrown out of the country a day later, and roughly handled at the border, as well as being detained for a number of hours. Samira took from him Arkan's contact details and a copy of Arkan's business card and then faxed a copy of this to Chris Lamb in Vukovar, exhorting Chris to track down this brigand to assist in the search for Peter and me. Samira, the fox terrier, she never rested.

The lights come on and wake me very early in the morning, at the first greying of dawn. Nobody comes to look in on me for hours, although there is a buzz of activity. Sounds as if food is being delivered to the cells. People are mopping the corridor. Food containers and buckets are clanging — the place is alive with activity. A stark contrast to my last three and a half days in the military intelligence interrogation centre and before that the police station. There is lots of chatter, people calling out all the time, but it sounds more like conversation between guards; I do not have a sense of prisoners calling out or chatting. My door rattles. I sit on the side of my 'bed', the door opens and in come the two young agents, with an interpreter. They bring 'breakfast', a loaf of tough bread and one boiled egg. They are incredibly friendly, stop to chat, asking after my health, whether I am OK. The interpreter is very shy and all smiles and reassures me that all will be well. They feel that I am going to be released soon. 'Back home soon to Australia, it has all been sorted out, perhaps some misunderstandings,' she says. 'You must realise, everybody is scared of this war, people are under pressure,' she continues candidly. Marlon, the guy who some twelve hours before had said that he was glad now that he would not have to kill me, stands close and nods agreement. 'A few days, a few weeks, a few months perhaps,' he shrugs, '... you will be out, do not worry.' I am relaxed with all of this, but not really at rest. I am deeply suspicious and feel a long road is yet ahead. Still, for the time being it does mean a respite, and I make do with what I have.

Whether the agents are genuine or even really themselves know what is really going to happen, at least their attitudes this morning are cause for optimism. And I am acutely aware that I have to rebuild reserves of that commodity. Hours pass. I sit there quite happy to listen to all the noise — oh, how I have missed the sound of people and their activity. About midday the two young agents return. Again they are relaxed and friendly; I still cannot come to terms with this incredible capacity Serbs have to swing dramatically and easily from one extreme mood to the next. I have seen this all through my Yugoslav experience. This knowledge is a warning call for me.

I am escorted down about 100 metres of corridor, again hooded, but this time without handcuffs. My arms are pinned to my sides. I get the impression we have left the zone which is the territory of the military intelligence and I am being moved to another zone within the prison. A door is opened and I am gently pushed inside. Hood removed. The cell is exactly the same size as that from which I have just come. The two agents motion me gently to face the end wall, away from the door. Red Jacket slaps me gently on the arm, says goodbye, and they back out of the cell, reminding me to face the end wall and not look around.

A minute passes. Murmuring outside. Suddenly I hear the pounding of boots and two strange guards come rushing in, flinging me up against the end wall. One of them thumps me heavily over the back of the head and my face slams into the wall. The scruff of my neck is grasped, then my hair is pulled to hoist my head back, nose up. There is blood on my cheek from the blow to the wall. I am sick and tired of hearing my ears ring! Nobody says anything and I cannot see them. My legs are kicked out into the frogmarch position. They frisk my body, search all of my clothes. They are brutal. They pull my handkerchief, my only worldly possession, out of my pocket, and throw it to the floor. Suddenly they back off, bark gutturally, motion to me to stand up straight to attention and face the wall. As they leave the cell, I glimpse them — they are very young men, tall and tense. Dressed in the blue uniform of the Interior Police — baggy trousers with side pockets, waist jacket, black military boots, light blue shirts and dark blue berets. The door crashes shut, and there is a rattling of keys. I stand there dazed, but tell myself that I should have anticipated that; it's routine, expect it, do not worry about it. Simply clumsy Serbian administration.

On 5 April, and regularly over the next week, Charles Tapp contacted Samira by telephone and questioned her about my earlier movements and habits. He was taking no chances, covering all bases. He asked Sam to list all the things she could remember that we had con tingency packed for possible evacuation and which I could be expected to have in my vehicle when I departed. He asked Sam to list anything else that she may guess, from my habits, I might be carrying — equipment, personal effects and documents. Samira, then as busy as ever — a good thing, I am to reflect much later — wrote a lengthy fax which she forwarded to Tapp's hotel in Vukovar. A number of briefing notes of this type were to be prepared and sent by Sam to Charles over the next few days. Like Chris Lamb, Charles Tapp seemed to be in high spirits; clearly, he was behaving optimistically.

Samira was having terrible nights. She was constantly jumpy, suffered a racing heart and cried herself to sleep. Except she did not really sleep. And she was pregnant, which added to her stress. She woke frequently through the night and had to breathe deeply to calm herself. When I eventually heard of Sam's ordeal it nearly broke my heart.

This first fourteen days of not knowing our fate was torture for Samira and that she got through it so well was an incredible testimony to her great strength and courage. Charles continued to call Samira to 'gee her up'. He was very supportive. Samira wanted to know more information, felt at times that the CARE senior staff and the embassy staff were not as forthcoming as she would have liked. She conceded, though, that they were well intentioned and probably sought to protect her. Charles organised for Liz Miller, wife of Graham, CARE International's liaison officer in Geneva and an Australian, to come down to Budapest to keep Samira company. We remembered Graham and Liz with great fondness from previous CARE missions around the world and Samira was grateful for Liz's company.

The cell has a lino floor, the lino crumbling at the edges, and a small table half a metre square in the corner; next to the door is a squat hole surrounded by white tiles, with a tap and cistern over the top. White cement walls and no bed, just a bare floor and a blue door. Very stark, maybe 1950s vintage. Two guards come in sweating and carrying mattresses and blankets. I am told to stand rigidly to attention. I sign a receipt for the bedding, which I am told to make up, and the mattresses are put on the floor. The guards come back, open the tiny visor in the door and hurl through the gap a plastic cup, which goes bouncing across the floor. One of them grunts and motions, quite seriously, that this is for drinking. I thank him mentally for his giant intellect. The bed takes up almost the width of the cell and most of the length. There is very little standing space. I am told never to lie or sit on the bed by day. To do so means beatings, motions the young guard. (I am a little jealous when I find out three months later that Peter Wallace has been granted these privileges from day one, the bugger! Allowed to lie on his bed by day, to sit and be comfortable? An outrageous privilege! Gee!)

These guards do not speak much English and make no attempt to speak any of the few words they do know. They are very firm and not friendly in the slightest, barking orders all the time, although in time they are quite well behaved with me. For the most part, that is. Out of approximately thirteen junior officers and guards some nine or so prove to be civil. The other four are to be forever surly, contemptible and unremittingly tough. Two of these four are to be, in the first four weeks, occasionally brutal with me and, along with two other guards, regularly brutal with other prisoners.

For the first eight weeks I am rarely out of the cell and, unlike other prisoners, I am given no exercise walks. In this period I never see the other prisoners, nor do they see me. I only see guards, three of whom speak some English. I do not talk to any prisoners for the duration of this solitary confinement; not, that is, until late May, when I am reunited with Peter and Branko. Other than my interrogators and two or three brief meetings with Australian embassy staff and my lawyer, I am to have no conversations for two months. No news is brought to me, and it is about six weeks before I see my first letter from outside. I am deliberately shut off from the world. I am totally theirs. In comparing notes with Peter later, I am to find that his conditions were much the same, although fortunately he is considerably better treated by the guards and the interrogators.

For the first week I settle into the routine. The beard comes off straight away, then the hair. When the coast is all clear two guards whisk me out of my cell and take me about 10 metres down the corridor — for me a great and relieving journey out of my box. I am seated in a room and shaven to the skull by a grumpy and bad-tempered guard. The other guard, whom I now name 'Psycho', watches as my hair is massacred, and giggles, points and laughs. Small things amuse what is obviously a small mind, but I am to learn that an amazing number of the guards, including those in their late twenties and even early thirties, are just as immature. Shaved, I am hoisted to my feet by a shouting Psycho, and many orders are given for the simple action of my walking back to my cell.

On the very rare occasions on which I do venture from my cell, usually with about ten guards rehearsed and co-ordinated to ensure that no other prisoners bump into me, I walk hands behind back and head sharply tilted down. A breach of this usually results in a belt over the head, although I am to find that most guards, while liberally cuffing other prisoners, do not cuff me. Two of the mongrels do, however, take great delight in cuffing me, depending on who is watching. We do not have prison uniforms, and I live in my jeans, one shirt and one jumper, freezing day and night. It is now coming into spring, but it is still bitterly cold in Belgrade. There is no heating oil, no doubt due to the war shortages or rationing. This old concrete mausoleum is an ice box. I ask for but am not allowed contact with the outside world, am told that I am in the hands of the Military Prosecutor and that he is my only contact. I seek communications with the International Red Cross and the Swiss and Swedish embassies, but this request is met with much hearty laughter. Oh well, I muse, at least I got a laugh out of them.

During my first week in jail Branko Jelen is arrested. I am to find out much later that he was picked up about 8 April by the secret police in Nis and brought to Belgrade. His initial interrogations occur in the Central Belgrade Prison, carried out by the same Military Prosecutor staff who initially deal with me in the prison. I had been anticipating that Branko would be arrested, and now that I am in here, I still believe that some other Belgrade key staff will be arrested. So the task I find myself focused on this first week is to listen intently for any signs that any of my colleagues, particularly Branko, may have arrived in this prison. I also listen for signs of Peter Wallace, and on the second day determine that he is in a cell about six down. (I recognise his unique throat-clearing habits, habits which used to distract me. As deeply imprinted on my memory banks as my nose-blowing honks no doubt were on his.) Towards the end of the week I think I detect Branko further down the corridor — again I feel the lead weight of responsibility on my shoulders. His voice is unique, and I believe I would recognise it. I think he is there, but hope not.

I cannot seem to hear anybody else familiar, although for a few days I believe I can detect the voice and well-known sniffing sounds of one of my other Belgrade staff. I am delighted to learn later — he is named by the guards — that this person is somebody else. The guards in these first four weeks rarely call names, certainly not mine or Peter's. All the guards come to gawk at me, as do any visiting policemen. The small door slide is often slammed open, and I see gazing eyes and hear much chatter. It is usually one of the guards showing off his new charge. I am like a rare panda bear at the zoo — there is much 'arr, aha, aha', usually a small smile of satisfaction on the visitor's face and then the slide is slammed shut. Cigarette lighting occurs every two hours, the time the guards also check on the prisoners. The guards are beside themselves that I do not smoke and that over time I am not forced into taking up the habit. It becomes a big talking point in this cerebral place. How can this crazy Australian do nothing all day? He must be severely nervous, must be screaming for a cigarette. Peter and I are to develop some serious questions for these guards over the months, over a number of behavioural issues.

I am in these first few days 'hopping to', with new instructions, new drills to learn, daily cleaning routines and inspections, morning supervised shaving, all done at double pace, with stern guards presiding and much shouting. The days are incredibly slow and boring, but also bitterly cold. I am forever walking up and down the cell in a vain attempt to keep warm. A great pleasure is on a rare sunny day to stand up on my small table and stare through my window at the window across the corridor, which will on such days reflect the sunlight. I imagine that I am warm and take solace from this. Bored, freezing and intimidated by bullying guards I may be, but compared to week one of my Yugoslav arrest experience, this is a piece of cake.

On about the fourth day of my prison experience, about 8 April, I am treated to my first significant journey out of the cell, a hurried 200 metre walk, head bent, arms behind back and harried all the way by two shouting guards. From the corner of my eyes I can see the ogling guards, those in the adjacent prison sections who have never seen me. There goes the NATO spy! I am rushed along another corridor, not daring to look up, through large doors opened by sentries, and pushed quickly up two flights of old sandstone steps. The stairway chamber is built of stone, and it is cold, dark and dank, like something out of a medieval scene, reflecting the age of this old communist-era institution. On the second floor I am whisked without preamble straight into an office that overlooks the inner prison courtyard.

I am made to sit facing a large wooden table. It is a starkly furnished place — a few chairs, the table, little else. A portrait of Slobodan Milosevic adorns the place. Wire-meshed windows, the scenery beyond totally depressing. Dominating the courtyard of the prison I can see about four floors of three building wings, all decorated by the grey crumbling concrete so typical of older 1950s communist institutions. All the windows are wire-meshed, adding to the depressing feeling. The courtyard, when I am able to quickly peer out the window behind the guard's back, is a dirty, grey, disgusting-looking place. I quickly gain the impression, judging by the number of rooftops I can make out and by the memory of the number of corridor junctions I passed on the walk up, that there are probably about three or four courtyards — about five prison wings in parallel and two bracketing corridor ways — making up this fine institution.

In strides a tall, swarthy man, impeccably dressed in a green corduroy three-piece suit. The two guards with me stand to attention and I am motioned to my feet. The man immediately waves me to my chair. He has a broad strong-boned face, prominent cheekbones and one of those wild, flourishing jet-black moustaches prominent among Central European army officers at the turn of the century. He has deep and fierce brown eyes, he affects the mannerisms of a gentleman. He looks Asiatic to me and reminds me of some sort of East European plains marauder. I see him as possibly among those Serbs with a strong Turkish heritage, of whom there are many. But I remember him as 'Genghis'. He is accompanied by a young female interpreter, a law student, as it turns out. She explains this is in a friendly way and she actually sits next to me. Like most officials who have dealt with me, Genghis does not speak English, although he seems to understand it reasonably well and occasionally will break into English phrases to emphasise a point. His voice booms, and he clearly prides himself on his appearance and his presence. The girl certainly seems intimidated. I ask some questions about what the hell is happening — what is the routine, can I see an embassy or the Red Cross? He shakes his head, tells me nothing, but drearily and alarmingly repeats the phrases I am so sick of hearing. Bending forward to lean over his desk and fingering his waistcoat pocket as if he were massaging a fob watch, he booms, 'Major Pret, you are in very serious trouble, of the deepest kind, and you must co-operate with us. If you do not you may not see your family and you can expect the worst!' He announces himself as the assistant to the military prosecutor 'investigating judge'. He says that he has been through the police and special investigators' statements and reports, and my so-called 'confession'. He does not refer to the military intelligence team, just to the 'special investigators'.

When I say that I have been psychologically tortured and beaten, with confessions forced out of me, Genghis scoffs. He impatiently waves away these responses of mine. It seems that we are sitting here in a judicial institution; people are dressed in civilised ways and speaking in legal and civilised language. Nobody is standing over me, I am not being bashed and yet I learn in these first two meetings over the next three days that nothing has changed. The 'rules of the game' still apply, even though I am supposedly dealing with people who are working in the justice system, as opposed to the preceding wild elements, who were operating out of dingy hidey-holes. I am raced back to my cell — enough for one day.

Over the next two days a number of guards are to say to me that I am going to be shot after the trial. Pyscho leads the pack in this exercise. He comes to my cell, and I am told to stand to attention at the back. Accompanied by another guard he lectures me, occasionally prodding me with his billy-club. I am lectured about the evils of the West and about my own evils — Major Pret, the NATO spy. He sometimes comes to the cell after the evening meal when he is drunk, and singles me out for attention. He revels in his descriptions of my execution — the make-up of the firing squad, the formal process of execution by firing squad, the wall, the pole for lashing against. Probably no blindfold, he says, not like the movies. 'We want to see your eyes, we want to see you shitting yourself,' he laughs, actually giggles, through an interpreter, one of the guards. What am I to make of this babble? I start to dream it, to relive Psycho's lecturings. I now awake frequently, with a racing heart and very bad dreams.

Samira received a surprising telephone call from Chris Lamb, out of the blue. He reported that he was calling her from Belgrade and had finally arrived there on Thursday, 8 April. She was mightily relieved and hoped that effective action now could occur. Samira got the impression Chris was trying to contact the Yugoslav Foreign Office, but still doing it tough. Chris asked Samira whether I was carrying a British passport, discreetly or otherwise. He was very keen about this question and pressed Samira closely. Samira replied adamantly, 'No, he does not have one,' and added that Steve had only been once to the UK in his life, in January 1999, to attend a CARE International human rights conference and workshop. Lamb seemed to be mightily relieved. 'Thank you very much, Madame!' he concluded. He told Samira that 'there is a rumour running around that one of the Australians was carrying a British passport.' This was the first subtle indication to Samira that somebody Lamb was talking to must know something of the two Australians. Lamb continued to seem optimistic, joking as always, having a laugh or two. Samira felt he may have been trying to cheer her up, as his cheeriness felt somewhat at odds with the situation. During this telephone conversation Chris Lamb stated that he was not getting any clear information about Peter and me. All the 'official' people he had managed to speak to did not acknowledge that we existed, alive or dead. Knew nothing. However, Samira gained the impression that through his unofficial contacts Lamb had been advised that it was believed we were being held in a police station at Sremska Mitrovica, a small town some 20 kilometres from the Croatian border, not far off the main highway to Zagreb. Indeed, the highway that Peter and I had followed that fateful day.

Charles Tapp in his daily calls to Samira also spoke very optimistically, and hinted to Samira that he believed we were alive and in prison. Samira felt that Charles was sharing Chris Lamb's 'unofficial source' information on this issue and therefore sharing Chris's optimism. Samira marvelled at how buoyant and adventurous both Chris and Charles seemed to be. Was this some adventure? Feeling a little awkward about it, a little puzzled by this odd demonstration of enthusiasm, she nevertheless was grateful for their morale-boosting updates, irregular though they were. Yes, they were probably skylarking a little to keep her spirits up (maybe theirs as well?). Charles Tapp, unable to get over the border and indeed threatened at the border post, remained in Vukovar. He was treated aggressively and with much abuse by the border guards and officials. While I did not know anything of this at the time, it occurred to me during the first week that Charles Tapp would be trying to get into the country and I deeply feared his attempting to do so. He would be walking into a trap and was likely to be arrested, as my 'espionage boss'.

Two days later, about 10 April, I am taken back to the interrogation rooms. Genghis is there again with the interpreter. I am amazed at how the junior prison guards slouch around, berets pushed back on their heads, talking so casually with Genghis and the interpreter. Could be any old bunch of sociable Serbs, the Serbs being probably the world's greatest 'coffee housers'. I find this bizarre. I sit here quietly on my chair, with all this idle chatter going on around me, waiting for proceedings to commence.

A none too subtle threat is made. This hangs over me for the next four weeks. Indeed, it lingers for two months, until I can actually clear the matter up. Genghis immediately commences his proceedings at this second interrogation by stating that if I do not co-operate the state may take the most extreme measures in their punishment of me. He does not say 'state execution', but this is implied. When I seek a straight answer from him on this question of maximum punishment he shrugs his shoulders. I tell him of Psycho's nightly lectures and warnings that I will be shot. He shrugs again, eyes boring into mine, and says, 'The judicial investigation is not completed yet.' What the hell does that mean? I am not familiar with Yugoslav law, in peacetime or in war, and for all I know special provisions exist in war for capital punishment. The gravity of my alleged offences could attract the severest punishments, I think. Genghis nods gravely, says that now is not the time to discuss such issues, and simply repeats that the interrogations so far point to my extreme guilt. He again stresses that it is imperative that I 'co-operate' and, using the same language as my previous tormentor, Chief, says things may go easier for me 'if I follow the rules of the game'.

It is at this time that I make a significant mistake, which is to have some bearing on my further interrogations and trial. The mistake I make is to listen to Genghis's summation of my five days' worth of statements and not vigorously challenge it. Under the pressure of the moment, with Genghis reminding me of the need to co-operate and the 'extreme gravity of my position', I sign and witness his interrogation summary. Later I think that I should have refused, should have at least pressured for the presence of a laywer. But I was at my lowest ebb and just signed the bloody thing. It was a terrible, weak moment of which I am not proud. It comes back to haunt me — the investigating judge was to continually refer to Genghis's document, to harangue me about it, over the following three weeks of interrogation. As I grew physically and mentally stronger and was able to assert the truth about some of the investigating judge's statements of interview, he was still able to point to the 'continual inconsistencies'. Eventually the 'trial' will point to such 'inconsistencies' as a major factor in their so-called 'deliberation'.

On reflection, however, it seems that such a mistake is inevitable, given the state I am in at the time. Days of little sleep, psychological torture and beatings, eating little, suffering dramatic weight loss, being subjected to sheer terror and listening to threats to my staff — these have all taken their toll. There has been no respite, and now Genghis is bullying away. I am so cold that I am shivering violently. Some of the shaking is from fear. The interpreter inquires as to why I am shaking and I reply, 'because I am bloody cold'. They are testing me again, testing my resistance levels, and I am sure that I am about to enter a new phase of interrogation — over the same old ground, perhaps with a little more decorum, with an air of 'judicial process', I imagine. Maybe an absence of beatings, but I detect the psychological stuff will be the same, indeed worse, because now attrition is becoming a factor. My assessments that afternoon turn out to be correct, and for the next four weeks I am to go through a different type of hell.

I have been taken through the earlier coerced statements. I am interrogated with extreme threat by Genghis, and he makes it very clear to me that if I were to deny the statements prepared by military intelligence and those 'confession' statements of mine, 'your situation, Major Pret, will deteriorate'. He scoffs and laughs at my suggestion that the military intelligence statements were prepared under threat of death. It is a hearty laugh, a booming, angry response, and it is difficult for the interpreter to keep up and retain her composure. Genghis is singularly unimpressed and uninterested

14 APRIL 1999: The televised coerced 'confession'. (AAPIMAGE)

JUNE 1999: The meeting of 'the braves'. Samira in Belgrade, pictured here with Djeordje Durisic, my indomitable lawyer.

JUNE 1999: A lovely message from the children of Taperoo primary school, South Australia. (NEWS LIMITED)

JUNE 1999: Samira meets the very determined Dimitri Dollis (then an MP in the Victorian Upper House), who was attempting to seek our release through his very close connections with the Greek government. Here they meet in the Belgrade Intercontinental Hotel, my last place of residence before capture.

JUNE 1999: Samira with David Ritchie (second from right), Australian acting Ambassador in Belgrade, with the tireless embassy staff member John Casperson (centre), and Ross and Judy Wallace, Peter's parents.

JUNE 1999: Samira at the CARE Yugoslavia office in Belgrade with two Yugoslav staff members.

JUNE 1999: Dr Ivan Jankovic, Peter's brave and most effective lawyer, with my lawyer Djeordje in the background. Both lawyers were internationally well regarded for their human rights work and both had to withstand certain 'pressures' during our ordeal, which they did without complaint.

AUGUST 1999: Samira giving her international press conference, widely reported around the world, appealing to President Milosevic to exercise clemency. (NEWS LIMITED)

4 SEPTEMBER 1999: Peter Wallace and I, having just flown out of the Balkans, attend a press conference at Australia House, London. (NEWS LIMITED)

10 SEPTEMBER 1999: On return to Australia, meeting Samira and our new baby Yasmina at Canberra airport. David Ray of CARE Australia escorts us (left). (NEWS LIMITED)

SEPTEMBER 1999: A long-awaited visit to Taperoo Primary School, South Australia, to thank these students and, through them, all the children of Australia who sent diligently prepared messages of support to Branko, Peter and me. (NEWS LIMITED)

OCTOBER 1999: Samira and little Yasmina at friendly and hospitable Norfolk Island on a well-earned holiday.

JANUARY 2000: Catching up with old chums at the Duntroon College graduation, with Yasmina.

JANUARY 2000: Branko is free! Peter and I welcome him home at Canberra airport. (NEWS LIMITED)

MARCH 2000: With Malcolm Fraser in Canberra, both of us gratefully thanking the UN Secretary General Kofi Annan for his determined assistance in the release campaign of all three captives. (NEWS LIMITED)

in my CARE Australia work and the truth about our presence in Yugoslavia. He melodramatically waves away such discussion. He explains to me that the 'investigating judge' will now review all the 'evidence' of my case to see whether an indictment should be prepared and laid against me, to see whether I should 'go to trial'. When I ask about a lawyer, perhaps backed up by the International Red Cross, he takes this to be another joke and laughs a hearty laugh. 'We think you are a NATO spy, Major Pret, you are not entitled to privileges. This is a time of war, things are different now.'

And yet there are moments when he listens too, fascinated and interested, to the background story and facts of my work with CARE around the world and now in Yugoslavia. He seems quite capable of 'snapping himself out of it', though, and soon returns to what I now believe to be the 'state's script' in this charade of a play. It is now becoming abundantly and distressingly clear to me that the state has taken me off the 'missing' list, but is singularly hell-bent on cranking up a trial and, I feel, a conviction. Peter Wallace and I are now pawns in the Yugoslav regime's propaganda war. As part of the war effort I am now absolutely sure that Peter and I are going to be made examples of to the rest of the world. There will be an exaggerated effort by the Yugoslavs to 'exercise judicial process'; protocol is adored in this society, and 'process' will be demonstrated, as has already been made clear. I do not see how anything, short of an international diplomatic intervention, is going to save us from trumped-up convictions and some form of sentencing — perhaps, in my case, State execution.

CHAPTER SEVENTEEN

First Light

I am not to realise it at that exact moment, but it will dawn on me days later that the three-day session just completed with Genghis has cemented my fate, in terms of a conviction at least. But without a lawyer to assist, without knowledge of the Yugoslav legal and judicial processes and up against a system determined to convict, I am putty in their hands. Add to this that I am in no mental state useful to any clever self-defence. I am to learn much later that Genghis was not a military prosecutor — he was military counter-intelligence. He had cleverly sucked me in. About 12 April I am frogmarched up to the interrogation rooms. A new guard — young, tall, loud and very energetic — has my arm bent right up my back, his other hand on the scruff of my neck, bending my head down. In this position I am pushed at the double by this boot-stomping guard whom I now call 'Stompy'. Stompy is a very conscientious guard who likes to show off his prowess to the other guards. Bucking for a promotion, one would guess. I appeal to him to go easy on the arm gymnastics — he laughs, but actually does release the pressure.

Wheeled in, I am confronted by yet another new man, dressed neatly in a rather fashionable three-piece suit. He is about my height, sandy-haired and of slim build, and he introduces himself as the 'investigating judge' appointed, he says, to see whether there is a case to be prosecuted. What a laugh, I think. The same tall young female interpreter who had accompanied Genghis is here, and there is also a stenographer. All very civilised and correct, I'm sure. Looks great, designed to impress, I think bitterly. Out with the goons and in with the civilised trappings of 'democratic processes'.

This regime would not know democracy if they tripped over it, I reflect. I think it is clear to me now, and indeed it is confirmed in my own mind over the next three weeks of interrogations, that an elaborate play is put into effect. A show is made of Yugoslav national sovereignty and their so-called exercising of 'international judicial process', integral to the wartime propaganda effort. It is nothing but propaganda for both internal and international consumption. This cynical exercise is to overlay a predetermined, illegal and evil fabrication designed to justify innocent members of a neutral country being detained, arrested and cruelly treated. Weeks later the Australian ambassador is to compare notes with me and we are to agree that this is the scenario that we were confronting.

Malcolm Fraser arrived on Saturday, 10 April in Zagreb and was awaiting the issue of a visa for entry to Yugoslavia. Meanwhile Charles Tapp had travelled to Athens and reported to Samira that he had met the Australian–Greek Victorian state member of parliament Dimitri Dollis. Dollis was there and approaching Greek Foreign Minister Papandreou. He intended to raise our case, and request a bilateral government approach to the Yugoslavs.

So here I am facing the man who introduces himself as Major Dragosaveljevic of the military judiciary, prosecutors' office. Another major! If nothing else, this drama is studded with a broad cast of majors. He tells me that he is responsible for me, and that no one else will interfere with me. All my problems I must bring to him. Another joke! No, I cannot have access to the International Red Cross or to the neutral country embassies. Just in case I have missed the point lately, he reinforces, word perfect, '... you are in very serious and deep trouble and you must co-operate ...'. Head down, and with a sigh of 'here we go again', I sit freezing and shivering. At least this interrogation office seems about five degrees warmer than that bloody concrete box I have just been hauled from.

The next interrogation commences and I am actually impressed that the procedures are in line with those I am familiar with in the West. The stenographer, a pleasant lady who would be at home in any court in Australia, dutifully types away, occasionally asking for clarification. The judge's questions are recorded and so are my answers. The procedure is competent and relatively painless. The judge is firm, impatient, but likes to smile and demonstrate that he is a reasonable man, which he really isn't. He does not accept my story, although he seems to listen to parts of it with some interest. I swear that at times he is uncomfortable with the whole exercise, but he is a loyal and tough army officer, would have to be a party man, and so follows the regime's propaganda agenda. I am to come across people like him many times over the next few months — decent, professional Serbs in the military, the judiciary, the prison system, and some politicians, who are clearly uncomfortable with this 'frame up and bang up' exercise, but who will never say so. They are the people who will provide a little break here and there and silently wish us the best.

As far as the judge is concerned, though, the interrogation statements and false confessions are established and have sunk my case. Genghis's preliminary investigation of some two days earlier, he says, seems to have confirmed the police and military intelligence interrogation positions. For the first time I have the strength and presence of mind to vigorously protest the nature of the previous interrogations, the way the fabricated statement was taken and the accompanying death threats and beatings. He sits there at his large wooden table, daintily dressed, with overcoat draped over his shoulders, arms out of sleeves as if he were wearing a cape, blinking at me with feigned amazement. Where is the monocle and the cigarette holder, I muse? I think he is enjoying impressing the young ladies, something I cannot do, sitting there pathetically shivering in filthy clothes and with my shaven head. I check myself again for falling into that silly, distracted, flippant mood.

'These are very serious accusations Major Pret you are making,' he says, surprising me with a burst of passable English. I speak with gritted teeth and shake as I emphasise the point, with a hoarse and weak voice, 'Well, Major, you had better believe it. These statements were taken under extreme duress.' Unlike Genghis, he does not understand the concept of the 'rules of the game'. He expresses ignorance, looks to the interpreter and laughs, as if to say, 'how unlikely'. But he sagely says, with a deep frown, that he will look into it and take into consideration what I have said. I do not hold my breath for this.

These interrogation sessions go on for two more weeks, sometimes three to five hours long. They are about two to three days apart, although once there is a week between interrogations. I sit in my solitary confinement concrete box for that week doing nothing — no reading, no talking, and I am not advancing my 'legal position' in any way. Not that I have any illusions about advancing such a cause anyway. At each session I am handed a transcript of the statement taken from the previous session, for signing. I make a grievous mistake with the first two presentations, allowing myself to be bullied by the investigating judge. He tells me to co-operate by signing the statement, regardless of my protest that I wish to only sign an English copy. 'Pret, things may go easier for you if you sign. You will otherwise only severely inconvenience the investigation process and this will delay your resolution of the problem.' It is not until the fourth session, when I am stronger, more confident and have developed a better orientation, that I refuse to sign the Serbian texts, instead demanding English translations. Surprisingly, the judge co-operates, and the last two statements for signing will be in English, although I am to pay in the cells by night during that period for my impudence. Finally, with a lawyer belatedly in attendance, some order and decorum will be brought to the farce. However, it will be too late, as the damage accumulated over four weeks of interrogations by police, military intelligence and judiciary has already been done. And would it have mattered anyway? No, I am to decide, the state agenda was irrevocably in place anyway.

Samira was jolted into shock by a Sydney *Sunday Telegraph* story published on 12 April. While she did not immediately see the article, she was to hear about the essential details of the printed story and about the nature in which it had been obtained. She was deeply angry and deeply stressed by what she recognised immediately as the dangerous treatment of the so-called Steve Pratt story. The story, strongly implying that I must have been carrying out espionage activities in Iraq during the Gulf War in 1991 while working for CARE, is completely erroneous, reckless, based on dubious sources — the pressured questioning of my mother under cunningly contrived circumstances — and was uncorroborated. Both my brother Stuart and Samira respond with anger, and immediately. At that moment Stuart is convinced that the article will excite the Yugoslav authorities and could cause my death. Stuart very firmly tackles a senior editor in the newspaper over the article and the newspaper's cynical treatment of my mother. He receives from her an emotional acknowledgement that, 'perhaps things had got out of hand'. Stuart commences action against the newspaper through the Australian Press Council and, after fighting an effective campaign, is successful.

On one of the last interrogations I am told I must 'repent', and the investigating judge gets very agitated. I am told again that co-operation is essential otherwise there will be dire consequences. I am forced to 'repent' in my statement. I have no idea what 'repent' means in the Yugoslav context; nor, at this point, do I care.

About the middle of April a technical legal document is served on me in my cell. It is basically a 'commitment to trial' authority, and states in the heaviest language that I am accused of organising and supervising an espionage network, of passing secret military information to NATO through my parent organisation, CARE Australia, and of reporting on the outcome of NATO bombing. The surprise, because of the focus on this subject during the earlier interrogations, is that I have not been accused of assisting in the planning and guiding of NATO bombing. This does not hearten me. Stompy gets me to sign a receipt for the document after he shoves it through my door visor. He looks at me silently but with malice. The Serbian version is followed some three hours later by an English version. The document has been issued by the court of the 'First Military District Headquarters'. The legal document is a devastating and frightening thing. It is written in very emotive and aggressive language. Reading it knocks the entire stuffing out of me for the whole afternoon.

I am invited to submit an appeal within twenty-four hours, which I do. A senior guard brings me some prison paper and a cheap, inefficient pen. For the first time in three weeks of incarceration I am writing; I am doing something cerebral, and I am fighting back. I write a four-page statement appealing against what I suppose we in the West would call a 'prima facie case to answer' declaration. I write this squatting on the floor, in very bad light. I spell out my position, my duties in Yugoslavia and those of my staff, whom I assume have been co-accused. I spell out why I have briefed my CARE head office on the situation prevailing in my country mission refugee assistance program areas. At this point I still do not have a lawyer, but I submit my case as best I can. I have had some satisfaction in writing this appeal, and as I finish the document and seal it into a cheap prison envelope I wave an arm and gesture obscenely to no one in particular. The appeal is rejected, of course.

On the evening of the day I am given the legal pronouncement of the 'prima facie' finding I am visited by the guards for a bashing. This is also the period when I have started to become difficult with the investigating judge in terms of refusing to sign any more Serbian language texts. The prison has been quietly peaceful for the two-odd weeks I have been there — the usual shouting and abuse from the guards but no violence in the wing in which I am housed. I have heard beatings in other wings. Such are the acoustics of this place.

The door is banged open and three guards stand there staring and transfixed. Two are cursing in Serbian. I notice the younger, chubby guard with the baby face standing behind is silent and watchful. The sergeant I am to call 'Sarge' walks in, yelling in broken English, 'NATO spy, dirty spy, so you have been found guilty!' Psycho is with him, yelling so loudly he is frothing at the mouth. Psycho belts me hard across the face, a stinging round arm. He stands very close and abuses me unintelligibly. He repeats his often-issued threat of the firing squad. Another open-handed whack over the head. The third hit is a closed fist which he delivers, curiously, with half speed, landing it roundhouse style, on the jaw. Half speed or not I am propelled by the force of it into my little table, knocking my meagre eating utensils sprawling onto the floor with a great crashing noise. Sarge seems to rebuke him, I am not sure. I am standing to attention at the rear of my cell in the required position, standing firmly to try to weather the storm. Psycho goes outside, but swiftly turns and runs at me quickly, kicking high with his right foot. My instincts take over — I imagine I am an opening batsman facing a bouncer, and roll away from the cannoning ball at the last split second, something I used to be good at. As a result, Psycho's boot grazes the side of my head and simultaneously Sarge throws his arms across Psycho's chest, to prevent him from following through, or repeating the exercise. He actually pulls Psycho out of the cell. My head is throbbing again, after two weeks of relative peace. A lot of pain. Psycho is big and powerful and knows how to hit. Sarge shakes his fist at me and they leave.

Over the next two weeks there are intermittent beatings, and I am to be part of a wing-wide bashing campaign. For some reason a number of the younger guards are to be allowed random bashing excursions. This is to go on for two weeks straight, ten out of fourteen nights. The bashing program commences about 8 pm, an hour after the evening meal and just after the evening guard shift changeover. Four of the guards regularly participate, although none of the junior lieutenants or anybody any senior is ever present when these beatings occur. The many random light beatings that seem to be part and parcel of daily routine are another matter. The nightly beatings accompany the evening cell inspection.

The first indication is a shout from about 100 metres down the corridor, then a loud abusive call. Shit, it's on again! I brace myself. The bashing party is about twenty cells away and heading in my direction. I am in the last cell. The bashings will occur with no pattern: some prisoners will escape entirely, some will suffer short beatings, others will take up to twenty-five hits, by my counting. The blows to the other prisoners, judging by the sound of impact and by the responding grunt of expelled air and/or pain, will be severe and delivered by boot or fist. Some prisoners will throw up because of the force of the beatings. They will not fight back, of course, and must stand to attention to face each blow.

The guards usually laugh — they definitely enjoy what they are doing. Often other guards will accompany the bashing guards but will not participate, although they will giggle along with the basher at some misfortune the beaten prisoner has suffered, such as vomiting, or blood from a broken nose on his clothes. The bloodied prisoner will then usually be re-beaten for bleeding on his floor. Religious pronouncements will often be part of the guards' rantings: 'Bomis Porg!' (God be with you). Bash! Bash! 'Bomis Porg!' They are getting closer. I think I have worked out where Peter's cell is and I listen anxiuosly to see whether he cops it. It does not seem so, although I hear Psycho really giving Peter (if it is Peter's cell) a hell of a verbal pasting and, I am sure, all sorts of weird abuse. I have noticed somebody is always close to Psycho to pull him off when he goes too far, which is often. How grimly ironic that there are such 'standards' of behaviour in this prison. I pray to God to give me and the other prisoners strength. I steel myself. They are getting closer.

Somebody is moaning down the corridor. Somebody else hurls up dinner, which wasn't much anyway tonight. I am shaking and very afraid. I remember my days in the dressing room just before a battalion rugby match. I used to need a bit of geeing up, and I would buzz myself up to get ready for the first hard ruck and the inevitable belt in the side of the head. I prepare like that now. Deep butterflies in my stomach. The door is flung open. Stompy or Psycho, either one will let fly a stinging open-hander across the face to start proceedings. It is rare that I cop a closed fist or a boot, and in this I am much luckier than the others. I am a 'controlled bash': strict limits apply to how far the bashers are to go. Luckier than most, I escape two out of three nights, and on the third I get three to five open-handers. I suffer no broken bones or concussion, unlike many others. I feel ashamed to get this comparatively light treatment. This may be a really stupid and unfathomable response, but that is how I experience the entire bashing season, these are my moods.

This goes on and on for six or so weeks, with a couple of week-long breaks, during my early solitary confinement experience. The night after heavy bombing in the city the bashings get worse, and I usually get it. The guards' anger is taken out on the prisoners, and I am not to realise until much later that there are a significant number of Albanian Kosovar prisoners in this prison, in the same wing as me. I am generally left alone after the sixth week, and only have to endure the dreadful sounds of beatings. On such nights the guards come into the cell, calm and a little more respectful in these later months, as if butter would not melt in their mouths, even though they have just beaten the shit out of many prisoners. They will ask me how things are, compliment me on my neat, clean cell, salute me as they always do and politely say 'good night, Major'. And promptly move on to bash the next prisoner. In these later months the goons who would love to be bashing me will have nothing to do with me. If they cannot bash me they will not go anywhere near my cell; they delegate that task to somebody else. Spitting the dummy, I think, children. As best as I can determine Peter is not beaten, thank God, and when we are reunited he eventually confirms this, although he will describe harrowing close calls.

On 14 April Charles called Samira, who was still in Budapest at the ambassador's residence. He tells her of a shocking television broadcast about me. Samira and Ambassador Heggie watch 'Sky News' at 6 pm and see the so-called 'confession' which had been broadcast that day by Yugoslav television, around the world. As it turns out later, when we piece the details together, it is a televised account of the coerced (at gunpoint and threat of death) statement and so-called 'repentance' which had occurred on the fifth day of my interrogation. They were to see me, gaunt, tired, perhaps dispirited, dirty and unkempt, stumbling away over words they thought were not mine, 'confessing' that I had, 'gone to Yugoslavia to carry out espionage work...'

Samira is horrified, wailing strangely without tears and shaking from head to foot. Mark and Zoe Heggie do their best to comfort Samira, Zoe crying perhaps both in sympathy for Samira and in shock with what she had just seen. The ambassador and Samira's second reaction is that this statement is clearly a fabrication. A few hours later Samira finds the strength to call Haydon, Stuart and then her family to prepare them for the upcoming broadcast, to try to comfort Haydon and in so doing perhaps comfort and steel herself. Charles Tapp kindly calls Samira again to help comfort her, something that Charles has done and continues to be very careful to do over these months. Charles tells her that from his point of view the televised broadcast is a very good thing, because it proves that I am alive, and therefore so is Wallace.

About Tuesday, 20 April the door of my cell is flung open and Stompy steps in, turns me around, and handcuffs and hoods me. He and another guard take me down the corridor. Many doors opening and crashing behind me. Down the stairs and I feel myself being handed over to somebody else. The new blokes are much rougher and much firmer, if that is possible. I am, I think at the time, taken to the front of the prison. I am worried and feel most uncomfortable, as I had just got into a routine in the prison.

Small Yugo car again, back seat, head forced right down almost to the floor, excruciating pain in my right shoulder due to the odd angle at which my arms are being pulled up my back. Right wrist really clamped shut by the cuffs and unbearably sore. I protest and get hit over the head, told to shut up. Driving through the busy midday traffic and pedestrian crush, a sense of driving up into the city. Amazed to hear the number of people and amount of traffic on the streets. Sounds normal — NATO bombing has not slowed this city.

I am delivered to a large building in the centre of the city which I guess, much later, may have been the Department of Justice building. Taken upstairs, I wait for an hour, hooded, allowed to sit but with my head pushed onto a desk. I do not know what to think, and silly thoughts again rush through my head. The handcuffs are very sore. My right hand has been numb for about an hour, and my right shoulder is in muscle spasm shock. The guards are strong, very quiet, nothing like the rabble back at the prison. They treat me with a ruthless disregard. Is this my court case? Am I to be put on show? What is this latest threat? I think of Samira and my family. Finally I am on the move again, taken down about four flights in a lift. The handcuffs are removed, and I am taken out of a busy corridor and into a room where the hood is removed also. Another lovely historic room, with deep Persian carpets, ornate drapes, and period furniture. A feast for my eyes after what I have been looking at lately. The guards are tall, plain-clothes blokes who stay very close to me while we await entrance to yet another room. Two military officers, colonels, are seated on the period furniture near me, eyeing me off and muttering dreadful things. 'Humanitarna Pomoc!' (humanitarian organisation) scoffs one scruffy old bloke who looks as if he has left his band of Chetnik fighters behind in the mountains. Finally the guard is motioned to bring me in. Is this the courtroom, I wonder? I am motioned to a comfortable old red velvet chair next to the most gorgeous mahogany table. We are surrounded by television cameas and I have bright lights focused upon me. Gee, must be the Star Chamber, I think, trying to massage the pain out of my numb right wrist.

So busy am I admiring this impressive furniture that at first I fail to realise that the lovely suave tone murmuring away as I entered the room, that lovely burst of English I had heard deep in the fog of my brain, was the voice of Chris Lamb, Australia's ambassador to Yugoslavia, until recently out of the country. My head snaps up on recognition. Shit, it is! I am speechless anyway and do not have the strength or the composure to speak. Ambassador Lamb is his glorious smiling self — the man is famous for his charisma and cheek and here he is in his full glory, ruddy-complexioned and beaming a warm smile. As if he were on a picnic. Looking left, through the fog, I see assistant ambassador Don Foley, with all the colour drained from his face. Do I look that bad, I wonder?

The meeting is being chaired by the investigating judge Major Dragosaveljevic. He is nervous and very restrictive in what he allows to happen here. Did these blokes come in for the day from Budapest, I wonder? The embassy could not be reopened, surely, while the war is still in full swing.

I cannot speak. Just beam back to Lamb a smile which nobody could wipe off my face, not even with a backhander. I am afraid to speak at first. I do not want to break down in front of these two men, whom I have considered these last twenty months to be my and Samira's good friends. The meeting is short; only fifteen minutes is allowed, and we are not allowed to discuss the case at all. Discussion is restricted to my wellbeing and some news from home. Chris very nicely gives me the great news that Samira is well and strong, the pregnancy is going well and he tells me she is in good hands in the UK. I instantly know whose hands — our good friends, I am sure.

I am now ecstatic, as a great feeling of hopefulness washes over me. Chris says to the major that he would like to shake my hand, and is that alright? While doing this he comes very close and peers closely at what I know is an abrasion on the side of my head, a mark left by Psycho. I wink to him and he gets my message. I stammer out to Chris that he should tell Samira I am fine and that she is not to worry about me. I am also able to say to Chris, in a disguised way, 'Do not believe all this shit.' The only thing I could do was to profess my innocence. Chris nods, pats me on the shoulder; his warm, almost carefree smile at that meeting I will never forget. The major cuts off any further discussion, and the very brief meeting is cruelly over. A warm handshake with Don and I am whisked out of the room. Back to reality. Tough guards, rough treatment with the hood and handcuffs, sucked back into the dark and evil vortex. Nevertheless, all the way back to the prison I am able to smile my own warm smile beneath the hood.

About a week later, 27 April, the exercise is repeated: same plain-clothes guards, same ruthless treatment. Same long delays, handcuffs biting into flesh, right shoulder agonisingly in spasm. I think this must be another ambassadorial visit and am impressed that he has been able to organise access to the country weekly. I am not to know that he has in fact been in the country since 14 April. Wheeled in again, I find the same attractive red velvet chair and this time a microphone set up on the table next to my chair; perhaps these paranoid bastards intend to collect any further bit of espionage chatter I should attempt to pass on. Again it seems to take an inordinate amount of time for me to orient myself, to see what is happening. I am told much later by embassy staff that on these early visits I look bloody terrible, right out of it.

I am stunned to look up and see that with the Australian ambassador this time is the looming and massive figure of Malcolm Fraser. He is dressed in a dark blue pinstriped suit. Absurdly, I notice at first how large his bloody feet are! It is tremendous to see him, and for a fleeting second I fantasise that he is here to collect me and take me away. More than anything else in the world right now, I just want to get up and walk out that door with Malcolm Fraser. Malcolm is forcing a brave smile and I will be damned if I can't see just a small quivering at the corner of his mouth and a little moisture in one of his eyes. Shit, I must look pretty grim. He is as big as an oak tree and his presence for me that minute is very, very important. The room is full of the usual suspects: another investigating judge, translators, cameramen, Serbian journalists — all party mouthpieces of course — and an old rugged bloke who looks like a senior military officer in civilian clothes. He fixes the evil eye on me for the complete proceedings and never wavers. He does not look happy — he looks as if he is suffering a severe case of piles. If he could kill me he would do it there and then, I am sure. I ignore him for the most part, or at least try to.

This meeting is off to a blazing start. I know the rules about 'no discussion of case' but I hook in, somehow finding sufficient strength to do so. In a surprisingly weak voice I blurt out, 'Mr Fraser, Mr Ambassador (I glance right and notice the interpreter relaying all this concurrently to the stand-in judge), I would like you to know and to please pass on to Prime Minister Howard that I, my colleagues and CARE Yugoslavia are entirely innocent of any allegations of spying ...' Much shouting, the judge going right off his brain, the old bloke in the corner rising to kill me with his bare hands, an enraged growl rumbling from his old plum brandy-coloured lips. Concurrently, Malcolm Fraser interjects to tick me off, rather firmly (I smile inwardly), and says, 'Steve, we have promised to abide by the rules here, and we will not, you will not discuss aspects of the case, please. Do you understand?' And I imagine he winks.

We discuss family matters. He brings me news of Samira, and this boosts my morale. I now hear, for the first time, of the great depth of support and sympathy coming from the Australian people. Malcolm runs through a number of descriptions of the type of things which are happening back home, joined by the ambassador, who describes the type of press coverage he has become aware of. The Yugoslavs do not like this line of chatter, although the young dark-haired judge, who I am to meet many months later (he is another major), smiles quite pleasantly and listens with interest. Monster in the corner looks disgusted and would prefer, I think, to machine gun us all —including the judge major, for smiling.

Malcolm and Chris promise that they will do everything possible to expedite matters. Malcolm asks for and gets the judge's permission to take a list of my immediate clothing needs and is told that he will be allowed to arrange a clothing delivery to me in prison. A small victory. I find the strength, from memory, to crack some sick joke about wearing the same underwear for three weeks, saying I have not been game to remove them lest they run off of their own accord. The judge, despite my earlier breach of protocol, seems a professional fellow, reasonable and compassionate. A firm handshake from Malcolm, who tells me to keep my chin up, and a warm hug from Chris, who, taking the Yugoslavs by surprise (was the Western dolt passing secret messages?) tells me, as he is often to do in the weeks and months to come, that under instructions from Samira he is passing on her hug. He draws the line at passing on kisses. We all laugh, except Monster, who look as if he would rather see me at the bottom of a dungeon without any privileges.

I am then suddenly whisked out and back to horrible prison reality, but when I arrive back at my cell I feel bloody good. There is hope, and it keeps building, centimetre by centimetre. A cold bowl of soup awaits me in the cell. It is disgusting and overlaid by a filthy layer of scum, but I wolf it down. The news about Samira and from home was fantastic; the extremely narrow world which I have occupied has been prised open, and my perspective is broadening again. It is a great feeling. A flash of light at long last, light at the end of the tunnel.

Visits from the ambassador are now to settle down to a routine of one per week, and they are a flash of light in a world of evil as far as I am concerned. Chris Lamb is candid, positive, and as the meetings continues, able to tell me, and then both Peter and me, just a little more of what is happening and what we can expect in preparation for the inevitable trial.

It is about the last week in April. On one of my visits to see the ambassador things suddenly become a lot more civilised. I am taken in a police paddy wagon now, without handcuffs and with three companions. This is the first time I have been so close to other prisoners. We are accompanied by Stompy. It takes me five minutes to realise that one of the prisoners is Peter Wallace — he is thin, and with his shaven head I did not at first recognise him. In the dark at the back of the vehicle and with his head down in the time-honoured tradition of prisoner behaviour he is hardly recognisable. Peter is to tell me months later that he did not recognise me for the whole journey. Under the circumstances he does not look too bad though, and this is gratifying.

There are two other prisoners, and they look distinctly European to me. One is as old as me. He looks calm. The other is a slightly built man in his mid-thirties. He is in sheer terror; head right down, he is slumped into the corner of the vehicle, pointedly avoiding looking at Stompy. We are all put into separate solitary confinement cells at a small prison — the First Military Headquarters remand prison, as it turns out. At this place we are taken to see our respective ambassadors. Peter and I are taken together to see Chris Lamb and Don Foley, but Peter and I are forbidden to talk to each other. The ambassador continues to talk up the visit, to pave the way for subsequent visits. He subtly gets his way with the authorities. His laughter and general mirth do not endear him to the senior military judge chairing this meeting, and I am to wonder at times over the months whether Chris pushes the envelope too much.

Nevertheless, he is effective and tireless. It is always good to see him and his whacky humour is a tonic for us. At this particular meeting, I clear up with him whether the death penalty is applicable to the sorts of charges which are likely to be laid against me. He rather casually (I think at that moment) says 'No'. They had wondered themselves and looked into it, and, he says, the maximum I was likely to get was fifteen years. He then turned away and loaded his pipe. I describe the regular pieces of advice I am receiving from the prison staff and the inferences I make from Genghis's remarks, relative to a likely death sentence. Chris and Don both say that there is in fact no death penalty under Yugoslav federal law. In wartime are there special provisions I ask? No, says Chris, and he encourages me not to worry about that. I am mightily relieved, and on returning to my cell have a bloody good cry. My uncharacteristic tears also come because as a result of this visit I read the first letters I have received since my arrest, letters from my wife, my son Haydon and my brother Stuart.

On the way back from the ambassadorial visit I notice that there are German names on the personal items bags carried by the other two European visitors. I find out later that these are German journalists, arrested on suspicion of guiding NATO bombers, that both had been beaten, especially the younger man, who had been severely treated. The older journalist, Werner, is to tell the world of their ordeal and is interviewd by Mark Colvin on the ABC radio program 'PM'. Werner is to graphically describe life in the prison and his knowledge of Peter's and my ordeal. There are also three US servicemen who have been arrested after having 'strayed' across the border from Macedonia. (I recalled that during the bashings of one or more of the prisoners many derogatory references were made to Bill Clinton and to the USA in general.) It became clear to me retrospectively that the three Americans, also housed in my wing, were treated very severely. The Americans and the Germans are to win their releases through diplomatic pressure, and are out in early May.

CHAPTER EIGHTEEN

The Trial

After the fourth interrogation session with the investigating judge I meet my lawyer. Some sanity at last. I was asked if I wished to have him work for me. The answer was yes. Chris Lamb had advised me that this lawyer had worked for the Australian embassy and seemed OK. His name was Djeordje (George). Djeordje was not allowed to speak in these interrogation sessions and I not could ask him for any advice. He merely witnessed what transpired, but of course the most important sessions had passed. The investigating judge treated him rather indifferently, although not unkindly. It occurred to me that if the lawyer was not a stooge of the state, but a public defender simply provided to represent the 'guilty bastard', then he was incredibly brave. He was in a way taking on the state, during a time of war. Certain that Djeordje was no stooge and was indeed brave, I was to feel in his debt over the coming weeks for his efforts and courage, and continue to feel the same way much later, on quiet reflection, after returning to Australia. He was thin and in his sixties, but spritely, and with a fitness that demonstrated a good constitution.

In the first week of May the ambassador and Djeordje warned me that the indictment was soon to be issued, and that it would not be

THE TRIAL

pretty. It was not — a document in heavy legalese, approximately thirty-five pages long, spelling out the prosecution's case. Djeordje and Ivan (Peter's lawyer) were working through the Australian embassy and sometimes directly with the Canberra-based branch of the law firm Mallesons Stephens Jacques. Two lawyers, Justin Stanwix and Ian Johnson were specifically on our case and working hand in glove with a very diligent CARE Australia project team. Mallesons and CARE had committed themselves to long hours of frantic work, often working late into the night. David Gilmour, who I had known in East Africa (he had worked there with CARE Sudan/Somalia) very carefully and tirelessly co-ordinated our support project. It was his job to take a country director's experienced eye and look for all the angles, to investigate anything that may have been unusual about my country mission and which CARE should anticipate as a potential problem. He worked closely with Mallesons, in effect providing a layman's perspective to the mountain of documents that the lawyers waded through.

Mallesons, CARE Canberra, the Australian ambassador and our lawyers did not always see eye to eye and differed in their tactical approaches to tackling the prosecution case. But we were aware that the combined effort was impressive. They did a mighty job. What was disgusting and depressing was that all the language used in the indictment reflected the earlier military intelligence interrogations. The outrageous claims made by the chief and his team were now in full, formal print. It was uncanny to see this rubbish written up in such a way. I was hit heavily by the indictment document and fell into a depression for about two days. It was all I could do to snap out of it. I did that by undertaking 5 kilometre walks in my cell, 1000 laps, interspersed with readings of my wife's wonderfully inspirational letters and the calm, strong and irreverent letters of my great boy Haydon and my terrific brother Stuart.

Djeordje and I had our first private meeting. He had to agitate to get the meeting approved. There was a move by the authorities to limit the lawyer/client meetings — in fact they attempted to delay these until a week before the trial was due to start. I was told that we would have only two meetings, of thirty minutes duration each, before the commencement of the trial. I wondered how vigorously the lawyer and the ambassador were appealing against this. It was absurd that a man facing a fifteen-year sentence and who was not allowed to have a lawyer present for the most crucial phases of the interrogations was now restricted to two short meetings in preparation for his defence. Only because the authorities did not get their act together, with the trial consequently being postponed three times, was the program of meetings between client and lawyer extended.

Djeordje worked hard to get access to me. He was a hugely calming presence — his first words were, 'Do not let yourself be fazed or shocked by the indictment document. It is all rubbish, it is illegal and it is definitely based on a fabrication born from threats against your life. I know all about that. This is not the end of it. Do not focus on the fifteen years. This is just the beginning of your fight and you will win soon, one way or the other.' Djeordje is confident and very direct. 'Of course no matter what direction this unpredictable trial will take, you must never never plead guilty!' he said, staring straight into my eyes. Djeordje then coached me on the preparation of my defence statement. This would be the centre of our approach. He outlined his strategy to deal with the central issues.

Firstly, the prosecution would fail to prove that I allegedly passed 'secret military information', because we could prove by definition and by practice that no such information was included in any of my work. Secondly, he said we would prove that there were no agents recruited by me or paid by me for espionage purposes and that the prosecution could never prove anything to the contrary. Thirdly, he said the prosecution would not be able to prove that the safety information included in my SITREPs was sent to any NATO organisations. Fourthly, he said we would present to the court the details of and reasons for the monitoring and the reporting of the situation in the field — the increasing humanitarian need, the safety of CARE staff and the integrity of the humanitarian program. Finally, he said that sending SITREPs to my parent organisation — that is to my head office — and to sister organisations within CARE International did not, by definition and by Yugoslav law, constitute 'sending information to a foreign organisation'. By Yugoslav law

THE TRIAL

foreign companies are absolutely entitled to send information of any kind to their overseas head offices. These were the five basic tenets of my defence and that of my colleagues. I set about preparing my defence statement based on that framework.

It was now six weeks since my incarceration, and a little of the pressure had been eased, with more and more guards now behaving sympathetically. I noticed a distinct sea change. I was not to be beaten again, and although still badly and roughly handled, it was by no more than three of the fifteen in this prison, and by none of the guards in the other prisons that I was to go to later. The senior guard officer for my wing, a Krjina Serb in his mid-forties, a dark-complexioned man whom I call 'the Italian', was surprisingly helpful to me in my preparation period. The Italian brought me plenty of paper and new pens as I put together and then redrafted what turned out to be a sixteen-page defence statement. The Italian ensured that the light over my cell stayed on, on grey or dark days, as I feverishly wrote and rewrote my statement and my own court notes. He was a humane and very professional officer, and he did not allow the other guards to interfere with, or read, or inspect the many documents I had now put together. It was also clear to me that whenever the Italian was around beatings did not happen, although there was no reticence on the part of the bashing group to venture forth otherwise.

The writing of the defence statement was for me a cathartic experience, giving me great strength and faith and rekindling my hope. I was to pull no punches in the critical analysis of the interrogation, and indeed I was urged on by Djeordje. He was able to win two more meetings to read and correct aspects of the defence statement, and with the help of the Italian a couple of these meetings were actually extended. The trial was close upon us — we were warned it would begin on 15 May.

Last urgent meetings are held between us. On more than one occasion Djeordje finds that he has to reinforce to me that there is no death penalty, such is my fragility during those days. During those first four weeks or so in the central prison and the interrogation phase, some five of the guards, led by a sadistic, lanky lieutenant, had regularly promised me that I would be executed. They would tell me that under a special proclamation of state, due to war, a firing squad outcome for my trial was being arranged. I had raised this desperate question with the investigating judge. He waved me away with a sarcastic grimace, reminding me of the need for co-operation — though correctly indicating, as I learned later, that under federal law there was no capital punishment. But his brevity and casualness at the time, coupled with the guards' campaign, meant that lingering doubts had remained.

Given my fragility, Djeordje helps me immensely to remain focused on the task at hand: the preparation for the trial. He would confide in me some months later, under better circumstances, that he was shocked by my physical appearance — the great loss of weight and the strain showing in my face. I now bore no resemblance to earlier photos of me that he had seen. He could see that I had been subjected to continuous terror over many weeks and had been forced under the severest pressure to sign statements which had now driven me into a corner. I find out much later that Djeordje is experienced in these affairs, having himself been imprisoned over human rights issues.

The prison governor visits my cell. He is a large and deep-voiced man, rosy-cheeked, and I sense that in other places, he is a cheerful soul. He is firm with me but respectful; in the months to come I see that he also is a fair and humane man. Through May two of the guards who speak English, if only roughly, become a lot friendlier and more helpful, often stopping by for a couple of minutes' chat. One of them has a girlfriend in Australia. Psycho grudgingly leaves me alone. The lanky lieutenant, who is dark haired and about 2 metres tall, I call 'Farmer', because he has that look about him and is always walking around with a piece of straw in his mouth; he enjoys prodding me and continues to treat me roughly. He is a vicious idiot and clearly the instigator of most of the bashings in the place. 'Iceman', a sergeant, is tough, loud, full of invective and threats, and is a very cold customer in appearance. However, he mellows quickly during May, and while always tough and demanding, he becomes more reasonable and actually prohibits bashings.

In about the last week of April or early May I am bustled off to another meeting, thinking it was ambassadorial. By now the trips to the meetings are more civilised — I am transported in the back of police vans, with no hood and no handcuffs. I am very grateful for this small mercy, as those many trips taken in previous weeks, when I had been bustled, roughed up and hooded, had been ones of great anxiety and outright fear. The trips are now routine.

Instead of the ambassador, I join the prison governor. Seated with him in a small, rather pleasant room are two Serbian Orthodox priests; one was actually a bishop, from the province of Novi Sad, and responsible for an area including Sremska Mitrovica, where this ordeal had started. They are both Australian citizens, the bishop now residing in Yugoslavia, and the other residing and working in a parish in Paris. They are both very cheerful, and have visited on Malcolm Fraser's request. The meeting is relaxed and unhurried, the first pleasant affair I have experienced in six weeks. They are both very warm men, heavily bearded, both rumbling away with laughter in their black robes. It is infectious, and for the first time in weeks, I actually laugh. They hold worry beads, which they constantly knead between strong fingers, with hands more of farmers than of clerics, I think. At the end of the meeting I am handed a copy of an Orthodox Church book. I do not examine it until back in my cell, but I am excited, as it is the first item of reading matter I have been given, and was permitted on the spot by the governor.

When I look at the book I am horrified to find that it is an apocalyptic account of sin, death and the end of the world. Cemeteries and skulls adorn the cold grey cover of the book. It was a dismal wet day outside as I looked at the book. I am proclaimed, according to the title, to prepare myself for my death. It puts the wind right up me, and I shudder with a returning fear that I thought I had conquered. Have these men been preparing me for my execution? These silly thoughts race through my mind. On later reflection, I was very grateful to these men who had travelled so far to encourage me, which had been their only intention.

Samira has meanwhile been sitting in Budapest, where she has made a name for herself for her fierce and unrelenting pursuit of my case. By mid-May she had departed Budapest and moved to London to join her good English friends (out of Belgrade), who put in an incredible effort to support her, to keep her sometimes flagging spirits up and to advise her on all manner of affairs. They took her and her worried pregnancy into their charge. I was honoured and grateful to meet them later. I realised how much of an ordeal this was for them; they were true samaritans, the salt of the earth. Samira was by then heavily pregnant, though still happy to go on walks with her hosts, and still doggedly and determinedly pursuing the campaign to release Pratt, Wallace and Jelen. She tirelessly e-mailed the world looking for openings or answers, or else pressing ideas on people. She was relentless in her communications with CARE Australia, and with the Wallace and Pratt families.

By early May, ambassadorial visits were weekly occurrences, and much looked forward to. We were now permitted to receive press clippings from home as well as mail and books. Books were my saviour and my habit of ardent reading, a habit of years before, returned with a vengeance. Clothes had become available and I was now warm for the first time since my arrest. But air raids were also increasing around Belgrade, and there was a noticeable escalation of strikes close to Belgrade itself. I would often awake in the small hours of the morning to hear anti-aicraft batteries blazing away and the unmistakable crump, crump of falling bombs. For the first time I was able to actually hear the aircraft, so I knew that medium fighter/bombers and lighter fighter aircraft were coming in low to strike the anti-aircraft batteries. I would lie there on the floor, tightly cocooned in my three blankets in that infernal, bitter cold, staring at the ceiling and just listening to the unfolding drama.

I had enormously mixed feelings at the time: sad that in bombing random semi-military and civilian targets across the city, NATO could be so stupid as to continue an action that would only further unite the people behind Milosevic; supportive in a 'give those batteries hell and go for it, brave pilots!' sort of way; and then fearful that, given the closeness of some of the strikes, the prison itself might be bombed. On more than three occasions the whole prison was to shake violently with that terrible sound of the shock wave and rush of air from a nearby strike. After a night of bombing when civilian targets had been hit and civilian casualties allegedly inflicted, I would often hear other prisoners suffering abuse and beatings.

Prison walks had been on the agenda since the third week in April, and after four weeks of total isolation I began to see other prisoners. We would all walk, heads down and hands behind our backs, in a long line around a dirty, dingy courtyard, bracketed by four-storey-high dirty, uninspiring concrete walls. I was surprised at how filthy the place was; the whole courtyard was littered with discarded take-away food and associated rubbish. I wondered who got to eat that stuff — it was at least more exotic than my soup and bread. We could not talk, but often would nod to each other.

I found myself treated as a real curiosity and was to find a great deal of quiet sympathy from the prisoners — although a small number gazing at me would have killed me with their bare hands given half a chance. At least that is what their expressions said.

I see Peter, and I see Branko for the first time. Both are difficult to recognise, both are walking very carefully. We were on some occasions able to furtively swap smiles of encouragement. The walks are my tonic, and I eagerly look forward to them, walking briskly and talking vigorously to myself: 'Chin up Pratty, chin up (per my wife's exhortations via her sweet letters), you can do it! Fight the bastards! Going to be out of here soon!' That was essentially my chant, which rang in my head day in and day out.

On 27 May the trial began. I dressed for the occasion in my best blue long-sleeved shirt and a pair of dark green dress trousers held up by a strip of white, torn cloth. I also wore for the occasion my battered, unpolished brown shoes, with no laces. The rough treatment was back on again. Handcuffed, bent forward at the waist, arm wrenched up my back, hustled out to the police wagon and again from the wagon up into the court building. The Serbs were reminding me who was boss on this trial day and encouraging me to keep things in perspective. The message transmitted was: 'NATO spy, we are the boss, you are our pawn. Do not get excited about any notions of court justice, and seeing your accursed Australian friends near the court, for you are fucked!'

The building is in town, on a busy road. It's in a modern building of about five storeys, and we appear to be on the top floor. There is a bustle of people in and out the courtroom environs. It is a good feeling to be sitting in a place surrounded by perfectly normal people going about their everyday jobs. I can recall at that first moment shaking my head at the surreal atmosphere. What the hell was I doing sitting here in a chair in an open-door courtroom, still handcuffed, head shaven, skinny and miserable, with pleasant-looking smartly dressed Serb civilians and busy young women walking in and out? It took a supreme effort to remind myself of my circumstances, and to focus on the battle close at hand.

The court tribunal was made up of five military officers, dressed in their combat fatigue uniforms: a major as president, two lieutenant colonels sitting either side of him, a navy commander (a lieutenant colonel equivalent) and a major on the other end. The five looked at me in an almost resigned and bored fashion, although two of them were mildly interested in some of the issues. These two, as it would turn out, were to rigorously question the prosecutor on some aspects of the case and to even agree with the way I had done my job with respect to security measures and information reporting. (This was Djeordje's feeling, confirming my own instinct, he told me later.)

Nevertheless, through the entire proceedings of the trial, given the bored, 'let's get this over with' expressions, the total lack of interest by members of the court board in reading any of the evidence, or indeed to bother reading anything, and their never taking any notes, my overwhelming feeling was that I and perhaps my colleagues were as good as sunk. This trial was merely ritual. The Australian ambassador, the Australian press, UNHCR, CARE observers and Branko's family were denied access to the trial until verdict and sentencing time on the fourth day.

My moment of truth had arrived. I was on my feet reading my defence statement, occasionally prompted by my lawyer, who for the most part was forced by the president to stay out of that phase of the proceedings, an incredibly strange thing, it seemed to me, for a court of law. I was to be essentially on my own for that first and second day, reading my statement and answering questions for eight hours, six straight on day one. I was not to be allowed to sit at any stage. Peter and Branko are out of the courtroom for this, and their defence presentations are to be far shorter affairs: Branko's is about an hour and thirty minutes and Peter's is forty-five minutes.

I began shakily. It took about twenty minutes for me to compose myself, to stop my voice breaking at times. I stood with my feet widely planted, shoulders back and head up, as if I were on parade. I left my feet planted like that, giving the bastards no chance of gloating over my discomfort. From that point on the emotion of controlled anger settled in. This would sustain me for the next four days. I was castigating in my evidence concerning the circumstances surrounding the life-threatening interrogation, the ridiculous assumptions made by the prosecution case and the ignorance demonstrated by the state about the duties of an NGO mission head in matters of safety, security and incident reporting.

I had no intention of holding back. And as I frequently looked over to Djeordje, he nodded encouragingly — it was clear he did not think I was going over the top. I think I was being realistic using this kind of approach, on the basis that if I was going to go for a row I might as well throw every punch I had. At no stage did anybody on the bench or at the prosecutor's table pull me up or object or counter any of my arguments, not even when I accused the prosecutor and the so-called special witness, a colonel in intelligence, of being 'incompetent liars'. This was the tenor of the trial for the next four days.

After my initial shaky start, I delivered these verbal blows with a feeling of great relief and catharsis. The president was a curious fellow — cold, sour and terribly, terribly serious. There was some irony in that he was a Krajina Serb refugee, as I was to find out much later. He had a Milosevic-style haircut and the same sort of broad, frowning face. His four colleagues on the bench wore perpetually grim expressions, although the commander and the rather dainty cavalry officer-like colonel did crack a few smiles during some of my more sarcastic moments. The prosecutor was a portly, middle-aged major who, over his ample belly, his shirt stretched to breaking point, wore camouflage trouser braces, the first I had ever seen anywhere in the world. He peered, not in an unfriendly way, at me over half-glasses. As far as I could translate his pronouncements, he made no sense, and never sounded confident. My assessment was that he was reading from somebody else's script.

The courtroom was carpeted, had comfortable chairs and nicely timbered walls, and overlooked a pleasant valley view of a greener part of Belgrade. It was a beautiful sight for my weary eyes. And the weather, now in early summer, was clear and warm. The atmosphere though was to be severely damaged by the falling of two bombs in the centre of Belgrade, near enough to shake the courtroom. When asked by the president if I cared to continue or wanted to retire to a shelter I replied with a shrug, 'I will as long as you will.' This drew a deep laugh from the navy commander and a suppressed giggle from the colonel — but only a frown from the president. The interpreter was a lovely lady in her early fifties, with a strong, deep, beautifully enunciating voice, and her English was perfect. Her job these four days was hell, and she had no respite, translating everything back and forth — the judge jurors (as they were called) did not speak English, although most of them clearly understood the language. She was to break down in tears twice during the proceedings, apparently in sympathy with Branko's plight. At the back of the court, apparently to ensure that I did not charge the bench to throttle these fair gentlemen, were six army guards, all young men with whom, during short breaks outside on the sunlit stairwell, all three of us were to strike a strong rapport.

The president ran a court which had barred all observers, 'for security reasons'. The 'star chamber trial', which is exactly what it was, was closed to the outside world, because the regime knew that the proceedings, prosecution evidence and bench pronouncements would not stand up to international scrutiny. Apart from this, the court was run to strict procedure, and the regime went to great lengths to exercise its idea of correct protocols. Branko and Peter were to give their evidence in turn, with two very short so-called cross-examinations. Cross-examinations of defence evidence were extremely paltry affairs; there was no interest or conviction demonstrated by the prosecutor or the judge jurors. Djeordje's, Peter's lawyer's and my attempts to cross-examine the one and only prosecution witness and to tackle the prosecutor's pronouncements were for the most part blocked by the president. On one occasion the two seemingly sympathetic judge jurors pointedly sought to follow up on two of the four allowed (out of twelve) cross-examination questions

I put to the special witness about the nature of 'secret military information', very crucial to the prosecution's case. The inept special witness was left floundering, but this prosecution failing had little bearing later anyway.

Peter, Branko and myself were reunited during the court case. We were for the first time in months allowed to mix and talk freely, although these sessions were short and occurred during breaks. It was terrific to meet them and be able to speak freely and in a friendly atmosphere again. The guards with us wanted to know all about Australia, so these interchanges were pleasant. Only one guard caused trouble, but he was consigned to the outer court and we were not to see much of him through the day. After hours he gave us hell, threatening Peter and Branko often. We were to see more of him later. Because of his shaven head, almost nonexistent neck and short, squat, powerful stature I was to dub him 'Pitbull'. He was a very nasty son of a bitch.

On one afternoon after the day's proceedings had come to a halt and we were being bundled up and handcuffed, to be taken back to the prison, Pitbull came looking for Branko. He personally escorted him back to the prison. Such was the casual way things were done in this prison and military system that a strange outside guard, who had nothing to do with the prison, was free to jump aboard and take over escort duties. On return to the prison he severely beat Branko in his cell, delivering about twenty-five heavy blows. The useless and sad lieutenant 'Farmer' wandered up and down the corridor outside whistling; if it was not for intervention by one of the better and more humane guards, 'Flat-top' (a big simple country boy, named for the shape of his haircut), I fear the beating would have gone on much longer.

Branko was in a lot of pain the next day in court. He gave his evidence and was very emotional throughout. He was clearly shattered that the country he loved should have turned its back on him. It came out in the evidence that statements had been forced from Peter and Branko, or misconstrued to further implicate me. The defence lawyers had restructured their clients' defence statements to rectify those fabrications. Peter's lawyer Ivan, like my lawyer, was outstanding in his defence. He was particularly good in technical law and impassioned from a human rights point of view. Both Djeordje and Ivan were fearless in their presentations, and while reminding us throughout of the absurdities of the trial and the shallowness of the prosecution, they still quietly prepared us for the worst. They knew what was coming. Djeordje's comforting comment to me was to remind me that this was merely the beginning of the fight; I shouldn't take to heart the severe sentence which was approaching like a steam train.

Throughout the trial we received messages of support from the Governor-General, Sir William Deane, Prime Minister John Howard, Foreign Minister Alexander Downer and Deputy Prime Minister Tim Fischer. These messages were tremendously important and reminded me that, although tied to the tracks of an approaching steam train, I would eventually recover and would win my freedom. Messages from these four gentlemen were greatly valued. The Governor-General and Tim Fischer had been regular in their messages of concern. I was now aware of Sir William's personal interest in our cases, including Branko's, and of his personal interest in my son's wellbeing. Tim Fischer had also taken our cause to heart. He, too, impressed us as a man of intelligent compassion. These leaders of Australia communicated to me a genuine warmth and reflected what I was beginning to understand as a remarkable but genuinely warm groundswell of support for our cause.

The convictions and sentencing came easily. For the president and his judge jurors the boring and arduous time was over. It seemed to me they simply opened the envelope which had been sitting before the president since day one. The observers were allowed for the first time into the court, and as I walked back into the courtroom to face sentencing I noticed that Greg Wilesmith and Katy Cronin of the Australian ABC were present. Wilesmith was one of the last Westerners I had seen, some two days before my arrest. Like Don Foley on our first meeting, they both looked a bit ashen-faced. The ambassador was his normal florid self and gave me a wink. Standing next to him was the beautiful and elegant Jelena, a Serb worker with the human rights group, Helsinki Watch Committee. She was in a bright yellow miniskirt, deeply tanned and wearing a splendid hat that would have won first prize at the Melbourne Cup. Surreal, I thought, as I walked back in. This time the guards were stern and flanked the three of us.

The sentence of twelve years flattened me, regardless of its having been predicted; and so too the sentences for Peter and Branko, four and six years respectively. Two of the guards turned to me and apologised. Branko's mother, in the back of the court, wailed loudly. The ambassador gripped me by the arm as I was being marched out by two guards, hissing quickly, 'We will get you out of this.' I just nodded. On the way back to the prison Peter and I tried to console a shattered Branko. I can remember saying, 'Just a few months Branko. You will be released, stay strong, stay strong.' On return to Belgrade Central Prison even the prison guards were shocked at the outcome. They whistled incredulously.

That afternoon Peter and I were taken to see a visitor, a member of the upper house of the Victorian parliament, Dimitri Dollis. He had somehow travelled all this way and got into the country, and accessed us. It was a pleasure and a comfort to meet him, particularly after this wretched verdict an hour or so earlier. Dollis was to continue pressing very hard. He and Samira became good telephone friends, and they compared strategies. He was, I think, underestimated by the Australian ambassador in Belgrade, who seems to have had little time for him; I was to wonder whether Dimitri and the ambassador had been able to co-ordinate their efforts effectively.

Peter and I were reunited when Peter was moved into my little cell. The sharing of our experiences was to continue non-stop for two days, before we both ran out of energy. It was a relief just to be with each other and talk after our confinement. We were to be transferred to the military prison and were surprised to see that our guards were to come with us. They donned new uniforms, discarding the civilian blue for their old military uniforms. We discovered that the military prison inmates and staff had actually been transferred into one wing of Belgrade Central Prison. I asked the Italian and the governor of the prison whether Branko could be included in our prison cell in the military prison. He was.

Things are much easier for us. The prison is a better place; the living conditions have improved and our treatment is significantly better. Branko is never beaten in the month that we are together.

Pitbull comes onto the scene as a regular guard — an army sergeant, it turns out — but he is kept away from our cell and confined to another wing. When Branko and Peter see him on walks he threatens them, but he tends to leave me alone.

Despite the incredible tensions of the last few months and the chaotic nature of things we three got on well over these four weeks. Of course there were and will always be questions about who was supposed to have been pressured to say what about whom during interrogations. I think this was in each of our minds. But it seemed to me at the time useless and insulting to press my colleagues on these very private issues, and I decided to let sleeping dogs lie. We did, however, talk about our experiences generally and put together parts of the mosaic over those weeks.

Samira stunned me by appearing in Belgrade shortly after we were transferred to the military prison. She had actually arrived two weeks before the bombing and the war ceased. Of course I was both apprehensive for her safety and tremendously glad of her presence. I was so proud of this brave woman, who had made the journey despite the turmoil and the dangers. Samira was very experienced in the realities of war and had no illusions about these things.

She lumbered into the place, hugely pregnant. Our first meeting, in the visit room at the front of the prison, was very emotional and exciting for us both. We were both grinning broadly, and for me this was a hugely relieving moment. I was stunned at how healthy she looked. I had expected that she would be tired and drawn because she was pregnant and had superimposed an assumption that she would be additionally exhausted and stressed by these events. She was either a good actor, covering up for my benefit (which is Samira's style), or superbly strong. I suspect it was a little of both, but am to soon realise that Samira is even stronger and more remarkable than I knew.

On our visits we were left in peace by the guards, most of whom seemed to take a shine to Samira. She befriended them and the prison governor, all the time angling for more visits and improved entitlements. Samira made as much progress on these issues as the embassy staff had earlier. She found herself in disagreement with the ambassador over some issues. For him it could not be easy, dealing with a dynamic and determined wife; he would also have been cognisant of other, broader issues relevant to the prisoner issue, which he could not have confided in Samira. She forged strong bonds with various members of the embassy staff. She would work tirelessly during the month she was in the country to improve our conditions and to improve the management of our prisoner support activities. Her arrival unexpectedly at the CARE Belgrade office, rolling in cheerfully to say 'Hi!' seemed to catch the staff by surprise. While receiving a warm response from many of the staff, particularly the women, she noticed some hesitation on the part of others. This would soon evaporate — she was well supported by the Belgrade office in that extraordinary month.

Samira went to our apartment at Banavo Brdo. She did so with embassy and CARE staff and found that the place had been well and truly searched. This should have been no surprise; the secret police and intelligence agents would have investigated the place, no doubt looking for secret transmitters, or batmobiles or whatever. I was actually surprised to hear that Samira and the Australian embassy were allowed near the place. The apartment had not been wrecked; indeed somebody had gone to the trouble to return it to some sort of semblance of order.

Samira found that a number of domestic items, including our better clothing, had been removed or stolen, whereas the many private papers and work documents left in the place had not been touched. Domestic items and clothes seemed strange items to support a prosecution case. I thought bitterly that the people in the military judiciary were nothing but a bunch of thieves. If not they, who else had access to the place? Samira thoroughly packed up what she could recover and this was removed to the ambassador's residence for safe keeping.

There were occasions on the appointed visiting days, depending on which of the officers was on duty, when Samira was held outside the prison in the waiting area before being allowed to see me. The Wallaces, who by this time had also come to Belgrade, got the same treatment on occasion. Farmer was the mean officer concerned. Clearly he did not agree with the way in which we prisoners were being specially treated. It is a moot point, but he failed to understand that unlike Serbian prisoners, who would see their families routinely over the months or years to come, we would not. Our families would not be allowed to live in Yugoslavia for the duration of our prison terms.

Branko Jelen was not afforded the same type of treatment and Peter and I were to agitate for improvements constantly, but with mixed success. The ambassador was able to improve Branko's position with regard to visitations and food and other items, and CARE Yugoslavia was eventually allowed to see Branko.

Meanwhile the Wallaces had arrived. They are very pleasant and strong in their support for all three of us. They too look after and encourage Samira and I am grateful to them for this, given their own obvious distractions and worries for Peter. We were now able to also see CARE staff, and it was bloody good to see them. Hurried (all visits were short and conducted in a feverish atmosphere) discussions with Mikhail, and later the colourful and robust Sophia, are really welcome. I crave more of their visits but we are severely restricted. In these meetings, time is too short to discuss serious matters, and in any case we have to be very careful. There is a reluctance anyway to discuss issues such as anyone's degree of culpability at the time of my arrest. This and other subjects are skipped over on these otherwise brief, joyous occasions. The Belgrade office staff were trying very hard to be supportive, under extremely challenging circumstances, and we were greatly impressed with their visits.

Samira brought me greens for the first time, which I was craving. She managed to get fresh peas, bags of muesli and the like past the guards. Quality books were also being arranged, and CARE USA, via the wonderful Sue Aitken, provided some magnificent titles and various pieces of news from CARE USA, who were marvellously supportive. Samira remained in touch with her on these issues. Branko and his family received all manner of items from CARE USA, who would never be forgotten for their thoughtful generosity. The National Director of CARE USA, Peter Bell, wrote very supportive and appealing papers to top USA journals crying our defence. Sir 'Hooky' Hughes, that silver-haired old gentleman who was the president of CARE UK, gave strong media interviews on our behalf, and like Peter Bell, highlighted the absurdity of the

Yugoslav charges and their ignorance regarding NGOs operating in dangerous places. Samira worked hard to collect copies of press releases from the largely supportive and very sensible Australian press, who were reporting quite responsibly on our plight, as far as I could make out. Between Samira and the other saint in the pack, the very experienced and calm Vesna of the Australian embassy, we were showered with material. We were beginning to realise the staggering depth of support from around the world for us in our plight. The groundswell of support from schools in Australia also overwhelmed us; gratefully, I noticed that they were all very inclusive of Branko.

Samira and the Wallaces revelled in bringing the news of this support. Samira was to also pass on strong and brave messages of support she had received over the phone from my son Haydon and brother Stuart. Her networking was vigorous, the enormous telephone bill a small price to pay, I was to reflect, for increasing morale all round. It was a dreadful time when Samira had to leave. Samira and I took great joy in feeling the now kicking baby. Samira would giggle in that girlish way of hers and I would grin like a Cheshire cat. To watch Samira looking down and talking to the little antagonist booting away was such a great tonic. Typically, she left with grace and without a fuss, warmly thanking the prison staff. They had been pretty good with her, I thought, particularly the prison governor, who showed her a deal of kindness. On our last meeting she said, 'Keep your chin up, Pratty.' In the month that Samira was in Belgrade my health and spirits improved dramatically: I put on some weight, and even experienced a revival of my sense of humour. I would be in my wife's debt forever.

We received a visit from Foreign Minister Downer. There had even been speculation from our guards that this visit meant our imminent release, but I discounted this because I was now convinced the regime was committed to our running the full legal cycle of appeals etc. Poor old Alexander Downer looked as flat as we were. He was blunt with us, which I appreciated, playing down any chances of immediate release. I went back to my cell both flattened and hopeful. I saw the visit as a good sign for a medium-term resolution.

Djeordje visited me as much as any lawyer was permitted to, and kept me up to date on all issues, as well as preparing my appeal. I had to get another defence document ready as part of the appeal process. Meanwhile I heard through one of many visiting sources, that an infamous Serbian mafia fellow of Italian origin had been involved in the intrigue surrounding our case. He had met Malcolm Fraser, as had Arkan before him, seeking to discuss the issue, perhaps to assist. Fraser and CARE Australia had a strict position on all discussions, meetings and negotiations about us, no matter at what level, ministerial to mafia. Firstly, they would meet anybody. Secondly, they would state outright that no money was to be involved. This situation and the CARE position was explained to me much later.

Di Stefano had some sort of connection with the colourful Sydney lawyer John Marsden, who I was to read to my amazement in prison about this time (in a copy of the Australian *Bulletin* magazine provided to me in prison) had absented himself from a scheduled appearance in court in Sydney (a defamation case against Channel Seven) to fly to Europe, apparently to assist in the free Pratt/Wallace campaign. Di Stefano was apparently speaking on his behalf from time to time. Di Stefano was to proclaim our innocence, as indeed even Arkan did at one point, to the international media. It would not become clear to me to what extent Marsden had actually become involved, nor quite what was motivating him. Apparently he had failed to gain entry to the country. Nevertheless, the reports reaching us about such colourful characters getting involved raised our morale. Later, I was to wonder whether we could possibly have become pawns between various mafias and political factions.

On a number of occasions after Samira had left I experienced spells of depression, often lasting a day to a day and a half. I had not suffered these so much in previous months. I would occasionally despair that I might not be released for some years, although logically I knew that pressure must eventually bring about an early release. I worried a great deal about Samira's health and pregnancy and about the wellbeing of my son and mother. During these tail spins, worry for my family was paramount. Five days a week for the rest of my incarceration I would be supremely confident that I was soon to be released. On the other two days I would just have to walk up and down that cell like blazes, in order to motivate myself. On these occasions, about four in all as I recall, I appreciated Peter's support. He would bring me back to reality. 'C'mon Pratty, you know we will be out soon,' he would say. There were times when I was reduced to plain old whingeing, and the company of my colleagues was comforting. I tried to reciprocate the support. There were times when Peter too would get frustrated and go into a quiet spell, and I like to think I helped him out.

Peter and I were both busy with Branko, who was often sad, and very frightened, understandably, for his family's safety. To make matters worse, there was a nonsense about the organisation and the sustaining of support needed by Branko's family. The nonsense, involving some members of CARE staff and other people working in co-operation with the embassy, got me extremely angry, and letters were written and appeals made to embassy staff to do something about it. Things improved eventually, but only after much heartache had been suffered by both Branko and his family. This was one of the gloomier aspects of this saga. He was under immense pressure, more so than many prisoners. It was to his credit that he withstood that pressure, as did his brave wife. He was to face more severe ordeals in the months to come.

David Ritchie, senior officer at the Australian embassy in London, came to Belgrade to stand in for the temporarily absent ambassador Chris Lamb. Ritchie's no nonsense style of doing business appealed to us. He skilfully assisted the lawyers and the three of us in preparing our appeal documents, and we went to the appeal court with David and newly arrived John Scott (deputy ambassador) attending. I recall David sitting behind me 'cooling me off' during a short, heated exchange I had with the bench. Our sentences were reduced — mine by four years to eight, Branko's to four and Peter's to one.

In the First Military Headquarters prison brutality on the part of a minority of guards continued, mainly aimed at Albanian Kosovar prisoners. An incident during one of our 'shaving parades' best characterises this brutality. On one warm evening we were all lined up, shirts off, shaving kit presented to us and in hand (kit was not allowed to be kept by prisoners). The hall and rooms were half-lit, but from the corner of my eye as I faced the wall I could just see Psycho antagonising and brutally toying with a tall young prisoner. Egged on by Pitbull, Psycho, who appeared drunk, motioned to the prisoner to stand still, bragging that he could knock him down in one hit. The frightened and shaking prisoner stood stock still. A very fast straight punch connecting with the prisoner's face crashed him straight to the floor, but he quickly scrambled to his knees, whimpering and crying, bleeding profusely from a badly injured nose. Psycho was enraged because, he said, the prisoner was bleeding on the just cleaned floor. He then kicked the young man viciously in the ribs, rolling him across the floor and through the blood. The twenty or so prisoners remained dead still, nobody moving, nobody game to help the prisoner. So although our treatment and conditions had dramatically improved, every three or four nights hell would return.

In the last week of June Branko was to be transferred to a new jail about 80 kilometres east of Belgrade. We had made approaches, by letter and personally to the governor, for Branko to remain with us and go with us when we were transferred to Sremska Mitrovica, which we had been told would be occurring soon. But the authorities were keen to show the Australian Government, CARE and the rest of the world that Branko's sentencing, fate, or whatever else, was none of the world's business. We tried to convince Branko that this was, simply another phase on the way to freedom. I was by now convinced that CARE's strategy for the release campaign was, and had to be, a two plus one plan. It was clear that the Yugoslavs would retain Branko for a further period, no matter what — it was a case of them exercising their sovereign rights.

The day of departure was traumatic; Branko was extremely emotional and very unhappy, with everybody. He seemed to be feeling let down by everybody. It showed in his eyes, and it is understandable. He said that he would be mistreated at the Poljuvec Prison and he was right. He is to have a hell of a time there, far surpassing our arduous and frightening experiences. Branko and I embraced as he left, heads down. There was nothing Peter and I could do. We heard a little about him over the next few weeks through the ambassador, and the news was not encouraging. CARE

Belgrade office staff were to battle mightily to get in to see him, being put under pressure themselves for their persistence. CARE Belgrade played an important and very effective role in Branko's support — and in fact his salvation — over the coming four months of his terrible ordeal.

Peter and I were to be transferred about the end of the first week in August to Sremska Mitrovica. Thus I had come full circle, at least geographically, as this was the town where I spent my terrible first twenty-four hours. This time, however, we go to a state penitentiary, not the country jail where we had been initially held. Sremska Mitrovica is the prison to which all foreigners go. It is the ambassador's belief that release could occur soon, that this transfer is an automatic phase in that process. While many are sceptical, Ambassador Lamb turns out to be right. Since the end of the trial he more than anybody else seems to have read the signs right, no mean feat in this totally unpredictable country. I was apprehensive about the transfer and did not look to the move as being a positive one; it seemed to me that my predicament was only being cemented into place. Peter would soon be eligible for parole, and I realised I had four years, minimum, to wait for that honour. But I was wrong, and soon we were to detect a new mood and subtle signs that release might be a possibility — even then, I still thought a best case result for myself would be six to twelve months.

On reception at Sremska Mitrovica, we immediately noticed the more relaxed and mature mood of the guards. One of the guards who had family in Australia said to me, 'Hey, one month, maybe six, you will be free.' He was kind; indeed all the guards were at least approachable or at worst harmlesssly indifferent. There was absolutely no sign of random rough treatment, bashings or verbal abuse of the sort we had had to contend with for four months. The prison was a clean, well-organised place, with beautifully kept grounds and gardens the size of two football fields. Discipline was firm but not tight. There was an air of low-key friendliness about the place. Perhaps my lawyer was correct: this may well be some sort of model prison. The ambassador reckoned I would be asked by the prison governor to design and assist in the building of a golf course, to be sited somewhere amongst their thousands of acres. He did not seem to be joking. I reminded myself that nothing the unpredictable and unorthodox ambassador came up with would surprise me.

Peter and I were placed, for our 'protection', in the high security wing, in an isolated two-man cell. The door was always locked and we had no dormitory area freedom of movement, unlike the high-risk prisoners in that wing. They were all hardened criminals, mainly murderers, many of whom had been in the place for a very long time.

A trustee prisoner was allocated to interpret between ourselves and the guards; again, few of them speak passable English. He is extremely kind and gives us all he can. He seems to supervise the place in terms of its daily routine and seems well liked and trusted by all the guards and prisoners. The war has just finished and he and the guards talk openly of their great disappointments and their hopes for the future. For a while there are rumours of a possible uprising in the country, and in the immediate aftermath of the war we hear from our embassy visitors much talk and speculation about this.

One of the guards points out to me a cheerful prisoner in the wing who had murdered and then cut up his wife, storing her in the home freezer. Peter and I look around us in wonder.

Peter and I have morning walks in the garden on tight exercise courses, with up to eight prisoners who have been sentenced to death. These poor souls, ashen-faced and understandably introspective, walk their circles in these beautiful gardens not as men who might be seeing mother nature for the last time, but indifferently.

The governor of the prison is an impressive man. He is physically large, as it seems to me are all prison governors in this country. He is strong, very broad-faced, ruddy-complexioned, a big-framed but fit man, not out of shape. He is apparently a party man with close connections to Milosevic. He does not seem at all nervous about the reported deteriorating situation in the country. He takes pride in his prison and indeed it seems his was a well-organised and well-run place, at least on the surface. His staff are well dressed and comfortable in their roles, not slouches like the guards in previous places.

Peter and I settled down into a routine. We had our cleaning tasks and did these routinely each morning, rising at about 5.30 am. Meals were the normal prison fare slop (but under the sanction conditions in the country this was probably reasonable), and we sustained ourselves with food from the consular visits. Peter suffered badly from an asthmatic condition and had long coughing fits which kept him awake and further tired him. Otherwise our health through this period was fair, as it had been generally since the end of the trial.

The wonderful Sophia from the CARE Belgrade office, she of the colourful and cheerful language, visited us, as did our wonderful admin assistant. Vesna, too, was a warm and tireless supporter. The three of them would be reduced to tears upon seeing Peter and me in our grey prison uniforms. The signs were definitely getting better, although most of our visitors seemed exasperated and exhausted. Their sometimes open distress was a little off-putting for me.

On 2 September, Peter and I are summoned to the governor's office. Very unusually, he invites us both to sit down, actually on his plush chairs. We are handed glasses of Coke. The governor is in a sombre mood and says that he believes I will see my new baby soon; that will not be too many months away, he says. He requires us to fill out new applications for clemency, which is puzzling, as we had not been advised by the embassy or our lawyers that this was necessary. The governor asks that we mention in the clemency letter how we feel about the treatment we have received in the prison. Of course we write that we have been ecstatic.

Peter and I had been through so many exercises in speculation and had had so many false hopes destroyed that though puzzled, we went back to our cells and did not reflect much on what had happened. I was quietly confident that something would break. At 10 am the following morning, 3 September, our trustee, Dooley, came to the cell and kicked some empty boxes through the doorway. He had a broad grin on his face. He simply said, 'You are going home.' My first strange reaction is to feel sorry for Dooley, he who has been so kind and helpful, but who has got another eight years to run.

The feeling of relief slowly sinks in, but we both instinctively hold off on any celebrations, lest this be some monstrous trick. At the same time I doubt it, as it had seemed to me for some weeks now that any appetite for cruel teasing, hoaxing and the like (which I had lived with regularly for three months) had disappeared. Still unsure, we quietly enjoy the business of packing. We are taken to the governor's office. More drinks and kind words and he has Dooley call our families in Australia.

It is at this point that I know that this is no game, it is fair dinkum. Speaking to Samira, who by chance is with the Yallops late at night in Canberra, my voice breaks just a little as I hear over the phone great howls of relief in the house, from a number of people, it seems. Peter talks to his delighted folks and I can imagine his exhausted and worried mother sagging with relief.

About two hours later, close to midday, after new passports have been hastily cobbled together by the embassy staff there in the prison, we emerge through the towering front doors, into brilliant sunlight. We see four cars and a gaggle of people waiting. Most prominent among them, and fittingly I think, given his dominating role in this long rescue saga, is the towering figure of Malcolm Fraser. He is as pleased as punch, warmly shaking our hands and patting our shoulders. He is a bloody sight for sore eyes. With him is Ambassador Chris Lamb, chortling away as usual, and I greet him and thank him profusely too. With them are five members of the Australian Serb community, who it seems have travelled to the country just to work on our case. I am deeply honoured to meet them. They have played a pivotal role all the way through the arrest saga, I am informed by Malcolm Fraser. As we quickly get into the cars (quickly blokes, before they change their minds! I am thinking), we cast one last look back at the prison. We speed off, Peter and I in the back seat of an embassy vehicle driven by Ambassador Lamb, with Malcolm riding shotgun. The convoy follows. This is a surreal experience, and I am very light-headed, in a plush, comfortable fast and quiet car, whose acceleration is forcing me back into deeply padded seats. A beautiful sunny day, vast flat green fields, the odd farmer with a tractor. I'm trying to concentrate, trying to see whether I can observe the police station where I was first interrogated. But I cannot. Nobody talks. There is still much tension, and it doesn't ease until we cross the border.

Twenty minutes later we arrive at the border. This is about the same time it took five months earlier when I took that first horrid drive in the other direction. I have a deep feeling of satisfaction at this expereince of contrasts. Deep and warm. We are 50 metres from the border, but I am no longer afraid of 'missing out'. As I head for the toilet while we wait for the processing of our passports (without our attendance), one of the Australian Serb delegation says to me warmly, 'Listen, it doesn't matter to me what you might have done, I am just glad you are out.' I can only smile broadly back at him, thank him again for his and his community's support and reiterate, 'My colleagues and I did nothing wrong.' We separate, smiling, waving. They will return to Belgrade, while we pass through the border. I remember Branko, and the moment is soured.

As we crawl up to the border, we are the second of two cars. I will be damned if I do not see the little fat policeman with the scar on his chin, who had searched me that first day and who had tried to terminate my telephone call with Samira. Nobody else at the post is recognisable. I point this man out to Peter and to Chris. As we draw level, slowly moving past his checking window I ask Peter to lean back and in slow graceful passing I give him the big finger. He cannot believe his bulging eyes.

We speed up, are quickly processed, and go through to the Croatian side. This time we have made it. As we move on, we look ahead, and about 100 metres further on we see Charles Tapp waiting for us. We pull up to him, I get out of the car and we bear hug each other. He and Malcolm Fraser have worked like crazy for us. The day is wonderful. We take off down the long, deserted freeway towards Zagreb, and now I relax and begin to drift off into some sort of dozing sleep. We are out and away. We are free.

CHAPTER NINETEEN
Duty of Care

Speeding across the Croatian countryside, the four hours it takes to get to Zagreb, I found the realisation of release had yet to sink in. I was feeling a little numb and very tired, but at least — for the first time — a little more relaxed. It would be days before I would really begin to unwind and enjoy my freedom. Thoughts about Branko's plight were taking the shine off things for me. However, as one who naturally enjoys travel I found great comfort the first few days in just moving around, revelling in seeing something other than prison cells and courtrooms for a change. The first night of freedom is spent in a luxury Zagreb hotel, at dinner with Malcolm Fraser and Charles Tapp. The ambassador has had to return immediately to Belgrade. We wish him a fond farewell — he looks drawn and very tired, and has clearly put in a marathon effort all the way. Hotel staff ensure tight security as there are press already lurking around, ready to become the new ill-wind of my existence. No doubt, I think as I gaze around the beautifully decorated dining room, we would also be the subject of strict government control; there would be no aimless wanderings in the garden tonight. Malcolm demonstrates his familiarity with a good red; he enjoys a couple, while I manage only one — all my lousy constitution can withstand this night. He has a strong constitution for a man of his age, I muse, but he maintains his control and composure. He is clearly enjoying the moment.

Charles and Malcolm brief Peter and me on the program for the next week or so. I am impressed by the lengths CARE has gone to, particularly in arranging a counselling program at Ticehurst Hospital in the UK with Dr Gordon Turnbull, renowned for his treatment of high-profile hostage/imprisonment victims. The gentlemen also brief me on many of the background issues relevant to the war and to our arrest and imprisonment. It is a time of long-sought and eager catching up. Good too to be brought up to speed on news of CARE Australia's work in Macedonia as part of the CARE International team operating in Kosovo. We talk well into the night.

Still in the same clothes and still without shoelaces and belts, we arrive in London late on the morning of 4 September, ducking the press at every transportation terminal. We were even filmed on the plane by a pursuing journalist, although I noted that her attitude was respectful rather than pushy. We were to find in the immediate weeks ahead, in London and then Australia, that while the press pursued us eagerly, they were generally supportive and gave us our space. It had been a good feeling to fly out of the Balkans, to put the whole distressed region behind me as we winged it to the UK.

The press conference we attended that day was a nervous affair. I had had second thoughts about saying anything, not being a good public speaker at the best of times. I was at this time well and truly out of practice and my confidence was at a low ebb. Staring into the battery of lights and the very large gaggle of press was more than a little daunting. A number of faces I could recognise, one being Katy Cronin. I judged that what I could see were essentially looks of sympathy, not suspicion. Not a bad interrogation setting, I thought.

The short presentation I gave was pretty rough, but as good as I could do in the circumstances. I figured the press had to be told something of the ordeal and a little of the stark truth of the worst of it, although I was in no mood to go into any details and it would be weeks before I could open up — I never have fully, even to this day. I had been determined, though, to let the world know immediately that this ordeal had involved deadly serious acts and threats and that this was still the situation for Branko, whom I was concerned that the world should not forget.

Peter and I were immediately transferred to Ticehurst Psychiatric Hospital and placed into the hands of Dr Gordon Turnbull and his partner, Dr Walter Busuttil I was still in my scuffed, unlaced shoes and wretched too-big jeans without belt. The piece of dirty white cloth spanning two belt loops in a vain hope to hold the jeans up was observed with amusement by more than one passer-by. At a Marks and Spencers in a delightful country town not far from Ticehurst, the ladies at the sales counter, where I presented my new trousers, shoes, laces, belts etc, were much diverted by my prison garb demonstration and associated flippant antics. They seemed to know who I was, which surprised me. I enjoyed it immensely when these dear ladies, a gaggle of four, joined in the tomfoolery and began hooting away in that lovely English country way. We ceremoniously got rid of the prison garb, every bit of it; I could no longer stand the sight of it. That fine summer afternoon down at Marks and Spencers was a most cathartic experience.

The psychiatric nurse travelling with Peter and me was a sweet and patient woman. She decided that first night that while I should be observed through the night, drugs were not needed, and I was unlikely to hurl myself from the window. We were housed in a wing remote from the rest of the hospital patients. It was a very pleasant place. The building was an old, traditional country affair, surrounded by large, well-groomed grounds and woods; it was very roomy, and the hospital services were excellent. I was impressed that a significant number of staff should be warmly fussing over us — the attention was very welcome after the five months we had been through. The staff at Ticehurst were a professional and lovely lot, their general demeanour and basic caring attitude doing much to get me quickly back on the road to normality. CARE Australia had prepared and booked us for a five-day program.

There was much urgent debate between Gordon, Walter and myself on the first day, with Charles Tapp listening in and monitoring, as to whether I should immediately fly back to Australia and join Samira. At this point she was four days overdue to give birth. Charles and I had already discussed the possibility of my going direct to Australia, and I had also spoken to Samira on the phone to gauge her feelings. She was in very good hands with my ex-wife Kaye and the Yallops and Doolans, so I was confident about that aspect of things. Conventional wisdom was that I should not fly at this point unless it was an emergency. Samira had taken this position as well, and it was her point of view, supported by strong Turnbull advice, which I accepted. I would continue with the program.

On the second day, after we had spent time being introduced to the counselling program, including a background brief on why we needed help, Peter decided he would not continue and would instead spend the rest of the scheduled week in London. I believed he was badly mistaken and for the first time in five months donned my ex-country director's hat and told him so. We agreed to disagree and off he went for what he thought would be a better time. It had always been my practice as a CARE manager in emergency missions to send outgoing CARE staff off to the CARE-appointed counsellor, and this was no exception; indeed our circumstances in this case clearly needed to be very carefully assessed, I thought. Peter was also anxious to get on with investigating book and media opportunities, but for me at this time, and for many weeks to come, this would be the furthest thing from my mind. Regrettably, it was in London that Peter and I were to begin disagreeing on the approaches to the subject of writing books and generally dealing with media.

Gordon Turnbull was an ex-RAF wing commander and Walter too had been an RAF officer. They had both been deeply involved in the psychological debriefing of the Gulf War soldiers who had become prisoners of war, and had dealt with the caseload of Beirut hostages as well: Terry Waite, Brian Keenan, John McCarthy and others. They were extremely experienced and sensible men. They had a leisurely and relaxed approach to the business of counselling, yet their work was extremely effective. Gradually, over the five days, Gordon would slowly pull the poison from me, getting to the nub of what was pressuring me, what would or could develop to eat away at my inner peace later. We would sit relaxed in the study, or wander through the grounds and woods, even deal with the smaller issues over lavish English breakfasts, bathed in the late summer sun streaming through tall windows. There were many times when I just had to postpone a subject for later discussion, and to this day some are still postponed. I would often struggle through a session with a sweaty brow, yet on other occasions I would sweep through a difficult issue as if I were standing outside my body and commenting on somebody else. It was a very difficult time, although interspersed with moments of pleasure. Unfortunately the group sessions that Peter and I should have had were not to be.

Turnbull was a big, happy man with a deep grumbling laugh. He enjoyed my irreverent sense of humour, and I his. As an ex-serviceman similarly aged to me and with a Rugby background we had a lot in common, and that bode well for my program. Walter, his dedicated partner, acted as a good foil for the lurching Turnbull. Turnbull gently but firmly put me straight on a number of issues. He was very well acquainted with the details and circumstances of the ordeal.

On the afternoon of 5 September the mobile phone rang with the news that Samira had gone into labour and into hospital. There was nothing I could do, although I had a great deal of confidence in Samira and the baby. They had both inspired this confidence in me for many months. I waited and waited. Into the evening Gordon and I were continuing our therapy over one or two amber pints in one of those snug little country pubs I had only ever read about before. It sat at the bottom of the hill, just away from the hospital. Over the next few hours we waited pensively. Gordon had never met Samira, but after many phone calls with her, he felt that he knew her well. Samira was closely attended by two wonderful saints, fellow CARE workers Melissa Hall (Robert Yallop's wife) and Cathy Esposito (Brian Doolan's wife). In my mind's eye, I knew that these ladies would look after my wife as if she were the last soul on Earth, and they did.

At about 9.30 pm local time that night, via a message on my answering machine, I learned from a happily weeping Melissa that all was well and we had a beautiful baby girl. Samira had been in labour for eight hours and, as recalled to me later by a laughing Cathy, during the penultimate phase of labour, wild with pain, had screamed, 'I am never going to have sex with that bastard Pratt ever again!' While feeling very disappointed at being absent, I was hugely relieved that I had been released in time and Samira had delayed just long enough to have the baby in the full knowledge that I was free and safe. That snug little pub was awash with my champagne and littered with cigars well into the night.

The counselling continued, and while many devils were still lurking inside, many had been exorcised and the rest exposed, put on notice. It would be many months before I would begin to really settle down, but thanks to Turnbull and Busuttil I was in pretty reasonable shape. More importantly, I believed that a solid foundation had been established, and that because of it, my recovery would be faster and more complete over the months to come. Towards the end of the program I had the great honour to meet Brian Keenan. This had been arranged by Gordon. This man had spent five incredible years locked away, often bound by chains, in a number of Beirut secret cells, in unspeakable conditions, physically and psychologically. He was now a successful author. He was a calm and peaceful man, exuding great strength of character. He humbled me; my own experience was paltry compared with what this poor devil and his colleagues had been through. I was also to meet Andy McNab, the SAS sergeant, commander of the now famous 'Bravo 20' patrol. The patrol had fought with distinction behind enemy lines in Iraq during the Gulf War, then was captured and spent some weeks in captivity, suffering severe brutality, with a number of the patrol dying in prison, under torture. He too displayed an inspirational calmness. These were men I thought had a lot to teach society about adversity and about what really matters in life.

After four days of counselling I finished my time in London with a day's shopping. I bought a few more of the essentials of life: some more clothes, a watch and a suitcase. I had lost everything that I had been carrying at the time of the arrest, from vehicle to watch, and six years and more of personal papers. Peter and I joined Brian Doolan in London and prepared for the return journey. We gave two media interviews about the ordeal.

Qantas was truly fantastic, donating as they always do to CARE a number of seats for essential mission travel. Peter and I were upgraded to first class with sleepers, and there was much consideration by CARE and Qantas for our welfare during this very fragile time. The flight attendants talked with us well into the night and were extraordinarily caring with us both. It was a small world: an attendant from Ocean Shores on the NSW north coast told me that she regularly played golf with my brother Stuart and his wife Mary-Lou at the country club there. She amused me greatly telling stories of the errant behaviour of my colourful brother. I was beginning to find that I had now become a member of a very small world, and increasingly uncanny coincidences were occurring everywhere. Qantas and airport officials all the way through to Canberra also went to enormous lengths to safeguard our security and were ever watchful for any signs of distress on our part. They need not have worried — we were both doing fine, readjusting quickly. I was enjoying the homecoming for other reasons as well. For me it had been six years away on the trot, with only short visits for business and two short leave breaks home in that period. At that moment I had had enough of travelling and working in very difficult places. When we landed, on a resplendent morning, I felt myself lucky to be in the greatest country in the world. A tired old cliché it may have been, but it was absolutely relevant at that moment, as I basked in the glory of Sydney's sunshine and freedom.

On to Canberra. I could not wait to see Samira and my boy Haydon. I knew that there would be no awkwardness at all in being reunited with my wife and son. Despite our ordeals, there would be no difficult scenes, simply a warm and reviving experience. I wondered a little about Haydon, particularly about how he had been handling the stress and the worry of my incarceration. I was very much aware now of the media speculation he would have seen, firstly about my safety in those first crucial and dangerous four weeks and then later the irresponsible speculations from some media quarters, strongly implying that I had been some sort of a disreputable, reckless spy. What impact had these things had on my son (never mind the rest of my family, friends and colleagues)? His letters, though, had given me a good indication. He writes well, had developed nicely and, just like my father and brothers, expressed himself succinctly, bluntly and with a dry sense of humour. Haydon had seemed to be coping well, and the caustic and amusing comments he made had confined to the dustbin the negative and ridiculous media stories. Kaye later told me that he had coped well, never losing his confidence that I would (a) live and (b) get out of prison soon. He simply rolled over all negative stories — and, apparently, other people's fears. Kaye also proudly told me that Haydon's already good school performances had even improved a notch or two; he had clearly decided to hunker down and fight the ordeal in his own way. Through this experience my son was growing up very quickly; I hoped it had not hardened him too much.

Nervously, but in a state of high excitement, I approached the VIP lounge in Canberra, escorted by a couple of CARE Australia officials who had met us in Sydney and also by Sue Aitken, the Australian of CARE USA whom I had never met but with whom Peter and I had regularly corresponded while in prison.

I fall into Samira's arms, lots of laughter follows, Samira's trademark giggle out of control, beaming Haydon is blushing because he gets a hug from Dad, brother Ian is grinning broadly. And baby Yasmina. Beautiful little bundle. I am surprised at how bright and alert this cute little girl is. I kiss her, afraid of breaking her. There are more laughs, and I am aware on the periphery of my vision of a lot of old CARE friends warmly smiling. Robert Yallop, the man to whom I had last spoken by mobile some thirty minutes before reaching the border that fateful day, 31 March 1999, the man urging me to get out, not to delay another minute in that country. We greet each other affectionately. Other CARE staff join us, they too relieved that the end of what has been a long and punishing corporate administrative saga has come. Smiles, but flashes of shock too in the eyes of some as they take in my gaunt and still thin appearance. My shockingly stunted and chopped hair reduces Samira to giggles and Haydon teasingly joins in, punching me playfully on the shoulder and muttering 'skinhead'.

A hurried telephone call then follows with my mother, still in Casino, unable to travel. She shrieks delightfully, and then adds her customary good-humoured touch: 'Where have you been, son? When I see you I am to going give you a good belting.' I laugh, good old Mum. A call to Stuart as well. I know that beneath his strong, competent and quite public performances over many months in organising support for me, he has done it tough. Stu and I share the same characteristics: we try to demonstrate calmness and strength but beneath the surface we worry like hell. It's good to see the Wallaces again, too. Samira and I revel in their great relief and happiness as they greet Peter. We all depart the place, pushing through the large but respectful media scrum, and giving them a few short comments on the way out.

Over the next weeks I take a number of opportunities to speak to the press in order to send out to Australia an expression of the depth of Peter's and my thanks and gratefulness. My family and I have found the press to be largely responsible in their reporting of the ordeal, and they continued during this time to be respectful. These thanks to Australia seem insufficient, though — Samira and I cannot thank Australia enough. As we settle back into life in Canberra, and during our frequent travels to Sydney, it dawns on us how broad and deep that support was for Peter, Branko, our families and me. While proudly aware and deeply comforted in prison by the knowledge of that support, I had not realised the scope of it. I am humbled time and time again, and Samira and I always thank the many people who kindly say hello to us. It becomes a little distressing later, when sensational and negative media stories begin to doubt my character and suggest espionage behaviour on my part. I wonder then whether people who had so generously invested so much support in me and my family will feel betrayed. However, I am convinced that commonsense will prevail, and I know the Australian people by and large will not believe such unfounded innuendos.

On that first day in Canberra we were invited to Government House, where the Governor-General greeted us and cut those famous yellow ribbons flying from his balcony. Samira, still struggling through her postnatal phase, bravely gets through that first, hectic day. She finds immediately that our little pearl of a daughter, whom Sam and I nickname 'Luli' (Arabic for 'pearl'), is fast becoming a media star. Haydon joins me for the ribbon cutting. It is fitting that he is here: it was the Governor-General who very thoughtfully invited Haydon, many months earlier, on the day of the Governor-General-inspired Pratt/Wallace supporting ecumenical service, to join him in tying up those yellow ribbons. They are joyfully cut down, but soberly we put back a ribbon for Branko Jelen.

In the springtime, sun-drenched gardens of Yarralumla we meet many people deeply involved in our cause, and again I get this feeling of awe, and wonder whether I should apologise to all of them for the inconvenience caused by my capture and imprisonment. These people cared for us and were still doing so, regardless of the controversies surrounding my continued presence in Yugoslavia after the start of war and the arrest. The people here in the garden, it occurred to me, had been at the heart of the saga. We meet the Department of Foreign Affairs and Trade people, the secretary and his crisis team, and church leaders (representing various faiths) who were significantly involved. Among the church leaders we meet the Serbian Orthodox church leaders, the Bishop himself and the robustly happy Father Dragosavljevic, whom I was to meet again in the months to come. Many of these people felt a strong sense of duty about caring for our families and resolving the arrest/prison saga. Having wondered all these years where Australia's spirit had gone to, I found myself impressed that the old Australian willingness to fight for its people in dire straits was alive and well, both in terms of the individuals who had struggled for us, and in terms of the Australian people as a whole, who had rallied so strongly behind us. Here, truly, was our duty of care in action.

Along with the Serbian Orthodox church leaders in the Governor-General's gardens that day were other Serbian community leaders. There were members of the various Serbian welfare organisations, such as Nick Gotavec of the Serbian Orthodox Welfare Association, a man I had met during his travels to Yugoslavia and with whom I had worked to deliver Australian-sourced aid. My wife and I had had meals with Nick and his people whenever we could during visits to Australia on CARE business. Samira had spoken to Nick during my ordeal and Nick had agreed to help. Samira had in her own way helped Nick to assist the Serbian community during those first difficult and emotional days when tensions were running high between the Serbian community and the general Australian community. Present too was Mr Glisic, who had made an outstanding effort to marshall community support from the Serbs in Australia and had himself travelled with colleagues to Yugoslavia to help Malcolm Fraser in subtly and carefully building agreements with the Yugoslav government towards clemency and subsequently release.

The Australian Serbian community, I was to learn, were understandably demonstrative in Australia against the NATO campaign against Yugoslavia, but perhaps naive about the actions of the regime of that country. At first they were also understandably angry with Pratt and Wallace, perhaps naively believing all they heard from the Serbian government, reinforced by the irresponsible and sometimes dangerous stories in some of the Australian press and negligent stories in other media later. However, the Serbian community seemed to have come around to lending its support and then indeed taking a leadership role in the campaign for our release. This demonstration of national solidarity on the part of one of our more significant ethnic communities can only be beneficial for the whole nation.

Over the days of settling back in, it becomes clear that CARE Australia has exhausted itself in many of its functions and departments in the quest to release Peter and me. The organisation has been singularly focused on this saga since 31 March 1999, and indeed continues to be for Branko. It is staggering and humbling to me to see the extent to which the staff in Canberra, individually as well as corporately, had committed themselves to getting us out, and worried about our wellbeing. They had ridden the rollercoaster all the way. I saw the ABC's 'Four Corners' program on CARE from May 1999 and was quite moved by this story. There is a joy among the staff as we visit head office that is sometimes hard for me to come to terms with.

I go through a period of deep circumspection over the first months after my homecoming. CARE is at that time also going through a period of circumspection as to whether to continue the mission in Yugoslavia, but decides, for overriding humanitarian reasons, to continue. Such a continuation will also be essential in terms of underwriting CARE's efforts in the release of Branko Jelen, so I am happy to see this go ahead.

On Christmas Day I received a telephone call from Bernard Barron, the new country director for CARE in Belgrade. I had briefed Bernard about the mission some weeks earlier, before he left to take up his new appointment. Although I had met him, I did not know him well. On this occasion he was very concerned and worried about Branko, still in prison and doing it very rough. The feedback had not been good; indications were that he was being badly beaten by other prisoners, although he seemed to be getting reasonable prison administrative and counselling support. Bernard had been concerned about Branko's state, and was now fairly much in a state of despair. Bernard had visited Branko that day and was frustrated he could not contact anybody in CARE to voice his extreme concerns.

I called Malcolm Fraser and relayed Bernard's report. Mr Fraser had been aware of Branko's fast deteriorating condition and was familiar with the details of Bernard's concern. He was forever the tireless campaigner, and had been agitating vigorously for Branko's release with international contacts, usually through the eminent persons group, that order of distinguished ex-international leaders. However, what we didn't know was that at this point the Yugoslav authorities were considering a release, in the national interest. I was thankful to hear the latest news from Malcolm (although he did not discuss with me the Yugoslav position and did not seem know what it was), and somewhat frustrated and annoyed that I had not been informed by CARE Australia staff on either the progress on Branko's case or the deterioration of Branko himself.

An hour before midnight on New Year's Eve, with our friends Trish Lake and Ben Hawke, watching the fireworks herald 2000, I heard from Charles Tapp that good news was imminent. At ten minutes before midnight I received a telephone call that Branko had been released and was on his way across the border. I felt as if a great burden had been lifted from my shoulders. I wondered whether the Yugoslav Government had hastened its release date because they dreaded the possibility of being saddled with a dead Branko. I was able to contact Bernard by mobile — he was travelling in the car with Branko. It was a great and hugely relieving moment. I leaned on the apartment balcony and just let out a long whistle. A mixture of emotions flooded me. I was ecstatic that Branko was alive and safe and on his way to his family.

EPILOGUE

Since I have returned I have frequently been asked how was it for me during those periods of great fear, during those periods of adversity. This is still a difficult question for me, but I feel others deserve as much of an explanation as I can provide on these issues.

The environment into which my colleagues and I were suddenly hurled was volatile and very unpredictable. Firstly, the people we were dealing with were frightened for themselves and their families. They were in the first days of war, with rumours running wild — they were flying blind too. However, it must also be said that these secret police and military intelligence men were ignorant individuals, and did not much care what the truth was. They did not — at least in the early period of terror, the first four or so days — care who I really was nor what good work my organisation had done in their country. That period of close interrogation by these people, then by the man I have termed Genghis, and the quite casual terror treatment of some of the guards in prison, confirmed for me that these types of groups and others like them across the Balkans are capable of extreme levels of irrational cruelty and destructiveness. My ordeal was nothing compared to that experienced by those poor wretched souls feeling the terror in Kosovo, however, nor of the still unaccounted for thousands who had fled Srebenica before them, or of so many other communities across the Balkans. This is a very sobering thought.

I had a 'close-up' glimpse of the machinery. My fears were several — for my life, for the wellbeing and safety of my wife and the unborn baby, and for my staff. The psychological terror was maintained through constant references to the safety of my family — 'even now as we speak, Major Pret …' — and continual references to capital punishment later in prison, at a time when I did not have access to anybody except the regime and its soldiers. Then there were the references to hanging, to the building of the gallows in the courtyard, and later to the 'training and rehearsal that the firing squad was undertaking'. The terror varied in form but included 'mock preliminaries' to pistol execution, in the garage, in the cell, and outside in the small hours of a wet and cold night.

When you are at the bottom of a huge inverted prism, pinned beneath the point, and the world beyond does not exist, you cannot assess the risks to yourself or to your colleagues, the ones for whom you are responsible. After five days of severe sleep deprivation, forced to live in unbelievably cold conditions, fed a diet of fear and then beaten sufficiently to feel ashamed and to constantly carry some pain, you have to fight to maintain a grip on reality. Were they seriously considering killing me if I did not co-operate (or even in the first seventy-two hours, before other players came into the business, if I had co-operated)? I have no idea. Such regimes are unpredictable and irrational. The jury is still out and may never return. And I no longer care, because life must continue.

How I coped with all this is very difficult to explain, and I am not sure I did cope, except that I always managed not to completely break down. While they would see me shaking, I am sure my teeth were gritted, to stop me crying out and begging for mercy. I silently prayed very hard and would totally focus on Samira. I would pray for her to stay well, to carry on without me, and I would pray that I would see her one day somewhere. I do not believe that I had any deep faith, nor that it suddenly materialised to sit at my right shoulder — I have a healthy cynicism that would not have allowed that to happen. But yes, I have faith in God, casual and a little erratic, perhaps, but sufficient to help me in those circumstances. It was my wife's strong Muslim faith, and my deep familiarity with that, which I think was the primary engine for my strength, as well as the faith of my old Presbyterian grandmother, a strong and wonderful lady whom I had loved and respected all through my formative years. I reckon I had two dear angels riding with me and helping me keep it together. Backing this up was my military training; once a soldier always a soldier, they say. Twenty-three years of regular army service and before that some six years of junior military training had inculcated a belief in the worth of personal discipline, and that, I feel, was very important in my mental survival and subsequent recovery. Silent praying and cell pacing became routine activities for me and helped me build a mental box in which to survive those first twenty-odd days, the worst part of my ordeal.

Finally, recovery has been greatly accelerated by expert and experienced counselling, by professional but compassionate people who have worked with some of the toughest cases of personal ordeal. Counselling in these circumstances is essential. Some people instinctively claim macho status and decry the usefulness of counselling, but in my view this is not wise. You must be prepared to trust yourself and seek help from others, and not underestimate the ordeal. One must look to the long term, not the immediate comfort zone — you owe this to family, friends and the wider community. CARE Australia is to be applauded for their preparation and co-ordination of the counselling program and the release preparations for all three captives. Their diligence and good leadership, particularly Charles Tapp's, were outstanding, though the whole affair was debilitating and very draining for the organisation and its people.

For many weeks after returning to Australia, my total concentration was on my wife, my new child and restoring my health. Indeed the first two and a half months were entirely taken up with this and with catching up with family. We had avoided many media requests for either interviews or more substantial stories, although we did eventually undertake a number of interviews over late 1999 and January 2000. Initially I had given no thought to writing myself, although I was pretty clear about what the 'story' should be, in what

EPILOGUE

manner it should be treated and the type of people who ought to be involved in it. Peter Wallace and I had gone our separate ways with respect to writing a book; we had different approaches in mind to the way the story should be told. I wished him the best of luck. Trish Lake was the literary agent my wife and I chose to help us. She is a truly literary person and quickly demonstrated a passion for and commitment to the story and its effective presentation. We talked to a number of publishers and were very happy with our final selection. I had a very strong desire to get onto the public record the truth of what had happened in Serbia, and the events leading up to it.

A number of community events occurred in the early months of post trauma settling in, which Peter and I, or sometimes I alone, attended. As every little bit helps, I have been keen to contribute whatever I can that is useful to the community and to the country. I feel I have a certain debt to repay the community, so wherever I may be able to help various organisations or government benefit from my experience, in terms of trauma counselling, dealing with adversity, human rights issues, humanitarian assistance, regional and ethnic conflict resolution, peacekeeping or peacemaking, I have been happy to help. However, I have had to postpone a number of personal commitments to these and other issues until later in the year. I was pleased to be able to organise a visit to the impressive Serbian Orthodox church at Hall, New South Wales, for CARE, Peter and me, so that we could lobby for Branko and thank the Serbian church for their help. We breakfasted with the priests of Australia, called to conference. Amusingly, I detected that a number, although very kind, still suspected that I was a spy.

Peter and I were also able to visit the Taperoo Primary School in Adelaide to personally thank the children for their lovely and substantial support to us. We had received from them a number of drawings and letters, as we had from dozens of schools around the country. The drawings, with their beautifully innocent notes and messages, were very uplifting for us, and I would like to think that the authorities who had vetted them had been affected as well. It was a great contribution from these kids, and this example was repeated over and over. Community groups right around the country went to equally extrordinary lengths to cheer us up, to give us hope.

My old high school chums, led by the incredibly energetic Marika Souri, cranked up a very substantial support campaign, and I received stimulating and very caring letters from thirty ex-students. The Northern Rivers regional community, especially the people of Casino, rallied to my mother's and my family's side.

The great pity is that in these first seven months of return I have not been able to scratch the surface in terms of thanking people, particularly in writing; there are so many friends to catch up with who have not received a reply to kind letters or to telephone calls, so many groups which have invited me to visit and talk. From adversity and the horrors of a terrible ordeal my life has pretty much turned to being about a whole new positive experience. The duty of care that I have understood lives in so many Australians' hearts, and which I have personally experienced in action, is a way of relating to others which I will try to live up to for the rest of my days.

INDEX

Abelede, Eduardo, 171, 178, 180–82
Aden, 48–9
  battle in, 50
  landmine clearing program, 55
Ain-Kawa, 26, 35
Aitken, Sue, 292, 309
Al-Gahin, 52–3
Al-Kalah, 28
Albanian Kosovars, 132
  civil disobedience, 101
  KLA, uniting behind, 102
Amman, 24
'Arkan', 108, 176, 294
'Arkan's Tigers', 108, 177, 238
Army Office, Department of Defence, 17
Arrest, 170–86
  first twenty-four hours following, 187–200
  interrogations following *see* Interrogations
Australian Regular Army, 12
  headquarters, 17
AVIO, 20–22
Banyumelenge, 81
Barron, Bernard, 312
Belgrade, 2
Belgrade Central Prison
  campaign for Pratt's release from, 12
  imprisonment in, 245–75
    bashings in, 265–66
    return to, following sentencing, 289
Bell, Peter, 292–93
Blake, Lieutenant Colonel Murray, MC, 15
Boutros Boutros-Ghali, 43
Boyd clan, 7–8
Butare, 67
  displaced children centre, 68
Cambodia
  CARE Australia's deputy project manager, 12
  de-mining programs, 58
  UN Transition Authority, 20
Campbell, Liz, 92
CARE Australia
  job interview, 24
  Middle Eastern Office, 24
  Operations Manager, 23
  responsibilities of staff, 30
  stringent requirements, 30
  Yugoslavia, in
    closing down Kosovo, 144–56
    country director, 4
    'ethnic cleansing', 110
    human rights issues, 105
    Kosovo emergency appeal, 113
    neutrality, 106
    new office in Pristina, 108, 112
    war emergency plan, 159
    'Winter Relief' Appeal, 105
CARE International, 4, 63, 114
CARE Serbia/Montenegro, 96, 102, 104
CARE Yemen, 47
Carling, Col, 82
Clinton, President Bill, 43, 275
Colvin, Mark, 275
Confession, 1–5, 229–42
  broadcast of, 268
Cosgrove, Captain Peter, MC, 14
Cronin, Katy, 288, 303
Davies, Phil, 14
Deane, Sir William, 288
Dohuk, 28
Dollis, Demitri, 261, 289
Doolan, Brian, 149, 231, 244
  Canberra point of contact, 175
  London, meeting in, 307
  Samira Pratt contacting, 196
Downer, Alexander, 288
  visit by, 293
Dragosaveljevic, Major, 261
  judicial interrogation by, 261–63
  meeting chaired by, 270
El Grain, 60
El Khoud, 47, 52
Erbil, 25–6, 28–9, 35
  CARE Erbil Club, 34–6
Esposito, Cathy, 306
Ethnic cleansing, 110
  rumours of, 173
European Union's emergency agency (ECHO), 129
Feed the Children (FTC), 71
Fischer, Tim, 288
Foley, Don, 148–49, 185
  ambassadorial visits, 270–71, 274
  twenty-four hours following arrest, 192–95, 198
Fraser, Malcolm, 15
  Branko Jelen, campaigning for, 313
  dinner with, following release, 302
  escorting Steve to freedom, 301
  formal negotiations by, 231
  meeting with Steve, 271–73
    release from jail, following, 300
  Zagreb, in, 261
Free Papua Movement, 16
Free Pratt/Wallace campaign, 294
Gillett clan, 7–8

Gilmour, David, 277
Goma, 77–8
Gosford High School, 12
Gotavec, Nick, 311
Great Lakes region
 CARE Australia, 63
  shutting down operation, 93
 CARE International in, 63–4
 workshop, 64
Great War, 7–8
Guild, Ian, 15
Hall, Melissa, 306
Harris, Ian, 70
Hawke, Ben, 313
Headquarters First Task Force, 15
Healey, Harry (Damian), 12
Heggie, Mark, 197
 broadcast of confession, watching, 268
 Samira dining with, 247
Heggie, Zoe, 268
Hiddens, Les, 12
Holsworthy, 14
Howard, John, 19, 288
Hughes, Sir 'Hooky', 292
Humanitarian aid
 contributions to, 22
 moral dilemmas, 84–6
 tough and demanding, 30
Hutu
 displaced children centres, 65
 Kibeho refugee camp, in, 66
 Tutsi clashes, 86
 war, 87–94
Imprisonment
 Belgrade Central Prison, 245–75
  bashings in, 265–66
  Branko Jelen, reunited with, 289
  Peter Wallace, reunited with, 289
  return to, following sentencing, 289
  Samira, visit by, 290
 First Military Headquarters prison, 289
  brutality in, 295
 release from, 300
 Sremska Mitrovica, in, 297–99
Interehamwe, 68, 75, 81, 84, 132
 raids, 85
Interrogations, 204–17
 Branko Jelen, about, 207
 family, thoughts of, 223
 first twenty-four hours following arrest, 189–92
 judicial investigation, 257–59, 260–63
 military non-intelligence, 218–28
 Samira, thoughts of, 211, 216, 223
 SITREPs, about, 219–21
Irian Jaya, 16
Jelen, Branko, 103, 106, 108, 112, 165, 177–78
 alleged espionage network, in, 214–15
 arrest of, 237, 252
 defence presentation, 284

 evidence by, 287
 interrogation about, 207
 prison, in, 283
 release from prison, 313
 sentence, 289, 295
 support needed by family of, 295
 transfer to new jail, 296
 trial, reunited during, 287
Jordan, 24
Jurash, 24
Kahindo camp, 78
Katale camp, 79
 CARE Australia, 79
 fleeing refugees, 93
Kathleen Gillett, 8
Keats, Norm, 8
Keenan, Brian, 305, 307
Kibeho, 68
 Hutu extremists, 66
 massacre in refugee camp, 74–6
 refugee camp, 66, 74–6
Kigali, 64, 67
Kitney, Geoff, 247
Korean War, 12
Kosovo
 crisis and response, 112–130
 deteriorating political situation, 101
 emergency appeal, 113
 'ethnic cleansing', 110
 evacuation of CARE Australia team, 144–56
 guerrilla war, 108
 landmine incidents, 108, 111
 programming opportunities, 100
 threat of war, 131–43
 war in, 155
Kosovo Diplomatic Observer Mission (KDOM), 127
Kosovo Liberation Army (KLA)
 Albanian Kosovars uniting behind, 102
 genesis, 101
Kosovo Verification Mission (KVM), 142
 vehicles, 126
Kurdish Coalition Government, 27
Kurdish Iraq, 26–46
 provinces, 28
Kurds, 24–5, 34
Labani, Muhammad, 49, 54, 59
Lake, Trish, 313, 314
Lamb, Christopher, 195–96, 231, 249
 ambassadorial visits, 270–71, 274, 282
 Belgrade, in, 255–56
 Croatia, in, 246
 meeting following release from jail, 300
 Steve Pratt taken to see, 274
Landmines
 clearing program in Yemen, 55
 Drenica, 111
 Katale, in, 80
 Kosovo, in, 108, 114–15, 128
 Landmine Awareness program, 115
 Malisevo, 111

INDEX

Zaire, in, 85
Lawder, 53
Liberal Party
  joining, 18
  preselection, 19
Lipovac border crossing, 183–85
Major, Prime Minister John, 43
Makalla, 59
Marsden, John, 294
McGee, Tony, 95, 98
Melham, Darryl, 19
Miller, Graham, 250
Miller, Liz, 250
Milosevic, Slobodan, 138, 155
  Madame Marcovic, 179
  Serbian Socialist Party (SPS), 179
  Serbs unifying behind, 102
Ministry of Interior Police (MUP), 106
  arrest by, 186
Mobutu guards, 81
Montenegro, refugee centre support program, 96
Morina, Madame Buba, 179–80, 195
Mugunga camp, 78
  food distribution program, 79
  Nairobi, 66
NATO air strikes
  threat of, 135
NATO bombing
  commencement of, 157
  war, 157–69
Northern Iraq, 24
  CARE Australia objectives, 27
  CARE operations in, 28–46
  food distributions, 30–1
  security procedures, 32–4
Oaten, Richard, 89
O'Brien, Kerry, 174
Officer Cadet School, 12
O'Keefe, Margaret, 137, 149, 151–54, 159, 168, 171, 178
Organisation for Security and Co-operation in Europe (OSCE)
  peace monitors, 107, 111, 136
  visit to, 126
Oxfam, 111
Pacific Island Regiment
  2nd Battalion, 16
Papua New Guinea, 8, 16
  Defence Force, 16
Peshmerga guards, 25, 28, 32, 36
Phnom Penh, 21
Platt, Greg, 12
  Cambodia, in, 12
Pratt, Bede, 7, 8
Pratt, Ben, 6
Pratt, George, 7
Pratt, Haydon, 4, 18–19, 83, 167, 268
  birth of, 17
  Government House, at, 310
  letters from, 274, 277

messages of support from, 293
reuniting with, 308–9
Pratt, Ian, 9, 309
Pratt, Kaye, 16–19, 309
Pratt, Liz, 9
Pratt, Old Tom, 7
Pratt, Samira, 4, 106, 147, 170, 231–32, 249–50
  Belgrade, in, 290
  broadcast of confession, watching, 268
  Budapest, in, 168, 180
  CARE Yemen Aden office, 51
  family of, 59
  friendship with, 58
  letters from, 274
  London, in, 281
  marriage, 83
  Nairobi, 92–93
  packing belongings, 160–61
  pregnancy, 4, 148, 290
  reuniting with Steve
    Belgrade prison, in, 290
    Canberra, in, 308–9
    telephone conversation at border, 184–85
    thoughts of, during interrogations, 211, 216, 223
    twenty-four hours following arrest, 189, 192, 194–99
  Wadi Duwan visit, 59–62
  Yugoslavia, 95, 138–41
Pratt, Steve
  African experience, 63–76
  arrest, 170–86
  first twenty-four hours following, 187–200
  confession, 1–5, 229–42
  early years, 6
  freedom, 301
  Government House, at, 310
  imprisonment *see* Imprisonment
  into CARE, 23–46
  Lipovac border crossing, 183–85
  Northern Iraq, 28–46
  Operations Manager, 23
  release from prison, 300
  return to Australia, 307–16
  threat of death, under, 201–17
  Yemen, 47–62
  Yugoslavia, 95–169
Pratt, Stuart, 9, 308, 309
  Australian Press Council action by, 264
  letters from, 274, 277
  messages of support from, 293
Pratt, Yasmina
  birth of, 306
  Steve meeting, 309
Press conference, UK, 303
Pristina, CARE Australia office in, 108, 112
Rambouillet talks, 110, 136–37, 142, 149
Raznatovic, Zelko, 108, 176, 247
Ritchie, David, 295
Robertson, Ted, 113–26

INDEX

Royal Australian Regiment
  5th/7th Battalion, 14
  6th Infantry Battalion, 13
Rwanda
  CARE co-operation in, 66
  CARE International multimember team, 93
  displaced children, 69, 71–4
  massacre, 63, 132
  war, 87–94
Rwanda Patriotic Front (CRPF), 66, 75–6
  war, 87–94
Said Sadiq, 37
Sana'a, 48, 57
Scott, John, 295
Sentence, 289
  reduction, 295
Serbia
  refugee centre support program, 96
  Serbian Police Milicja units, 106
Serbian regime
  escalation of crisis, 102
  'ethnic cleansing', 110
Serbian Socialist Party (SPS), 179
Shabwa, 60
  floods, 61
Singapore, 6th Battalion in, 13
Singh, Bob, 21
Somali refugees, 47
  support program, 52
Souri, Marika, 12, 315
Srbica, 118–19
Stefano, Di, 294
Suleimaniya, 25, 28, 34, 37
Tapp, Charles, 231
  allegation regarding espionage network, 206, 213
    Athens, in, 261
    CARE Australia CEO, 149
    dinner with, following release, 302
    escorting Steve to freedom, 301
    information sought by, 249
    reports to, 154
    Vukovar, in, 256
Ticehurst Psychiatric Hospital
  counselling program at, 303–7
Tom, Edward, 133
Trial, 276–301
  appeal, 265, 294
  commencement, 283
  commitment to trial authority, 264
  conviction, 288
  cross-examinations of defence evidence, 286
  defence statement, 278–79, 284
  judicial investigations before, 257–59, 260–63
  lawyer, 276
  news of, 243
  sentence, 289
    reduction, 295
Truelove, Peter, 18

Turnbull, Dr Gordon, 303, 304, 307
Tutsi
  authorities, 68
  Banyumelenge, 81
  displaced children centres, 65
  Hutu clashes, 86
  war, 87–94
UN Development Program (UNDP), 57
UN High Commission for Refugees (UNHCR)
  implementing partners
    CARE Australia, 27, 47, 79, 86
    CARE Serbia/Montenegro, 96
UN World Food Program (UNWFP), 27, 79
UNICEF, 25
  CARE as implementing partner, 27
United Nations/Non-Government Organisations (NGOs)
  Ain-Kawa, in, 26
  Great Lakes co-ordination problem, 64
US Army Logistics Staff College, 17
  Vietnam War, 10, 11
  Wadi Duwan, 59–61
Wallace, Peter, 29, 112–26, 133, 135, 143–55
  defence presentation, 284
  prison, in, 283, 289
  release from prison, 300
  sentence, 289
    reduction, 295
  trial, reunited during, 287
Watson, A John, 113–26
Wilesmith, Greg, 174, 288
Yallop, Robert, 175, 244
  advice to leave Yugoslavia, 180–83
  Canberra, meeting in, 309
  director for Middle East operations, 35
  first twenty-four hours after arrest, 189
  fund raising program by, 113
  overseas operations director, 113, 180
  reports to, 154
  Samira Pratt contacting, 195
  visit to Kosovo by, 104–106
Yemen, 47–62
  CARE Yemen, 47
  landmine clearing program, 55
Yugoslav Army (VJ), 106
Yugoslav Military Intelligence
  English speaking agents, 2
Yugoslav Red Cross, 97–8
Yugoslavia
  arrival in, 95
  CARE Australia in *see* CARE Australia
  CARE International operations, 4
  refugee centres, 96–7
  refugee self-reliance program, 99
  Western bombing of, 102
Zaire, 77–94
  eastern, 63
Zairean Army, 81–2, 85
war, 87–94